Deterritorializing/Reterritorializing

BREAKTHROUGHS IN THE SOCIOLOGY OF EDUCATION

VOLUME 8

Series Editor:

George W. Noblit, *Joseph R. Neikirk Distinguished Professor of Sociology of Education, University of North Carolina at Chapel Hill, USA*

Scope:

In this series, we are establishing a new tradition in the sociology of education. Like many fields, the sociology of education has largely assumed that the field develops through the steady accumulation of studies. Thomas Kuhn referred to this as 'normal science.' Yet normal science builds on a paradigm shift, elaborating and expanding the paradigm. What has received less attention are the works that contribute to paradigm shifts themselves. To remedy this, we will focus on books that move the field in dramatic and recognizable ways—what can be called breakthroughs.

Kuhn was analyzing natural science and was less sure his ideas fit the social sciences. Yet it is likely that the social sciences are more subject to paradigm shifts than the natural sciences because the social sciences are fed back into the social world. Thus sociology and social life react to each other, and are less able to separate the knower from the known. With reactivity of culture and knowledge, the social sciences follow a more complex process than that of natural science. This is clearly the case with the sociology of education. The multiplicity of theories and methods mix with issues of normativity—in terms of what constitutes good research, policy and/or practice. Moreover, the sociology of education is increasingly global in its reach—meaning that the national interests are now less defining of the field and more interrogative of what is important to know. This makes the sociology of education even more complex and multiple in its paradigm configurations. The result is both that there is less shared agreement on the social facts of education but more vibrancy as a field. What we know and understand is shifting on multiple fronts constantly. *Breakthroughs* is the series for works that push the boundaries—a place where all the books do more than contribute to the field, they remake the field in fundamental ways. Books are selected precisely because they change how we understand both education and the sociology of education.

Deterritorializing/Reterritorializing

Critical Geography of Educational Reform

Edited by

Nancy Ares
University of Rochester, USA

Edward Buendía
University of Washington – Bothell, USA

and

Robert Helfenbein
Loyola University of Maryland, USA

SENSE PUBLISHERS
ROTTERDAM/BOSTON/TAIPEI

A C.I.P. record for this book is available from the Library of Congress.

ISBN: 978-94-6300-975-1 (paperback)
ISBN: 978-94-6300-976-8 (hardback)
ISBN: 978-94-6300-977-5 (e-book)

Published by: Sense Publishers,
P.O. Box 21858,
3001 AW Rotterdam,
The Netherlands
https://www.sensepublishers.com/

All chapters in this book have undergone peer review.

Cover photograph: *Representations*, 2016 © Kellie Welborn,
www.welbornimages.com

Printed on acid-free paper

TABLE OF CONTENTS

ACKNOWLEDGMENTS

Nancy Ares is indebted to Ed Buendía for thinking with her about schooling, critical geography, and ways that scholars can ponder the intricacies of reform. This is their second book around these issues, and each was a wonderful journey. She'd also like to thank Rob Helfenbein for his critical, creative thinking on these issues, and the way the three of us melded as a team. Shane and Adrian, my kids, are always a reminder of why I do this work – for love.

Ed Buendía sends sincere thanks to Finese for her unwavering support while writing instead of fishing.

Rob Helfenbein would like to thank the many colleagues and students (some represented here) that have helped, encouraged, and critiqued this project of thinking through the possibilities of critical geography and educational research and theorizing—thinking together has always been a joy. As always, special thanks to Kellie for the support and understanding of the time it takes to take up scholarly work.

The editors would also like to thank Loyola University Maryland students Matt Rossi and Vincent Liu for copyediting and formatting support in putting together this volume.

SECTION ONE

SETTING THE STAGE

NANCY ARES

1. ABOUT THESE TIMES

We decided to situate this book in the context of neoliberal policies and practices around education reform, given their widespread influence in the US and elsewhere. Such policies and practices have been pursued in a variety of places across the globe; a common denominator among them is their commitment to capitalism (for example, the United States, New Zealand, the UK, and Australia (Davis & Bansel, 2007). Among the many definitions of neoliberalism, one that seems to be widely agreed upon is: "An approach to economics and social studies in which control of economic factors is shifted from the public sector to the private sector" (http://www.investopedia.com/terms/n/neoliberalism.asp). In education in the US, we see marketization processes playing out in states and school boards being handed more responsibility and power in determining curriculum content and standards, as well as increasing privatization of public education through the rise of charter schools and for-profit organizations' incursion into managing schools (e.g., Edison Schools, others). In seeking to deepen educators' understanding of the effects of neoliberalism in education, we add this volume to policy analyses and demographic studies (among others) to examine the cultural geography of reform that results from the inevitable translation and appropriation of neoliberalism at various levels of education.

With this book, we seek to show how (critical) social scientists are translating geographical concepts of space, scale and place into studies of educational and community reform. Critical geography is a multidisciplinary field that,

> although valuing and acknowledging the important work in recognizing the ways in which language helps to construct spaces, a Critical Geography seeks to then take the oft-neglected next step of analyzing how … spaces change, change over time, and impact the lived, material world. (Helfenbein & Taylor, 2009, p. 236)

In addition, scholars working in this tradition have,

> a shared commitment to emancipatory politics within and beyond the discipline, to the promotion of progressive social change and the development of a broad range of critical theories and their application in geographical research and political practice. (Painter, 2000, p. 126)

Even with progressive and transformative motives driving intent, of course, power relations are implicated in research focused on politics, social change, and social

N. Ares et al. (Eds.), Deterritorializing/Reterritorializing, 3–25.

science research. No one of these is value-neutral or benign in its impacts on human activities and interactions. We come from the perspective that in this 'late' neoliberal/post-modernization era of education and land use policy, critical inquiry into both the hegemony of and resistance to the spatial construction of k-12 educational processes is crucially important. Specifically, we highlight work that reveals hidden inequities of race, class, ability, sexuality, and gender (among others), as well as inequities and underlying assumptions buried within often-used concepts such as community, identity, place, and space. Implications and consequences of policy responses that are quickly changing the landscape of educational and economic development across the US and other countries need to be unearthed to heighten awareness of and support action to counteract their potentially corrosive and oppressive effects.

Geography Matters: Translations Across Spaces of Schooling

Educational reforms in the 2000s in the US and elsewhere are, as always, highly contested. Since the 1980s in the US, moves toward increasing central control of curriculum, assessment, and evaluation (Au, 2007) vie with calls for increased rigor through creativity, "authentic"[1] curriculum and assessment, and student-centered pedagogies (American Association for the Advancement of Science, 2017; International Society for Technology in Education, 2017; National Education Association, 2017). States translated these calls in widely varying ways. For example, one of the most contentious issues, of late, is the Federal Common Core Curriculum Standards (CCCS, 2015), developed by,

> The nation's governors and education commissioners, through their representative organizations, the National Governors Association Center for Best Practices (NGA) and the Council of Chief State School Officers (CCSSO) … Teachers, parents, school administrators, and experts from across the country, together with state leaders, provided input into the development of the standards. The actual implementation of the Common Core, including how the standards are taught, the curriculum developed, and the materials used to support teachers as they help students reach the standards, is led entirely at the state and local levels. (http://www.corestandards.org/about-the-standards/frequently-asked-questions/)

In 2015, patterns of adoption and rejection of the CCCS across the country followed political affiliation at the state level, with many traditionally conservative states either never adopting, reviewing/revising, or repealing them (see Figure 1) (http://www.usnews.com/news/articles/2014/08/20/common-core-support-waning-most-now-oppose-standards-national-surveys-show). A large swath of the middle of the country is among those states. A mix of politically conservative (deep South), liberal (West coast, Northeast), and independent states (Maine, Vermont) have adopted the CCCS, with the vast majority not moving to review/revise or reject those standards. It seems that *geography matters*.

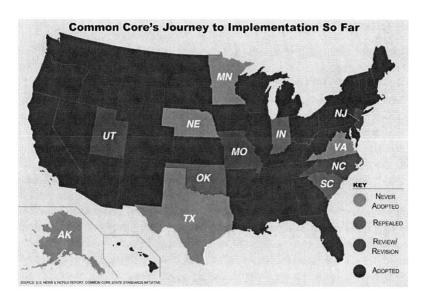

Figure 1.

More locally, states that have gone forward with adoption have addressed implementation of the CCCS in varying ways as well. For example, in 2013 the state of Kansas withdrew from The Smarter Balanced consortium, funded by Federal and State monies as part of a Race to the Top[2] grant, that was creating tests that aligned with the Common Core Curriculum Standards (http://cjonline.com/ news/2013-12-10/kansas-opts-create-its-own-common-core-tests). The Kansas State Board of Education decided to continue to use the CCCS, but after a yearlong effort, determined that the costs of implementing the testing would be too high. They decided to turn to the University of Kansas to develop testing at a lower cost. New York, on the other hand, has adopted the CCCS curriculum and testing with gusto, including providing teachers with an extensive website that provides the CCCS curriculum mathematics and English language arts modules by grade level and a Tristate/EQuIP rubric designed to help teachers evaluate modules that they modify (https://www.engageny.org/common-core-curriculum). In addition, the CCCS testing is linked to teacher and principal evaluations, with students' test scores accounting for 40% of teachers' scores (http://www.p12.nysed.gov/irs/ memos/2015/14-15-TSDL-Memo.pdf).

These two examples illustrate the effects of place on evaluation of teaching and administration in P-12 education, with teachers in Kansas and New York being subjected to markedly different evaluation systems based not on agreed upon standards, but instead on non-comparable performance indicators developed by groups with varying amounts of expertise in teaching and learning. They also illuminate how policies are enacted at the various scales of government involved in education reform.

Hand-Me-Down Responsibilities

Neoliberal policies result in downward pressures on responsibility for community development (economic, social, educational) from Nation-State to local entities (Entrena-Duran, 2009; Harvey, 2007; McCann, Martin, McCann, & Purcell, 2003) that construct people and spaces in part according to where they live, work, and learn. Federal and state-level mandates and policies are appropriated at smaller scales of activity, through which schools and classrooms, as well as communities, then translate these cascading demands into action at the most parochial levels where the variations are even more wildly different, including across schools (Ares & Buendía, 2007; Betts, Reuben, & Dannenberg, 2000), across classrooms (Harnischfeger, 2015; Rowan, Camburn, & Correnti, 2004), and across individual students and teachers (Kahn & Middaugh, 2008). Again, *geography matters*. The competing, converging, and multiple forces at play defy simplistic explanations but also result in multiple entry points for understanding how policies are appropriated differently and have material consequences for how teaching, learning, and reform are translated at local levels. Entrena-Durán (2009) reads these processes from a hopeful standpoint:

> The trend now is towards the search for development in specific local settings, a reaction to the current global processes of increasing competitiveness and transnationalization. These processes occur in a post-Fordist neoliberal context of socioeconomic deregulation, uncertainty and crisis … In this context, the search for local development can be viewed as an expression of the reflexive processes on a micro-social local level that, regardless of their explicit or conscious goals, are directed to give rise to ways of development led from and by individual or collective actors immersed in local-social structures. At the same time, inside these structures, class solidarities and antagonisms, … are changing due to the fact that they are suffering from maladaptive processes as a result of the current growing fragmentation, differentiation and diversification of class structures. A consequence of this is the reemergence of group and community links. (p. 526)

This points to activity that bridges scales of activity rather than a national versus global binary. It is a vector space of global/national/local production of people and spaces.

Similar processes of translation pertain to community development efforts that link to educational reforms, providing a broader context for understanding geographies of education reform. For example, Larson, Ares, and O'Connor (2011) describe how a collection of seven schools formed the initial impetus for a comprehensive community reform initiative that sought to provide "surround care" services to children and families (e.g., social service agencies, churches, local and State government, businesses). The goals and objectives for the initiative were envisioned to create networks of services centered on schools as sources of community health and wellbeing. Lipman's seminal work (2011) described a similar place-based landscape of reform in Chicago public schools [insert text on community reform. Further, Buendía and Fisk (forthcoming) also show how national educational reform movements involving the appropriation and integration of school districts into municipal governance structures can be molded by local nuances as state legislative and suburban mayoral stakeholders adapt and adopt certain elements of these national models and shun others. In all these cases, communities were seeking to respond to changing fiscal and political mandates requiring local entities to shoulder more and more of the responsibility for schooling and social health and well-being.

A Critical Geography Perspective

When it comes to on-the-ground work to negotiate the current economic and social policy context, coalition-forming around common issues (e.g., improving education) is the most widely employed (Alex-Assensoh & Hanks, 2000; Falcón, 1988; Lee & Diaz, 2007; Quiñones, Ares, Padela, Hopper, & Webster, 2011). However, the downward pressure on responsibility for economic development and provision of services brought to bear on local communities' coalitions results in a cauldron of sorts of competing demands, converging and diverging agendas, class and racial/ethnic conflicts, and exercises of power that are often premised on a zero-sum game around resources and agency to control outcomes, movements of people, and provision of resources. The dynamism and multifaceted nature of pressures can be overwhelming. Rather than succumb to reductionist efforts to reduce this complexity we argue in this book that critical geography approaches to studying and attendant understanding of the varied landscapes of reform can provide important and critical tools for researchers and policy makers seeking to make sense of these processes.

Understanding spaces and scales of reform. To contribute to research-based understandings and responses to neoliberal policies, we turned to critical geography to challenge simplistic notions of space that often accompany spatial transformations. Technologies such as zoning and rezoning, school choice, and charter schools and, more recently, GIS and asset mapping are being added to the tool kits reformers are drawing from that are influencing the movements and arrangements of people and things and that have implications for what kinds of people are allowed in which kinds of spaces (Freeman, 2010; Lipman, 2011). *But where are social science and education researchers?* Changes are racing ahead of us. A goal of this book is to bring together a variety of frameworks and methodologies within critical geography to help respond to new spatializing policies and practices with approaches that match the dynamism of educational reforms in current times.

The ways that varied social spaces are changing in response to population and policy shifts can be seen as waves of *de-territorialization* and *re-territorialization* (Deleuze & Guatarri, 1987; Lefebvre, 1991, described in depth below). Reforms

7

foster movements of resources and people, as well as shifts in curriculum, expectations, and accountability. Thus, when social, cultural, and material dimensions of space are treated as co-occurring and mutually constitutive (Buendía & Ares, 2006; Helfenbein, 2011), we recognize socio-spatial differentiations through which people are located within particular spaces and as inscribed with particular social orderings of who they are, what they can do, and how they can be (Anzaldúa, 1999; Buendía & Ares, 2006; Popkewitz, 1998). For example, in a study of a whole district reform focused on responding to rapidly changing student demographics in a large Western valley, Buendía and Ares (2006) found that literacy program choices were geographically distinct, with Eastside (white, monied) schools adopting a teacher-driven balanced literacy approach, Central City (mixed racial/ethnic and socioeconomic statuses) adopting a combination of prescribed and teacher-developed programs, and Westside (black and brown, lower socioeconomic status) schools adopting prescribed, lock-step programs. The locally defined terms Westside, Central City, and Eastside were recognizable to residents and educators as specific markers that masked the racialized meanings associated with people based on where they lived. Space and knowledge were intimately tied, as evident in the curricular choices made across the Valley.

Important and innovative lines of educational research have pushed the field to recast the processes of learning, knowledge distribution, and validation beyond the walls of schools. A range of different spatial metaphors has been proffered to urge researchers to explore the third spaces (Gutierrez, 2008), mobilities (Leander, Phillips, & Taylor, 2010) and networks (Lieberman, 2000) of learning and teaching– all alluding to new configurations of relationships, or scales. Such attention to the social and material aspects of space supports critical examinations of educational and community transformations.

We, too, embrace the recasting of frameworks and metaphors. Important to our perspective, cities and other spaces are not containers that 'hold' people and things; they are social constructions, as are notions of hierarchically ordered 'community,' 'city,' 'suburb,' and 'state.' Smith (1992) noted,

> Geographical scale is traditionally treated as a neutral metric of physical space: specific scales of social activity are assumed to be largely given as in the distinction between urban, regional, national and global events and processes...however, a considerable literature argu[es that] ... Far from neutral and fixed, therefore, geographical scales are the product of economic, political and social activities and relationships; as such they are as changeable as those relationships themselves. (p. 60)

Static notions of educational and community spaces as *containers* ignore that, as *social* spaces, they are actually dynamic and volatile. Dynamic remaking of relationships and the construction of spaces and scales are illuminated, as are the ways perceptions and assumptions around space have changed. Lefebvre's work on reconstruction and deconstruction of social space grounds our work, with reterritorialization/de-territorialization as analytical tools used to understand that dynamism.

Re- and de-territorialization of space. In analyzing and describing the ways that social spaces of schooling and communities are changing in this neoliberal, post-modernizing time in education, we find notions of *de-territorialization* and *re-territorialization* (Deleuze & Guattari, 1987) helpful. The manner in which processes of opening and reordering are captured in these constructs strikes us as a generative turn. Gordillo (2011) highlights these dimensions in noting:

> Deleuze and Guattari's use of the terms "deterritorialization" and "reterritorialization," ... broadly conceive of deterritorialization as a "decoding" of flows, a breakdown of the codes of control that regulate the flows of human action, setting them free. Likewise, reterritorialization is viewed as a "re-coding" or "over-coding," conducted primarily by the state, of what was previously decoded and deterritorialized, that is, a reassertion of domination over those flows. (p. 858)

Gordillo (2011) illustrates these concepts through research on Guaraní peoples' attempts to deterritorialize space in different regions of Argentina, an example of movements across political boundaries:

> ...in other areas of northern Argentina the demand for land titling by groups who identify as indigenous often involves spaces they already occupy, what distinguishes the conflict around La Loma is that the demands "for the rights of the Guaraní people" imply an attempt to move to a rural space under the control of more powerful actors. A similar spatial dynamic has defined the main Guaraní land claim in the neighboring province of Jujuy, ... As in La Loma, the people who fought for the lands in Vinalito aimed to move there from nearby towns and this mobilization also generated accusations by the regional elites that the Guaraní are Bolivians with no rights to land. These two struggles, in other words, have revolved around contradictory views about the type of presence that the Guaraní people have historically had in the region. (Gordillo, 2011, pp. 856–857)

Gordillo appropriated Deleuze and Guattari's concept of reterritorialization to account for indigenous Guaranís' realities of fluid memberships in various spaces. This is a productive move in that it acknowledges spatial transformations and reconstitutions produced by human activity, not just policies. He is also referring in some ways to the flat, horizontal spread of people that transforms spaces as they intrude (in the geological sense) into the existing matrix: "...rhizomic forms of connectivity [help] to examine these spatial reconstitutions as the product of multiple, horizontal, and expansive political practices" (p. 858).

An additional, related example involving education is of Roma people, who are traditionally nomadic in Eastern, Central, and Western Europe, moving across political boundaries and claiming their rights to inhabit those spaces based on historical attachments to space (Grover, 2007). Being designated as "state-less," the Roma deterritorialize space, breakdown codes of control that attempt to regulate their movements and sense of place-based identity. They also constitute a challenge to schools, as they are designated as a people in limbo, without official connections to place. Their presence disrupts what 'student' means, with often-negative consequences. Without a clear, state-sanctioned label, Roma children are over-identified as needing special education services (Hungary, Czech Republic, Bulgaria) or as unfit for school all together (Hungary, Greece) (Grover, 2007).

Border crossing within States is found in the steady increase of people of color moving into suburbs, breaking down of codes of control that designate those spaces as white and affluent (cite). In contrast, in cities in the US and Canada, Nielsen (2014, http://www.nielsen.com/us/en/insights/news/2014/millennials-prefer-cities-to-suburbs-subways-to-driveways.html) and the Urban Land Institute (Johnson, 2016)[3] report a trend in increasing preferences for city living among people born between 1979 and 1995. Convenience (living close to work, shopping), cheaper transportation, and the rise of charter schools are cited as causes for this shift. These shifting demographics are leading to major zoning changes, changes in property values, and demands for high quality schooling and manifest in decoding terms like 'inner city' and 'urban' so that they are no longer useful as shorthand to refer to people of color and those living with poverty. As De Lissavoy (2016), paraphrasing Peck, Theodore, and Brenner (2009) wrote, "At the same time that schools often abandon the students of color they ostensibly serve, their parents and communities are being driven from the city by a neoliberal urbanism that seeks to remake the urban core in the interest of White elites" (p. 353).

Re- and de-territorialization as dual processes have been in evident in many regions across the US. For example, a mayor in Western New York tried in 2003 to gain support for a countywide school system in a region that is highly segregated according to race/ethnicity and social class, creating stark designations of city and suburb (http://wxxinews.org/post/mayor-outlines-state-city). In Lefebvre's terms, his proposal would have led to a radical deterritorialization of space that surrounding towns and villages have claimed as separate from the City (decoding the City versus County/city versus suburbs distinctions). Those towns and villages' active resistance through voting and legislation was an example of seeking reterritorialization of their space (over-coding, reasserting their claims) that defeated the Mayor's proposal.

The relations of power that are implicated in such de- and over-coding processes may be seen as operating at multiple scales of activity. In present day circumstances that are characterized by new flows of information, increased connectivity across spaces due to technology and travel, and ongoing contestations over sovereignty and markets, we also turn to globalization as a phenomenon that is important to this book's project.

Globalization, localization, and the politics of scale. A strength we find in spatial theorist Henri Lefebvre's work is that while scales and spaces are hierarchically ordered, one doesn't supersede or subsume another. Building from Lefebvre, Brenner (1997) claims:

> Spatial scales (global, national, urban) and their associated forms of sociospatial organization (capital, territorial states, cities) are conceived as levels of the hierarchical geographical scaffolding through which globalization has unfolded historically: "Today our concern must be with space on a world scale [l'échelle mondiale] ... as well as with all the spaces subsidiary to it, at every possible level. No single space has disappeared completely; and all places without exception have undergone metamorphoses. (Lefebvre, 1991, PS: 412; p. 145)

> Globalization entails not only the deterritorialization of social relations into a worldwide "space of flows" (Castells, 1996) but their simultaneous reterritorialization into both sub- and suprastate configurations of sociospatial organization that are neither coextensive (identical in size) nor isomorphic (identical in form) with one another. This situation, and its massive consequences for transformative praxis, is at the core of Lefebvre's politics of scale. (Brenner, 1997, p. 159)

These authors' claims support work in this book that examines social space from multiple levels of analysis, as well as exploring relationships among those levels. Having provided definitions and examples of de- and reterritorialization as powerful analytical tools for understanding spaces and scales of education and community reform, we can now proceed to explore current geographies of school and community reform in the US.

Education Policy Driving Spatial Distributions of People and Resources

A critical geography approach has us explore patterns that have characterized the spatial organizations of groups of people. This approach challenges what social scientists have been asking over time in relation to the production of people, spaces, and divisions among them. The messiness that accompanies shifting patterns such as concentrations of poverty in urban and rural areas, hyper-segregation within cities and across city/suburban borders, movement of people of color into suburban areas, millenials moving into urban areas, etc. in the US requires theoretical and methodological tools that can help in making sense of such complexity. Policy and practice responses to these shifts in demographics in education and community reform are spatial in nature and entail complex politics of space and scale.

If we revisit the history of educational reforms leading us to the present day, we can see that legal signposts existed along the way that portended legislation and other policies around desegregation based on race in the US. Historical analysis can also illuminate how the re-segregation that we see today in the US has been an almost inevitable outcome of those same policies and practices. A little-known legal challenge, *Méndez et al v. Westminster School District of Orange County* (1947), serves as such as signpost, one that focused initially on one community in California, but that foreshadowed the infamous court case, *Brown v the Topeka Board of Education* (1954). That case, decided by the US Supreme Court, had an impact on a national scale.

Mendez v Westminster. A successful challenge to local level racial segregation that preceded the more well-known, national level *Brown* decision and set the stage for it was *Méndez v Westminster.* For over 50 years after the US Supreme Court ruled that "separate but equal" was constitutional in 1896 *(Plessy v Ferguson),* California school districts legally separated Chinese, Japanese, and American Indian children from white children. That ruling made segregation based on race legal as long as facilities were deemed 'equal' by administrators. Importantly, *Mexican Americans were categorized as "white"* in the 1940 US census. Still, more than 80% of Mexican American children in Orange County, California attended segregated non-white schools by World War II (Texas Bar Association, 2016). This pattern of physically separating Mexican American students was common in the southwest US, as educators judged that they were "not fit" for White schools based on their Latina/o surnames and their presumed lack of proficiency in the English language.

From a critical geography perspective, this case combined notions of place, designations of who was 'white' and who was not, and access to spaces of schooling. The lawsuit made its way through the California state court system until the appeals court's decision ended public segregation of Mexican Americans in the Ninth Circuit (covering most Western states, Hawaii, and Alaska). Some details:

> When the children of Gonzolo Méndez tried to enroll at an Orange County, California school in 1943, the school denied them entry because of their Mexican heritage. The same day the school administrators rejected his children, they admitted Gonzolo's niece and nephew, fair-skinned Alice and Edward Vidaurri. Administrators at the school district told the family that Mexican Americans needed their own schools because of cultural and language differences. … [This led to] the first class-action case in a Federal court in American civil rights history that would challenge primary school segregation….As the lead defendant, Gonzolo Méndez sued four school districts and superintendents on the grounds that his children and the children of other Mexican Americans were legally white, therefore entitled to attend white schools…. As a result, *Méndez v. Westminster* was the first Federal lawsuit openly to challenge "separate but equal" segregation in K-12 schools. (Texas Bar Association, 2016)

Interestingly, in 1947, the Ninth Circuit Court of Appeals affirmed the lower, District Court ruling but on different grounds that didn't challenge *Plessy v Ferguson* and its ties to equal protection as guaranteed by the 14th Amendment. Instead, this Court ruled on the basis of the school districts' implementing a practice that was not "specifically authorized by state law" (n.p). In effect, then, the Ninth Circuit Court limited the impact of *Mendez v Westminster* to California. It was not until after *Méndez* set the precedent that policies of segregating Mexican Americans in Texas and Arizona, also in the Ninth Circuit's jurisdiction, were struck down. Policy was linked to region, and was contained by political boundaries. As a result, in looking at a larger geographic scale, desegregation in the Southwest US unraveled and evolved in ways that were much different than in the South, as a result of *Brown v the Topeka Board of Education* that was decided in 1954.

Federal policy expands redistribution of bodies and resources. *Brown v Board* is a better-known case than *Mendez,* perhaps because of its wider reach, but also due in part to the Civil Rights movement of the 1960s being a largely African American-led movement. In this case,

> The Supreme Court's *Brown* decision was particularly important because it was not based on the gross inequalities in facilities and other tangible factors that characterized previous desegregation cases. In *Brown*, the Court dealt directly with segregation and ruled that even if tangible factors like facilities, teachers and supplies were equal, separation itself was inherently unequal and a violation of the equal protection clause of the 14th amendment. With *Brown*, the Court effectively overturned the infamous 1896 case of *Plessy v. Ferguson* which had permitted racial segregation under the guise of "separate but equal." http://www.civilrights.org/education/brown/?referrer= https://www.google.com/

The Court's opinion drew on an exhaustive review by the parties to the case of the history of education in the country since the ratification of the 14th Amendment to the US Constitution in 1868. The Court concluded that, even with that review:

> This discussion and our own investigation convince us that, although these sources cast some light, it is not enough to resolve the problem with which we are faced. At best, they are inconclusive … [Then, t]he curriculum was usually rudimentary; ungraded schools were common in rural areas; the school term was but three months a year in many states; and compulsory school attendance was virtually unknown. As a consequence, it is not surprising that there should be so little in the history of the Fourteenth Amendment relating to its intended effect on public education. (Warren, 1954, n.p)

Historical context was determined to be crucial in deciding the applicability of prior laws to present-day conditions of schooling. In other words, modern-day conditions had to be taken into account. Further, physical dimensions of space were not sufficient grounds for arguing equality:

> Here, unlike *Sweatt v. Painter*, there are findings below that the Negro and white schools involved have been equalized, or are being equalized, with

13

respect to buildings, curricula, qualifications and salaries of teachers, and other "tangible" factors. Our decision, therefore, cannot turn on merely a comparison of these tangible factors in the Negro and white schools involved in each of the cases. We must look instead to the effect of segregation itself on public education... Does segregation of children in public schools solely on the basis of race, even though the physical facilities and other "tangible" factors may be equal, deprive the children of the minority group of equal educational opportunities? We believe that it does. (Warren, 1954, p. 21)

In critical geographical terms, the spaces of schools involved not only material conditions and other 'tangible' factors, but social and cultural dimensions that had to be taken into account when considering access to quality public education. As a result, public schooling was to be equalized according to social spatial criteria, in recognition of the importance of mixed-race spaces of schooling for equal rights to education. Certainly, the focus of the Court was on African American students' benefitting from integration, not the mutual benefit for white students. Thus, public school policy and practices retained the assumption of superiority of white spaces of schooling.

Spatial aspects of de- and resegregation. Ladson-Billings (2004) traced cases brought by or on behalf of African Americans that, as she notes, made the *Brown v Board* decision all but inevitable. She wrote:

My argument here is that the case came at a time when the Court had almost no other choice but to rule in favor of the plaintiffs. Brown is not just one case, but rather the accumulation of a series of cases over a more than 100-year period. In 1849, Benjamin F. Roberts sued the city of *Boston* on behalf of his five-year-old daughter, Sarah (Cushing, 1883). Sarah Roberts *walked past five White elementary schools to a dilapidated elementary school for Black children.* ... Despite [Roberts' lawyer] Sumner's attempt to leverage the Massachusetts Constitution by arguing that school segregation was discriminatory and harmful to *all children,* the court ruled in favor of the *school committee.* ... Two cases in Delaware, Belton v. Gebhart and Bulah v. Gebhart (1952) ... won *limited local victories* that did *not have national impact.* (p. 4)

The highlighted text illuminates the spatial aspects of decisions that addressed where Black children could go to school and how the local context was favored over larger geographical political arenas. The connection to *Mendez v Westminster* is also clear: Contain the impact of desegregation geographically under the guise of favoring local control.

Brown v Board changed the geography of desegregation in its national sweep. Still, it put in place a policy that focused on 'end effects' (eventual redistribution of student bodies to reduce segregation based on race) rather than the production aspects of the law (the nature of the social spatial dimensions of school spaces). Attention to the ways that legal remedies unfolded in a context of overt racism and violence highlights the productive qualities inherent in judicial and policy approaches to desegregation. Viewed this way, *Brown v Board* addressed desegregation at a national scale, constructing it as a civil rights issue tied to multiple scales of activity. As such, it served as a remedy for local inequities, school district- and state-level policies and practices of exclusion, and federal laws serving the interests of the country as the Court interpreted their expression in the US Constitution. It is important as a policy/event that set in motion the social constructions of spaces/borders that we have seen in the last 50 years.

In actuality, *Brown v Board* was followed by a series of judicial and political decisions that shaped moves toward desegregation and that, over time, reversed them. Ladson-Billings (2004) wrote that, "Jack Greenburg (2003), one of the NAACP Legal Defense Fund lawyers who argued the Brown case, said, 'We knew there would be resistance, but we were unprepared for the depth of the hatred and violence aimed at Black people in the South.' … What the decision and its supporters could not account for was the degree to which White supremacy and racism were instantiated in the U.S. cultural model" (p. 5). Eventually, in 1973, the Court decided in the *Keyes v School District* that desegregation should be extended,

> in a limited way to the North and West and recognized the desegregation rights of Latinos. … [However,] The next year, the Court turned against desegregation for the first time since *Brown* in a 5-4 decision forbidding city-suburban desegregation … in Detroit and Michigan (*Milliken v Bradley,* 1974). The decision made full desegregation impossible in many large metropolitan areas. (Orfield & Frankenberg, 2014, p. 723)

The Supreme Court continued backing away from the goals of *Brown v Board* with decisions in 1991 (*Oklahoma City Bd. of Ed. V Dowell*) and 2007 (*Parents Involved in Community Schools v Seattle School District No. 1*) that allowed school districts to organize neighborhood schools regardless of demographic make-up, and forbidding voluntary plans at local levels that attempted to maintain integration, respectively. Further, the *Brown* decision and another lawsuit, *Sweatt v Painter* (1950), both focused on provision of desegregated schools for African Americans in the South; neither, though, addressed the rights of Latina/o students. As a result, states not identified by law as segregated and the rights of Latina/o students were unaffected. As Orfield (2014) said in an interview with USA TODAY, "Federal policy 'didn't do much outside of the South, and we didn't do much for Latinos ever" (as cited in Orfield & Frankenberg, 2014, p. 723). In critical spatial terms, large swaths of the US were subject through legal remedies to either forced movements of students and/or resources that shifted the demographic landscape or they were left to their own devices and the whims of powerful actors in school and economic policy.

History lives in the present. In an analysis of the lasting effects of *Brown,* Orfield and Frankenburg's (2014) work on re-segregation and education in the 21st century, with specific attention to access and equity concerns, provides a comprehensive analysis of federal legislative and judicial influences on where students go to school and with whom. They also examine the effects of those decisions/policies on contact among racialized groups. Their analysis gives an important picture of how reproduction of racial segregation has been maintained rather than dismantled and presents empirical evidence of what can be seen to underlie re- and deterritorialization in terms of policy and law that lead to physical distribution and redistribution of student bodies. The works presented in this book deepen their analyses by explicating processes at work, relations of power involved, and perspectives and experiences of people inhabiting spaces of educational and community reform.

In summary, the many examples explored in this chapter provide important new ways to understand space and scale as social constructions using theoretical and methodological tools of critical geography. We argue that this approach to the issues above illuminates research, policies, and practices in particular ways that afford scholars, students, practitioners, and policymakers invaluable insights into the processes at work. Having provided some background for the aims and timeliness of this book, we end this chapter with an overview of the rest of the volume.

OVERVIEW OF THE CHAPTERS

A central theme for the book is exploring critical geographies' methodologies and empirical studies as ways to address the new, changing landscape of educational reform and land use policy. In the sections and chapters that follow, researchers from a variety of fields and interdisciplinary studies (e.g., education, curriculum and cultural studies, feminist geographies, indigenous geographies, sociology) examine shifting social spaces to heighten understanding of a critical geography of education. They also show ways that relations among multiple scales of activity (local, regional; urban, suburban, rural; political, social, cultural) affect policies, communities, schools, families, teachers, and students and their educational experiences. Finally, the various methodologies employed serve also to highlight the ways that using the tools of critical geography can illuminate processes of reform and transformation currently in use. The summary of the chapters that follows introduces each chapter's unique contribution to our more general exploration of the geographies of education reform in the present neoliberal time.

Section One: Setting the Stage

The first three chapters in the book examine varied contexts of educational and community reform to situate the work in (1) the present neoliberal moment (Chapter 1, Ares), (2) in a critical geography theoretical framework (Chapter 2, Helfenbein & Buendía), and (3) in place – on Indigenous peoples' lands, with a history of slavery, and in the realities of the contested claims to space in the US as a site of settler colonialism (Chapter 3, Ares, and Tuck & Guess). Our goal with this section is to attend to multiple dimensions of social space and to the multiple perspectives and histories that are embodied in that space, and to orient readers to our purpose and point of view.

Section Two: Claims to Space

The four chapters in this section share a focus on ways that various groups navigated challenges to their rights to public and community spaces. In "Deterritorialization as Activism," Nancy Ares examines the role that space-as-social-construction played in the CCL, a community transformation initiative in upstate New York, with resident status being tied to a physical place that also embodied assumptions about who residents are, their associations to the initiative, and their relations to people in other parts of Lakeview. Understanding localized values, dreams, and historically derived relations of power opened up negotiations among the initiative's participants to scrutiny in ways that tie varied actors' motivations and histories together. Martin, McMann, and Purcell's (2003) three meanings of space – human attachments to specific locations, idealized images, physical organization in land use planning – provided a useful framework for making sense of residents' responses to the neoliberal policies of the CCL initiative. Further, this study foregrounds that these City and County level development policies were taken as responsibilities for economic development only. They were based in capitalism's emphasis on monetary capital to the virtual exclusion of human capital. Thus, urban planners treated the space, for the most part, as a very risky small business development zone, not one with particular strengths and resources. In contrast, residents and their allies' (but not all) attachments to specific locations and their idealized but still realistic images of the CCL focused on a variety of forms of capital, including human, relational, and cultural, as well as economic. Responding to the opportunity in neoliberal policies to take responsibility for and control of the CCL space, they fought to exercise their agency to shape the area in their own images and with resources and assets particular to their histories and communities.

Sophia Rodriguez, in *"They Called Us the Revolutionaries" Immigrant youth activism as a Deleuzian event*, draws on data from a critical ethnography of Latina/o youth activism in Chicago during the historic number of school closings in the 2012–2013 academic year. This chapter disrupts the dominant narratives of neoliberal policies and practices that are negatively impacting low-income communities of color by re-conceptualizing space as an entry point into excavating important narratives from youth as key stakeholders. Rodriguez uses Deleuze's (1990, 1993, 1995) relational space theory, through the concept of 'event," and critical geography theories of space (Buendía, Ares, Juarez, & Peercy, 2004; Ferguson & Gupta, 2002; Helfenbein & Taylor, 2009; Webb & Gulson, 2013) to understand how "youth cultural practices create social space" (Ares, 2010, p. 67) and contribute to recent materialist methodologies. Narrating "event" illuminates how minoritized and often silenced youth engaged in productive activism and developed positive identities in the face

17

of negative institutional labels. Youth experiences offer readers insight into how young people might "deterritorialize," and thus remake, educational spaces that seek to exclude them. Implications for how minoritized youth can enact positive, activist identities as they resist the forces of neoliberalism are discussed. Rodriguez argues that a Deleuzian theory of space enables educators and policy-makers to envision the positive contributions young people from low-income communities make in educational spaces as they defend the public institution(s) of education and schooling.

Mike Gulliver's chapter, *Seeking Lefebvre's Vécu in a 'Deaf Space' Classroom,* begins by outlining Lefebvre's three spatial moments—perçu (First Space; what we perceive through our senses), conçu (Second Space; what is planned, assumed about space) and vécu (Third Space; what can emerge in the contradictions among what we perceive and what we assume about space, transformation of social space)—exploring how the three combine to form a landscape that is constantly in roiling collision; reorienting, transforming, repeatedly opening up different vécu realities as new starting points… and then starting all over again. One such landscape is the UK's University of Bristol where an elite, hearing, Establishment university with hearing space based on the requirements of elite academia, housed a Deaf Studies Centre (CDS). The CDS produced spaces of a deaf perçu and conçu, by providing physical space, material resources, and symbolic support to deaf people. Gulliver examines what the spaces of that CDS looked like, and explores the ways in which tensions in exchanges between the CDS and the spaces of the wider hearing university hinted at the potential for vécu moments of transformation. He then drills down further to explore how one course and classroom within the CDS brought together students who were deaf and hearing. Although the confrontational situation between different spaces should have made CDS and its classroom places rich in possibilities for vécu transformation, in reality few arose. It is the lack of transformation (except at a personal level) that becomes the focus of Gulliver's analysis. What could have been transformative, he suggests—collisions between language, culture, academic prestige and priority, community accountability, and pedagogical method—were in fact beholden to the academic and administrative systems that had to be respected. Thus, conditions created to allow CDS to function and students to study and graduate, those different perçus and conçus spaces of the CDS and of the classroom, became invisible to the wider university. Opportunities for vécus were, effectively, defused by the larger University's (and therefore academe's) adjudication before they could have any transformative effect.

In the final chapter of this section, Nancy Ares explores story mapping as a participatory methodology for understanding constructions of social space. Returning to data from the Coalition for the Children of Lakeview (CCL) community transformation initiative, Ares and Pacifica Santos, a resident/activist in the CCL used a physical map and a walking interview to traverse two- and three-dimensional spaces so that Pacifica could narrate her embodied experiences in the CCL space and initiative. Story mapping helped make several dimensions of social space visible in this study. For example, Santos spoke about the significance of the CCL as a relational space, imbued with friendships, family ties among neighbors, and mutual responsibility for eachothers' well-being. She also spoke about it as a network of relationships. Santos privileged people over tradition, social over physical in talking about the prospect of razing an historic building, favoring job creation for residents over the physical-though-socially-valued building. In her work with the CCL, we examined the competing conceptions of the CCL space in Lakeview, as residents sought to claim central roles as people responsible for authoring and shepherding substantive reform. A critical geography perspective provided a powerful explanatory framework for what Santos and residents were saying and how they were 'performing' as resident/activists in the CCL space.

Section Three: Spatial Politics

The six chapters in this section address educational and community reforms in ways that illuminate the political dimensions of contests over social spaces. In particular, the authors uncover various stakeholders' struggles over the construction of people and relations of power involved in change.

In Chapter 8, Walter Gershon argues that U. S. schools have always been, and continue to be, neoliberal Jim Crow spaces that separate students and families based on color through racialized policies and practices. Building on foundational discussions of space and place in the field of critical geography as complex trajectories of history, geography, politics, and time, Gershon tacks back and forth between historical discussions of voting rights practices in the Jim Crow South and contemporary educational policy and practice. Examples include how annual standardized testing functions similarly to Jim Crow-era literacy tests African Americans and other people of color had to pass in order to vote and the ways in which school districts and schools within districts are gerrymandered along pathways that consistently favor more wealthy and Anglo families. Gershon similarly argues that schools have always been neoliberal spaces, applying allegedly universal ethics and practices in ways that at once avoid the exploration of contextual factors (e.g., institutional racism) and, in turn, place blame on individuals for systemic injustices.

This combination of already neoliberal and always Jim Crow makes it difficult for educators to more fully articulate the educational sea change over the past decade and a half. The same is true for the slow but incessant progression and further refinement of a system working with the efficiency of separation and segregation for which it was designed. Yet, framing the process of educational change through critical geography gives Gershon a measure of hope or, as he suggests, "if U.S. education is both a neoliberal and a Jim Crow space, they can be mapped" (this volume). And it is their mapping, the explicit cartographies of race, space, and place, that can be used as tools to at once call attention to and interrupt these patterns of injustice.

Gabe Huddleston brings critical geography theory to what he calls Zombie economics, a particular comprehensive school reform model, and school choice. This chapter is pulled from a larger qualitative study that uses a spatial theory and cultural studies framework to examine how neoliberal education reforms

19

interact with a Full Service Community School. More specifically, by deploying the theoretical metaphor of zombies to examine these reforms and their effects on those within the school itself, this chapter contends that static understandings of community work with and against neoliberal reform ideas such as "choice" and "accountability".

Buendía et al. report results of their study of Latino families' choices of where to settle as they immigrated to the US. The role of schools in the families' choices was their focus. Specifically, the authors examined the neighborhood selection processes of ten Latino families who settled into a suburban city in the Salt Lake metropolitan region. A burgeoning literature has explored parent residential choice and the relationship of these decisions to perceptions of school reputation and the expansion of segregation (Holme, 2002; Larreau & Goyette, 2014; Rhodes & DeLuca, 2014). Building and expanding upon this work, this chapter argues that school and school district reputation is not a factor in selecting a neighborhood in initial relocation for Latino suburban transplants. They show that process of neighborhood choice is facilitated and pre-determined by trust networks constituted of family members and friends whose geographical location in suburban cities defined the neighborhood and, ultimately, removed the school selection process from consideration. This stands in contrast to previous work that ties family decisions to school quality conversations, as federal policy requires school districts to publish annual yearly progress reports across community media. They also show that school attributes do eventually become a factor in Latino families' neighborhood selection processes, typically within a two-year window of resettlement for our sample. We show how parents' priority of seeking to maintain stability and continuity for their children within a particular school, not necessarily school reputation, was a key factor in selecting a home for purchase or for rental.

In *Developing a Critical Space Perspective in the Examination of the Racialization of Disabilities*, Adai Tefera, Cecilia Rios-Aguilar, Alfredo Artiles, Catherine Voulgarides, and Veronica Vélez examine the benefits of infusing a critical space perspective to address the persistence of racial disproportionality in special education in order to uncover and map enabling and (dis)abling geographies of opportunity. They ask: How can a critical spatial perspective advance the study of disproportionality in demographically changing school spaces? How can geographical mapping tools be used to supplement a critical spatial perspective to assist educational researchers and policymakers in understanding and addressing racial disproportionality in special education? The authors note the shifting racial demographics in historically white spaces—particularly suburban communities—raising new questions related to educational inequality.

Tefera et al. use the example of the suburban community of Middleton to set the policy context and illuminate the paradoxes in special education policy and the law as they pertain to racial disproportionality in special education, detailing how policies often reify inequities given the lack of consideration for the relationship between educational inequities and space. The authors then discuss emerging research that demonstrates the relationship between recent racial demographic shifts in suburban spaces, and the consequences of racialized or racially segregated communities on racial disproportionality in special education. The authors demonstrate how teachers and leaders contributed to material and discursive landscapes of exclusion shaped by a residentially segregated community. They then provide an outline of the possibilities and promises of infusing a critical spatial perspective with mapping as a powerful tool for researchers and policymakers to critically assess and address larger spatial and structural factors that influence educational inequities. Infusing a critical space perspective in research offers new insights into ways to address the persistence of racial disproportionality in special education in order to uncover and map the racialized consequences of (dis)abling geographies of opportunity.

Sandra Schmidt's chapter attends to redressing the inequitable school policies, arrangements, and curricular understanding of gender and sexuality through greater attention to the intersection of place and identity. Unfortunately, we cannot merely change the organization of space or create new policies and expect substantive impact on gender and sexuality inequity. The inequities themselves are not merely related to the distribution of resources but to the construction of the social categories and how they are used to organize schools. Foundational to the redress is altering the imaginaries of what is possible, specifically, the boundaries/binaries/divisions/ suppositions around categories of gender(s) and sexuality that mark the social arrangement of school. As such, this chapter proposes that these expanding horizons are very much vested not merely in the physical arrangement of but the symbolic/ perceptions of space, particularly as their gendered associations connect with and thus frame conceptions of gender/sexuality.

This chapter uses heterotopia as a conceptual place in which to reread the gendered play in schools. Reading particular school spaces and programs as heterotopia releases us from the binaries and characterizations that typically mark girl, boy, queer, and weird. The heterotopia supposes these spaces are the spaces of new formations of identities and attributes; thus, the analysis examines how, where, and when young people play with and (re)form their gender and sexuality imaginations. The work herein of young people, extracted from the regulatory functions of norms and adults, suggests that adults similarly need heterotopic places of encounter, wherein to consider how they organize and regulate gender and sexuality. Identities are not static; they change across time and space. Thus, policy and spatial reforms must be accompanied by attention to the concepts and constructs central to reform.

Finally, Edward Buendía and Paul Fisk's goal in the last chapter of this section is to expand the conceptual tools employed in research into mechanisms active in educational segregation by advancing a framework of scalar production. In its simplest form, scale is the bracketing of spatial relationships to define a level of resolution (Marston, 2000). Scalar production is a unit employed in human and physical geography scholarship and its adoption in educational research has the potential to allow researchers to attend to and represent the complexity of socio-spatial creation in forming educational segregation processes. The concept can attune researchers to the processes of interplay and realignment of local and national spatial relations of power that shift the political and educational landscape towards the reproduction of separate educational spaces. Importantly, it can move us towards identifying the dynamics at work prior to their coherence as durable structures.

To advance this framework, the authors analyze a suburban school district secession movement in a medium size metropolitan region in the western U.S. They explore the case of the Jordan School District (Utah, USA) secession to explore the methodologies of scalar production. The following questions drove the study: What socio-political elements drove the fragmentation of a large, multi-cited, suburban school district? In light of contemporary mayoral take-over movements in central cities, what overlaps and departures marked suburban mayors' roles in this case? Lastly, what implications do these initiatives have for continuing or rupturing patterns of segregation considering the demographic shifts taking place in these suburban areas? To grasp how processes of operational scale were destroyed and recreated we focused on the activities of mayors and spatial relationships with which they disconnected and connected in order to create a new order of operational scale that facilitated the creation of a new school district. As the authors show, school district secession movements are contentious, and involve the political fragmentation of an existing service unit. Members of a city or community seek to politically sever a relationship by redrawing district boundary lines as well as redistribute material resources of an established and, typically, large school district in order to create a new school district. While redefining school district boundary lines and autonomous governance structures are the objective of these initiatives, individual and group actors are involved in processes of redefining operational scale that involve the destruction and reconstruction of spatial relationships that expand beyond merely boundaries.

CONCLUSION

Given the complexity of education reform, we contend that critical geography theories and their focus on social, historical, political, cultural, and material dimensions of space add important explanatory power to work in understanding policy and practice. Neoliberalism, globalization, and growing demographic diversity are changing the landscape of reform in ways that shift responsibility for the education of children and youth to more local scales of activity. As such, opportunities to influence schooling are also changed, with both possibilities for transformation and dangers of entrenchment of existing inequities. This book covers a lot of ground – theoretical, methodological, topical, geographical – as part of that work, grounded in the knowledge that *space matters*.

NOTES

[1] Authentic takes on many definitions, e.g., real-world, connected to the world outside school (Newman & Wehman, 1993), integrated (Drake & Burns, 2004), related to professional practice (Salomon, 1997).

[2] Race to the Top is a Federal grants program that requires states to implement teacher evaluations based in part on students standardized test scores, to qualify for monies.

[3] However, see Forbes, 2013, www.forbes.com/sites/joelkotkin/2013/12/09/the-geography-of-aging, for contrasting analysis.

REFERENCES

Alex-Assensoh, Y. M., & Hanks, L. J. (2000). *Black and multiracial politics in America*. New York, NY: New York University Press.

Anzaldúa, G. (1999). Putting coyolxauhqui together: A creative process. *How We Work, 90*, 241–260.

Ares, N. (2010). *Youth-full productions: Cultural practices and constructions of content and social spaces* (Vol. 47). New York, NY: Peter Lang.

Ares, N., & Buendía, E. (2007). Opportunities lost: Local translations of advocacy policy conversations. *Teachers College Record, 109*(3), 561–589.

Au, W. (2007). High-stakes testing and curricular control: A qualitative metasynthesis. *Educational Researcher, 36*(5), 258–267.

Author. (2017). *Project 2061 – American Association for the Advancement of Science*. Retrieved from http://www.project2061.org/publications/bsl/

Author. (2017). *Student-centered learning – International Society for Technology in Education*. Retrieved from http://www.iste.org/standards/tools-resources/essential-conditions/student-centered-learning

Betts, J. R., Reuben, K. S., & Danenberg, A. (2000). *Equal resources, equal outcomes? The distribution of school resources and student achievement in California*. San Francisco, CA: Public Policy Institute of California.

Brenner, N. (1997). Global, fragmented, hierarchical: Henri Lefebvre's geographies of globalization. *Public Culture, 10*(1), 135–167.

Brown, V. (1954). *Board of education of Topeka*, 347 U.S. 483.

Buendía, E., & Ares, N. (2006). Geographies and communication. In C. McCarthy (Ed.), *Geographies of difference: Constructing eastside, Westside and Central city students and schools*. New York, NY: Peter Lang.

Buendía, E., Ares, N., Juarez, B. G., & Peercy, M. (2004). The geographies of difference: The production of the east side, west side, and central city school. *American Educational Research Journal, 41*(4), 833–863.

Davies, B., & Bansel, P. (2007). Neoliberalism and education. *International Journal of Qualitative Studies in Education, 20*(3), 247–259.

De Lissovoy, N. (2016). Race, reason and reasonableness: Toward an "unreasonable" pedagogy. *Educational Studies, 52*(4), 346–362.

Drake, S. M., & Burns, R. C. (2004). *Meeting standards through integrated curriculum*. Alexandria, VA: ASCD.

Entrena-Durán, F. (2009). Understanding social structure in the context of global uncertainties. *Critical Sociology, 35*(4), 521–540.

Ferguson, J., & Gupta, A. (2002). Spatializing states: Toward an ethnography of neoliberal governmentality. *American Ethnologist, 29*(4), 981–1002.

Falcón, A. (1988). Black and Latino politics in New York city: Race and ethnicity in urban contexts. In F. C. Garcia (Ed.), *Latinos in the political system* (pp. 171–194). Notre Dame, IN: University of Notre Dame Press.

Freeman, C. (2010). Children's neighbourhoods, social centres to 'terra incognita'. *Children's Geographies, 8*(2), 157–176.

Gordillo, G. (2011). Longing for elsewhere: Guaraní reterritorializations. *Comparative Studies in Society and History, 53*(4), 855–881.

Grover, S. (2007). Mental health professionals as pawns in oppressive practices: A case example concerning psychologists' involvement in the denial of education rights to Roma' Gypsy children. *Ethical Human Psychology and Psychiatry, 9*(1), 14–24.

Gutiérrez, K. D. (2008). Developing a sociocritical literacy in the third space. *Reading Research Quarterly, 43*(2), 148–164.

Harnischfeger, A. M. (2015). Identity construction in the margins: A case study involving non-conforming youth. *The Qualitative Report, 20*(8), 1141–1163.

Harvey, D. (2007). Neoliberalism as creative destruction. *The Annals of the American Academy of Political and Social Science, 610*(1), 21–44.

Helfenbein, R. (2011). The urbanization of everything: Thoughts on globalization and education. In S. Tozer, B. Gallegos, & A. Henry (Eds.), *Handbook of research in social foundations of education*. New York, NY: Routledge.

Helfenbein, R. J., & Taylor, L. H. (2009). Critical geographies in/of education: Introduction. *Educational Studies, 45*(3), 236–239.

Holme, J. J. (2002). Buying homes, buying schools: School choice and the social construction of school quality. *Harvard Educational Review, 72*(2), 177–206.

Johnson, S. (2016). Driving the reurbanization of downtown LA. *Urban Land Institute*. Retrieved from http://urbanland.uli.org/planning-design/driving-reurbanization-downtown-los-angeles/

Kahne, J., & Middaugh, E. (2008). *Democracy for some: The civic opportunity gap in high school* (Circle Working Paper 59). College Park, MD: Center for information and research on civic learning and engagement (CIRCLE).

Ladson-Billings, G. (2004). Landing on the wrong note: The price we paid for brown. *Educational Researcher, 33*(7), 3–13.

Larreau, A., & Goyette, K. (Eds.). (2014). *Choosing homes, choosing schools*. New York, NY: Russell Sage Foundation.

Larson, J., Ares, N., & O'Connor, K. (2011). Introduction: Power and positioning in concerted community change. *Anthropology & Education Quarterly, 42*(2), 88–102.

Leander, K. M., Phillips, N. C., & Taylor, K. H. (2010). The changing social spaces of learning: Mapping new mobilities. *Review of Research in Education, 34*(1), 329–394.

Lee, S. S., & Díaz, A. (2007). "I Was the one percenter": Manny Díaz and the beginnings of a Black-Puerto Rican coalition. *Journal of American Ethnic History, 26*(3), 52–80.

Lefebvre, H. (1991). *The production of space*. Oxford: Blackwell.

Lieberman, A. (2000). Networks as learning communities: Shaping the future of teacher development. *Journal of Teacher Education, 51*(3), 221–227.

Lipman, P. (2011). Contesting the city: Neoliberal urbanism and the cultural politics of education reform in Chicago. *Discourse: Studies in the Cultural Politics of Education, 32*(2), 217–234.

Mendez, V. (1946). *Westminster*, 64 F. Supp. 544 (S.D. Cal. 1946).

Nast, P. (2017). *Authentic assessment toolbox. National Education Association*. Retrieved March 15, 2016 from http://www.nea.org/tools/lessons/57730.htm

Obergfell, V. (2015). *Hodges*, 576 U.S.

Orfield, G., & Frankenberg, E. (2014). Increasingly segregated and unequal schools as courts reverse policy. *Educational Administration Quarterly, 50*(5), 718–734. doi:10.1177/0013161X14548942

Painter, J. (2000). Critical human geography. In R. J. Johnston, D. Gregory, G. Pratt, & M. Watts (Eds.), *Dictionary of human geography* (pp. 126–128). Oxford: Blackwell.

Peck, J., Theodore, H., & Brenner, N. (2009). Neoliberal urbanism: Models, moments, mutations. *SAIS Review of International Affairs, 29*(1), 49–66.

Plessy, V. (1896). *Ferguson,* 163 U.S. 537.

Popkewitz, T. S. (1998). Dewey, Vygotsky, and the social administration of the individual: Constructivist pedagogy as systems of ideas in historical spaces. *American Educational Research Journal, 35*(4), 535–570.

Rhodes, A., & DeLuca, S. (2014). Residential mobility and school choice among poor families. In A. Lareau & K. Goyette (Eds.), *Choosing homes, choosing schools* (pp. 137–166). New York, NY: Russell Sage Foundation.

Shull, C. (2017). *The American Latino heritage discover our shared heritage travel itinerary*. US National Park Service. Retrieved March 15, 2016 from https://www.nps.gov/nr/travel/american_latino_heritage/credits.html

Nancy Ares
University of Rochester

ROBERT J. HELFENBEIN AND EDWARD O. BUENDÍA

2. CRITICAL GEOGRAPHY OF EDUCATION

Theoretical Framework

The spatial turn is signaling what may turn out to be a profound sea change in all intellectual thought and philosophy, affecting every form of knowledge production from the abstract realms of ontological and epistemological debate to theory formation, empirical analysis, and practical application.

(Soja, 2010, p. 15)

Words fail. True in many ways, but particularly important as this volume takes up the question of what theories of critical geography might have to offer the study of contemporary education reform. In English, the terms space and place are used interchangeably and have multiple connotations from the specific to the abstract. This proves to be difficult as readers of the work are often unclear on important distinctions. Geographers, however, make an important distinction between the terms that proves to be a foundational starting point for the entire field of study. For these folks, one begins by conceiving of *space* as the physical, material attributes of the greater world that surrounds human experience or, perhaps more theoretically accurate, space represents the conjuncture of the spatial forces at work on people at any given time. While what most of us think of as geography has a distinct materiality—things like borders, capitals, mountain ranges, oceans, and rivers— an understanding of spatial forces also includes such socially constructed forces as economics, politics, and culture. A national border, for example, is certainly a spatial designation but, of course, represents nothing necessarily present in the natural world. It is a human construction that can change over time, may have varying levels of significance, and ultimately, holds different significance to different constituencies. We see then that space is both natural and man-made, holding both constraints and possibilities for the people that interact with it. As a result of this set of understandings and the failure of language, Shields (2013) proposes that it may be more useful to shift terms from space to "social spatialisation" in the hopes of highlighting the fluid and contested nature of spatial dynamics in theorizing and critical analysis. He suggests that particularly given the complications of how we make meaning of physical space, "it is not a concrete object, but a 'virtuality' or set of relations that are real but not actual" (p. 8). Emphasis here is again on the complexity of the interaction between people and spaces and provides a nuanced starting point for inquiry into the social.

N. Ares et al. (Eds.), Deterritorializing/Reterritorializing, 27–40.

The term *place*, on the other hand, has often been conflated with location but one can easily consider how various common usages trouble such a simple definition: "a place of one's own," "knowing your place", or "feeling out of place" for example. For geographers, the nature of place lies in a *localized* convergence of structural forces, experiential meaning-making, and a set of very real but often intangible relationships (see Shields, 2013, Helfenbein, 2015b). In this way, place can be characterized as a particular form of space—one in which meaning has been layered onto spatial characteristics and/or particular locations. Of course, this too is contested, subjective, and perhaps even contradictory as it is not difficult to think of particular places that bring forth special meaning to people for any number of reasons, both positive and negative. Theoretical work in geography and broader social theory—informed by parallel developments in marxist, feminist, and poststructural social theory—turns its attention to the processes involved in *space* becoming a *place* and the implications for the lived experience of the people involved in or excluded from that set of relations. Without question, any inquiry into such processes must consider issues of power and identity, socio-economic dynamics, and considerations of race, gender, ability, and sexuality (see this volume, Chapter 1); to take up social inquiry given these presuppositions is known as Critical Geography.

CRITICAL GEOGRAPHIES OF EDUCATION

In a growing body of scholarship, presenting geographic knowledge as scientific and objective—or perhaps more dangerously, that geography is somehow neutral or value-free—has been broadly challenged (Gregory, 1978; Harvey, 1973; Massey, 1994; Rose, 1993; Said, 1978; Willinsky, 1998). Insisting on the consideration of the ways in which humanly constructed discourse/s are impacted by and work to constitute the material world highlights that all forms of geography can either be reproductive, involve some form of negotiation, or potentially challenge particular formations of knowledge and/or identity (Helfenbein, 2015a).

> Seen this way, geography is inherently political and pedagogical, which provokes such questions as: what world does geography education make possible and intelligible, to whom, how, to what ends, and with what consequences? How does it position those it engages to inter/act (or abstain from it) in the world, at what scales, with what purposes? Who, in current societal arrangements, has the power to "name" the world and thus determine its meaning? What power arrangements underlie the discourses made available in geography education? Who does or does not get privileged by them? (Helfenbein, 2015b, p. 402)

The challenges presented here begin in questions of geography curriculum but additionally hold provocative potential for educational researchers writ large. As we question the categories and implications of geographic knowledge itself, the burden then lies within a new array of questions about the geographies, scales, and implications of those decisions on our analyses of educational contexts.

Critical geographers (e.g., Gregory, 1978; Harvey, 1996; Lefebvre, 1970; Massey, 1994; Soja, 1996) have challenged the fixity of terms such as space and place, suggesting a much more interrelated, entangled understanding that highlights how they function as sets of relations (Rose et al., 1993. As such, spaces and places are expressive of ideologies and relationships of power, processes filled with living politics and ideologies that shape who we are as people. Considered as coming into being through (and as) the intersection of "social practices, and structures, norms and values, power and inequality, difference and distinction" (Gieryn, 2000, p. 468), space and place become "the focus of critical social analysis" (Gruenewald, 2003, p. 628). For educational researchers and for the purposes of this volume, this theoretical framework holds the potential to open possibilities for re-examining how space and place are engaged in the lived world of education, education policy, and what they might promote and/or exclude as well as how they might be otherwise. That is to say, underlying questions for this approach might be:

- What are the understandings underlying current uses of space/place and what kind of understanding do they help produce and/or mitigate among students, parents, teachers, and the community?
- To what degree, and how, do they allow students to think, imagine, and be in the world as they negotiate a "sense of place"?
- How are schools *educative spaces* acting on and with those that inhabit them? How are larger spatial forces such as globalized economic shifts affecting the lived experiences of schools? (see Helfenbein, 2015b, p. 403)

Certainly, a good deal of work has taken up questions related to the role geographic understandings and representations have played in the West's project of empire-building and colonialism (Bhabha, 1994; Gregory, 1978; Jackson, 1989; Pratt, 1992; Said, 1978; Willinsky, 1998). What we are only now beginning to see is empirical research regarding the ways in which the legacy of imperialism and the colonial project is still present in educative contexts today (see this volume, Chapter 4). Scholars taking up a Critical Geography approach in educational research are exploring the lingering colonial concepts sedimented within the education system, both globally and specifically, in Western systems. For example, this work privileges an interrogation of the effects of European-generated terms such as the Middle East, Far East, the Orient, or Dark Africa and their role in determining a Western sense of center and the relations of power, culture, and language that continue to support it.

What do persisting European names of rivers, lakes, or mountains—ones appropriated and re-named in the effort to exploit, reconstruct, and control other lands (Crush, 1994; Edwards, 2001; Pahl, 1995)—both allow and inhibit in the construction of a "sense of place" (whose sense? whose place?) by different—say, European and aboriginal—students (Osborne, 1998)? Answers to such questions are important because how we divide and name the world within education has consequences for students' ways of seeing, for their mapping of identities and subjectivities, or the construction of their maps of meaning (Lambert, 2002) both inside and outside of the classroom. (Segall & Helfenbein, 2008, p. 273)

Here we see the implications of spatial representations within geography curriculum but, to carry the point further, rejecting the natural, or given-ness of these spatial categories and the processes that create them has additional impact in broader educational theorizing, research, and methodology.

Feminist geographers have also raised similar questions and taken up corrective analyses. Massey (1991) and Deutsche (1990), among others, highlight traditional geography's patriarchal view of the world. In an important work, Rose (1993) turns a feminist critique on Western spatial representation to note the existence of two types of masculinity in geographic knowledge: social scientific masculinity, which is characterized by a quest for abstraction—a detached objectivity which seeks to mask its value-ladenness—and, aesthetic masculinity, an assertion of male sensibilities to the human experience of place. Exploring the relationship between socially constructed gender relations and the social construction and perceptions of environments, feminist geographers have challenged the privileging of public over private spaces (Cope, 1997; Hanson & Pratt, 1995; Massey, 1994) the exclusion of the body as a scale of analysis (Butler, 1993) as well as a variety of binaries in geography such as man vs. nature, mind vs. body, male vs. female. Feminist geographers have stated that spacialities are both constructed and maintained by a variety of ideas about appropriate gendered behavior and values and that built environments are not only almost always surveyed, planned, designed and built by men, but that patriarchal assumptions about gendered identities are articulated through them. This, however, ecofeminists have argued, is not restricted to the built environment. Our notions of nature, they add, are also embedded in gendered relations, pointing out the relationship between the references to and treatment of women and nature under patriarchy and colonialism (Anzaldúa, 1999).

Similar issues pertain to race and the legacy of colonialism. While we have already touched upon how geography education operates in the division of "us" and "them," often along racial categories both in terms and representations used in geography and its education, attention to race also needs to become grounded in the racialized ideas and lives of students and how geography maintains and/or challenges them. This is because through the construction of race (as is true of gender and class), differences occur and are saturated in specific places, take shape over space, and "create spaces of inequality, fear, powerlessness, and discrimination" (Cope, 1997, p. 96). Issues to examine include how our conceptions of borders—both physical and imagined—work to separate groups, keeping some invisible as they are marked and stereotyped (Anzaldúa, 1999). In addition, we might re-examine how the places learned about within school curricula as well those in which students live (including their own school) are carved up along racial lines and how different groups construct identities (sometimes oppositional ones) within such places as they get "used." Similarly, attention should be paid to the role of landscapes as a "racial project" (Omi & Winant, 1994). That is, to how the "material quality of landscape—the tangible, visible scene/seen—makes it an ideal medium for making real and immediate abstract ideas in general, including ideas about race and racism" and the degree to which their use in geography education writ large "serves to either naturalize, or make normal, or provide the means to challenge racial formations and racist practices" (Schein, 1999, p. 189). In other words, educators make choices every day regarding the how places are represented, from whose perspective, and who gets left out.

In areas pertaining to the intersections of race and gender, possibilities lie in inquiry into "how gender, race, and other categories of difference are produced and reproduced through dominant understandings of what places and people are or should be and how ideas about nature, landscape and the built environment produce and reproduce difference" (Rose et al., 1997, cited in Segall & Helfenbein, 2008, p. 274). That is, critical geographies of education precipitate research on how education systems and the educators within them can either perpetuate or work against inequality based on race, gender, or other difference (De Oliver, 1998). Furthermore, as a critical approach takes as given the notion that cultural landscapes are formed and maintained by the views and interests of those in power to do so, sociological work emphasizing the way minority and marginalized cultures use, alter, and manipulate landscapes in order to express their own identities within the larger cultural landscape remains fertile ground for continued analyses.

SCALE AS SOCIAL CONSTRUCTION

In consideration of contemporary education reform, the question of scale often appears to be obscured amidst political rhetoric and lack of specificity. With the passage of federal legislation such as No Child Left Behind (ESEA) in 2002 and the Every Student Succeeds Act (ESSA) in 2015, one can infer that that the scale of education reform functions on a national level but, certainly, the burden of implementation falls to the states. An ongoing complication of U.S. federalism, education policy in general lies within the tension of federal and state control and compliance. Complicated by the historical notions of local control in education, the water is muddied further. For example, as part of the effort to train "highly effective teachers" and fill teaching vacancies in high-need areas, numerous alternative teacher education programs have emerged. Often proposed with global competitiveness as its rationale and with a national model that is presumed to be applicable in any context, one might see a college student in suburban Virginia recruited to Teach for America who is then trained in metropolitan Arizona to begin teaching at an urban school in Indianapolis. The implication of such a scenario is clear: context does not matter and the particularities of schools and communities are, at best, to be learned on the job and, at worst, not important at all. As part of a critical project, the assumptions that a national scale reform such as this one can be questioned along with the attendant considerations of who benefits, and in what ways, as well as what gets left out along the way. This leads us to consider scale as a concept and the ways in which it is socially constructed as well as constitutive of social space.

In geographical theorizing and research, scale has often played a prominent role and has been the subject of some debate, evidencing a tension between perspectives which highlight structural forces and those that focus on agency and human practice (see McCann, 2003; Martin, McCann, & Purcell, 2003). At its most fundamental level, scale refers to a form of measurement in the production of maps and spatial analysis—often referred to as resolution, marked from coarse to fine (Marston, 2000). Cartographic scale is similar in that it denotes the spatial bounds of the object of analysis and again often refers to spatial representation, while operational scale extends focuses on processes, relations, and interactions (Marston, 2000). Historically, scale as a spatial concept has been treated as not only given but immutable (i.e. a city is a city, a region is a region, etc.). In contemporary theorizing, notably with increased attention to forces of globalization, scale has been rethought in terms of social construction and rejected as an "ontologically given category" (Marston, 2000, p. 220). Brenner (2001) suggests:

> traditional Euclidian, Cartesian and Westphalian notions of geographic scale as a fixed, bounded, self-enclosed and pregiven container are currently being superseded—at least within the parameter of critical geographical theory and research—by a highly productive emphasis on process, evolution, dynamism and sociopolitical contestation. (p. 592)

Marston (2000) suggests that scale consists of three necessarily interrelated components: size, level, and relation. Coming from the perspective of social construction, her conception rejects the oversimplified consideration of size (e.g. census tract, zip code, county, etc.) and level (e.g. district, county, state, etc...) and emphasizes scale as relational within the complexity of space, place, and environment (pp. 220–221). This approach to the concept of scale then begins with three propositions: (1) there is no ontological given to scalar concepts as it is a human heuristic used to describe phenomena; (2) the stakes of the use of these heuristics have experiential and material impact on people—in other words, scale matters; and (3) these heuristics, as they are socially constructed, are complex, contested, and open to change over time. Marston suggests then that we come to understand scale in our analyses as rooted within a global capitalist set of relations. Again we see the turn toward complexity within a critical geography that recognizes that the study of the places we inhabit involves attention to forces at play, interactions, and the simultaneous blending of the discursive—meaning the way in which language provides the tools for social construction of spatial categories—and the material.

Certainly, Marxist approaches to spatial analysis have played an important role in the development of critical geography. Scholars such as David Harvey, Doreen Massey, and Edward Soja (while unique in project) all consider global capitalism to be the primary force with which to consider and reconsider spatial relations. A foundational body of work, Henri Lefebvre's theorization around the spatial within changing socio-economic conditions of post-Fordist globalism provides a way into understanding the connection of state power to the spaces of everyday life—in effect, applying a multi-scalar analysis that focuses on sets of relations. Lefebvre (1970) offers that as late capitalism coevolves with urbanization, social relations become more entangled, increasingly complex, and operating at multiple scales. He states "this space is occupied by interrelated networks, relationships that are defined by interference. Its homogeneity corresponds to intentions, unified strategies, and systematized logics, on the one hand, and reductive, and consequentially simplifying, representations on the other" (p. 167). For Lefebvre, this complexification results in increasing conflict for those left out of a social system only concerned with economic growth and the need for rethinking how these "interrelated networks" function. Operating merely at the macro-level scales creates the obscuration of lived impacts of such logics; which is to say, that marginalization and inequity persist outside of the analysis.

Brenner (2000) further summarizes the work of Lefebvre on state power and its integration with the construction of scale by delineating three strategies: (1) through regulation, planning and policy, and financial investment, "states operate to *mobilize space as a productive force*"; (2) in service of capitalist growth, the state serves as the "the most crucial *institutional mediator of uneven geographical development*" and intervenes at multiple scales; and (3) various types of state intervention by states serve to "*hierarchize social relations* upon different scales," creating a spatial logic around its practices (emphasis in original, pp. 370–371). As these processes become largely obscured, scalar categories tend to be seen as given rather than open to reconceptualization, ultimately limiting political agency. Interestingly, here lies the apparent contradiction and ultimate utility in the contradiction between both reifying scalar conceptions and embracing new forms in the service of state aims. Central to the analysis of the prescient Lefebvre and those that follow in this work is that, as globalized forces of capital expansion proliferate, state-based forms of power have been able to adapt and redefine the scale at which they operate.

The urban revolution

Cities happen to be problems in complexity, like the life sciences. They present situations in which a half-dozen or even several dozen quantities are all varying simultaneously and in subtly interconnected ways. Cities, again like the life sciences, do not exhibit one problem in organized complexity, which if understood explains all. They can be analyzed into many such problems or segments which, as in the case of the life sciences, are also related with one another. The variables are many, but they are not helter-skelter; they are interrelated into an organic whole. (Jacobs, 1961, p. 433, original emphasis)

Nowhere are the aforementioned processes more visible than in the urban context. Some theorists are intending to mobilize the urban—or perhaps, less problematically, the city as a productive unit of analysis. Certainly, the urban has been a historically important site for sociological work (i.e. Simmel, Weber, Benjamin, Park & Wirth) but it can argued that thinkers such as Foucault, de Certeau, and more contemporary critical geographers such as Massey, Harvey, and Soja consider urban space to be the frame within which to take on the study of broader social shifts and challenges. Sociologist Saskia Sassen (2011) has offered that we might consider the city as heuristic, or in other words, an analytic tool that enables a broader insight into much larger conditions. She, too recognizes the strategic inquiry into urban spaces as windows into the social, but intends to draw a much clearer line between urban processes and the state of a larger global capital. From issues ranging from housing and gentrification, access to finance capital, and political economy itself, she suggests that the political struggles of communities within cities are critical to understand, and represent, the risk/opportunities for people to participate in the shaping of the urban social fabric. However, urban spaces quickly become coded with the less theoretically efficacious study of social problems, noted clearly in the continued categorical struggle between urban and poverty, urban and economy, urban and globalization, etc. (Buendía, 2010). Once again, these obscurations provide cover for the actions of larger political forces and serve to limit possibilities for a broader public agency. Strategically taking up the city as an object of analysis—a move termed "toward the concrete" (Helfenbein, 2015a)—offers new understandings of the ways in which our social spaces are continually growing more deeply entwined in the process of being re/mapped and how material experiences are impacted by forces of the social, technological, economic, and political. Again, Sassen (2011) suggests an analytical approach to trends in this project,

> Among these trends are globalization, the rise of the new information technologies, the intensifying of transnational and translocal dynamics, growing inequality, and the strengthening presence and voice of specific types of socio-cultural diversity. Each one of these trends has its own specific sources, contents and consequences. The city is one stop in often complex trajectories that have many non-urban stops, and can in fact be global trajectories. But that urban moment is one where each of these trends (whether economic, technological, social or cultural) interacts with the others in distinct, often complex manners, in a way they do not in just about any other place. In that sense the city makes legible some of the most complex issues we confront. We can learn by just standing at a bus stop. (Sassen, 2011, n.p.; See also Sassen, 2010)

Suggesting not only an increasing level of attention to urban contexts but also a qualitative methodology that privileges the personal as well as the local, Sassen reminds researchers of the earlier calls offered by scholars such as DeCerteau, Lefebvre, and ethnography writ large.

The urban revolution then can be thought of as a shift in analytical focus as well as a descriptor for fast moving forces of global capital. It would seem that with this focus we can see the potential for identifying new capacities for the critical project of making the invisible visible, pointing to opportunities to build coalitions in response to these trends, and perhaps explore "leaky spaces" (Roy, 2003) and work towards new "spaces of possibility" (Helfenbein, 2009; Smith & Helfenbein, 2009). However, it remains important to recognize the function of much of contemporary urban policy (and perhaps even analysis) to obscure race and class relations within a structure of uneven development, the raced and classed underpinning and historical sedimentation of these forces, and to note the basis of its cartography in the scarcity required of the neoliberal order. In other words, take as *a priori* Fiske's (1991) descriptor of "the city is a mix of freedom and constraint" (p. 204) as well as Sassen's maxim: "the city talks back…[highlighting] the incompleteness of the city" (Sassen, 2011, n.p.). The urban then can be seen as:

constituted by opposing forces: on the one hand, there is the physical infrastructure of the city (streets, buildings, etc.) and on the other hand, there are the lived qualities of the urban experience that cannot be reduced to plans or maps. Making this (Bergsonian) distinction between quantities and qualities allows the thinker to recapture the very essence of city life: multidimensionality, unpredictability, irreducibility. (Fraser, 2009, p. 381)

For our purposes in this volume then, "Urban" as a term refers to more than a simple geographic category, it is "an elaboration, a search…a practice, *urban practice*" (Lefevbre, 1970/2003, p. 5). Certainly, some scholars have taken up this approach in educational research in various ways. A few examples would include: Tate's (2008) exploration of "geographies of opportunity" to explore racial disparity in K-12 education; Buendía and Ares' (2006) deconstruction of the ways "geographies of difference" are employed to both define schools and children as well obscure racial inequity in schools and cities; Haymes (1995) discussion of Black social movements and urban restructuring; and Fataar's (2013) examination the ways in which poor, Black schoolchildren in South Africa "carve" out strategies to navigate the social and educative spaces of the post-apartheid city. The implications of such moves lie not only in the theoretical but also in terms of the methodological as we consider projects within the changing formations of global capitalism. This claim however does not simply dismiss the ways in which the term urban is and continues to be racially coded; to ignore this reality runs the risk of further inscribing a social analysis that obscures the ways in race is foundational in the social construction of space itself (see this volume, Chapters 5, 8 and 11). This process also operates for other social constructions of difference including class, gender, sexuality, and ability/disability, although perhaps less explicitly than a deeply historical racial politics.

Globalization processes move through the process of disorientation (or deterritorialization), reorientation (reterritorialization), and mapping. For example, this volume offers that forces of globalization are at work on educative spaces— particularly urban ones—and the people that inhabit those spaces in new and consequential ways. Globalization can be seen as the pulsing extension of the contradictory processes of capital throughout the spatial realm. By offering the descriptor "pulsing" we suggest that these forces extend and retract—what Lefebvre calls the "incessant to-and-fro"—in the hopes of new markets, the reinscription of old ones, and the extraction of markets where there once were none, a point explicitly important to the connection to public education. Lefebvre (1970/2003) argues that fundamentally these processes follow the broadly conceived characteristics of urbanization. As these processes extend through the spatial, we see—sometimes slowly, sometimes quickly—the urbanization of everything (Helfenbein, 2011). This is to say, via Lefebvre, that the processes of global capital follow this trajectory in spaces that would not be considered cities *per se* but, as sets of relations become increasingly pervasive, finding spaces outside of those relations becomes difficult or ultimately impossible. Indeed, what is compellingly argued by Sassen (2014) is that we are increasingly seeing people and places expelled from access to economic systems as a result of new predatory formations within late capitalism. This expulsion results from the convergence of economic elites and the systemic structures—all originating in the urban centers of power—that enable them to determine who is "in" and who is "out" (see also Tsing, 2005). What then is at hand is indeed an urban revolution—both in terms of the intensity in which material experience is impacted by the convergence of global forces but also in the necessity for new analytics to make those dynamics visible.

On Spatial Justice and Scale

> *that the geography of the world is intimately entwined with the most fundamental of political issues: with inequality, with recognition and the evasion of it, with class and democracy, with—what we inevitably live within and are constantly remaking—maps of power.* (Massey, 2007, p. 23)

Soja (2010) argues that the project of spatial justice requires a multi-scalar approach that encompasses at least three levels. First, the politics of spatial distribution through borders, boundaries, and other legal and political tools can be analyzed through the lens of justice, access, and equity. Second, the localized condition is influenced through individual actors or institutions that may exacerbate discriminatory or privileged practices. And third, regional assemblages can both perpetuate and potentially work against processes of uneven development, necessarily attentive to both the global and local (pp. 8–9). Recognizing the spatial as relational therefore impacts how one takes up questions of justice and equity and rejects the binary of local and global within such concerns. Massey (2007) suggests that, "what is needed is a politics *of* place *beyond* place" (p. 15), intending to work on political projects that both recognize the contextual nature of the work while simultaneously seeing that context within sets of relations at other scales. She further states,

> Conceptually, it is important to recognize that the global is as much locally produced as vice versa, that an imaginary of big binaries of us and them (often aligned with local and global) is both politically disabling and exonerating of our own (and our local place's) implication. (Massey, 2007, p. 10)

Soja (1985) points to a critical social theory in which "being, consciousness, and action…[exist] not simply 'in' space but 'of' space as well. To be alive intrinsically and inescapably involves participation in the social production of space, shaping and being shaped by a constantly evolving spatiality" (Soja, 1985, p. 177). As Lefebvre (1970) observed, "we have forgotten or overlooked the social relationships (primarily relationships of production)" (p. 1) of urban contexts both historical and contemporary due to analytical work overly focused on time and history as opposed to space. By "spatializing" education research, the hope is to problematize, analyze, and address the contexts in which we work, hidden and otherwise, in new ways.

To return to education and education reform, two seemingly contradictory forces are at work in contemporary efforts at urban school reform that might be simply described as the global and the local. The global question in the discourse of reform is that of the global, or "21st Century", economy; in other words, how will students enter the workforce of the future? Pervasive to the current debate on schools and schooling is a rhetoric that revolves around the new conditions of a globalized economy and, although educational social theorists have commented on this for decades, that schools may be "behind the curve." Simultaneously, an increased rhetoric on teaching "urban kids" and, stated even more specifically, black and Hispanic students turns attention toward localized spaces and the particularities of certain populations. Small schools, community schools, a resurgence in vocational education, culturally relevant pedagogy, and charter schools are all offered as potential answers. Of course, education reform that embodies both an ear to the global workplace and the particular needs of the local community presents challenges that must be addressed by the "yes, and" as opposed to the "either or." In other words, the discussion presented here on critical geography and scale brings to light the failings of education reform analyses that choose the global over the local (or, less common, the local over the global) and resist the given-ness of such categories.

Critical geography—or, the geography of the "yes, and"—insists on the attention to both the global and the local but not only in the sense of assessing the needs of the future citizens and workers of communities, but also in the critical understanding of present conditions that students, teachers, and parents find themselves in. The localized context of job opportunities, obstacles to academic achievement, and even school funding are in no way separate from the responses to global economic forces by multiple levels of government and business interests. Urban settings provide the most condensed site for analyses of these processes and urban education reform exhibits all of the characteristics of a changing spatial ordering and prioritization, as well as the impact of new demographic and socio-economic shifts. A Critical Geography approach to education research attempts to translate these geographical concepts of space, place, and scale into studies of educational and community reform—a process that certainly has research methodology implications. Interjecting notions of space as dynamic social constructions rather than static containers, this work

> comes from the perspective that in this 'late' neoliberal/post-modernization era of education and land use policy, critical inquiry into both the hegemony of and resistance to the spatial construction of schools is crucially important. Specifically, we highlight work that reveals hidden inequalities of race, class, ability, and gender (among others) as well as inequalities and underlying assumptions buried within often-used concepts such as community, identity, place, and space. Implications and consequences of policy responses that are quickly changing the landscape of educational and economic development across the US and other countries need to be unearthed to heighten awareness of and support action to counteract their potentially corrosive and oppressive effects. (Ares, this volume, Chapter 1)

REFERENCES

Anzaldúa, G. (1999). *Borderlands: La frontera* (2nd ed.). San Francisco, CA: Aunt Lute Books.

Bhabha, H. (1994). *Location of culture*. London: Routledge.

Brenner, N. (2000). The urban question as a scale question: Reflections on Henri Lefebvre, urban theory and the politics of scale. *International Journal of Urban and Regional Research, 24*(2), 361–378.

Brenner, N. (2001). The limits to scale? Methodological reflections on scalar structuration. *Progress in Human Geography, 25*(4), 591–614.

Buendía, E. (2010). Reconsidering the urban in urban education: Interdisciplinary conversations. *Urban Review, 43*(1), 1–21.

Buendía, E., & Ares, N. (2006). *Geographies of difference: The social production of the east side, west side, and central city school*. New York, NY: Peter Lang.

Butler, J. (1993). *Bodies that matter*. New York, NY: Routledge.

Cope, M. (1997). Gender and geography: A political geography perspective. *Journal of Geography, 96*(2), 91–97.

De Oliver, M. (1998). Geography, race and class: A case study of the role of geography at an urban public university. *American Journal of Education, 106*, 273–301.

Deutsche, R. (1990, February). Men in space. *Artforum*, pp. 21–23.

Fataar, A. (2013). Students' bodily carvings in school spaces of the post-apartheid city. *Taboo: The Journal of Culture and Education, 13*(1), 11–20.

Fiske, J. (1991). *Reading the popular*. London: Routledge.

Fraser, B. (2009). Narrating the organic city: A Lefebvrian approach to city planning, the novel, and urban theory in Spain. *Journal of Narrative Theory, 39*(3), 370–386.

Gieryn, T. F. (2000). A space for place in sociology. *Annual Review of Sociology, 26*, 463–496.

Gregory, D. (1978). *Ideology, science, and human geography*. London: Hutchinson.

Gruenwald, D. (2003). The best of both worlds: A critical pedagogy of place. *Educational Researcher, 32*(4), 3–12.

Hanson, S., & Pratt, G. (1995). *Gender, work, and space*. New York, NY: Routledge.

Harvey, D. (1973). *Social justice and the city*. London: Edward Arnold.

Haymes, S. N. (1995). *Race, culture, and the city: A pedagogy for black urban struggle*. Albany, NY: SUNY Press.

Helfenbein, R. (2011). The urbanization of everything: Thoughts on globalization and education. In S. Tozer, B. Gallegos, & A. Henry (Eds.), *Handbook of research in social foundations of education*. New York, NY: Routledge.

Helfenbein, R. (2015a). Toward the concrete: Critical geography and curriculum inquiry in the new materialism. *International Journal of Curriculum & Social Justice, 1*(1), 164–185.

Helfenbein, R. (2015b). Geographical milieu. In M. F. He, B. Schultz, & W. Schubert (Eds.), *The Sage guide to curriculum in education*. Los Angeles, CA: Sage.

Jackson, P. (1989). *Maps of meaning: An introduction to cultural geography*. London: Routledge.

Jacobs, J. (1961). *The death and life of great American cities*. New York, NY: Vintage Books.

Lefebvre, H. (1970/2003). *The urban revolution*. Minneapolis, MN: University of Minnesota Press.

Marston, S. A. (2000). The social construction of scale. *Progress in Human Geography, 24*(2), 219–242.

Martin, D., McCann, E., & Purcell, M. (2003). Space, scale, governance, and representation: Contemporary geographical perspectives on urban politics and policy. *Journal of Urban Affairs 25*(2), 113–121.

Massey, D. (1991, June). A global sense of place. *Marxism Today*, 24–29.

Massey, D. (1994). *Space, place, and gender*. Minneapolis, MN: University of Minnesota Press.

Massey, D. (2007). *World city*. Malden, MA: Polity Press.

McCann, E. J. (2003). Framing space and time in the city: Urban policy and the politics of spatial and temporal scale. *Journal of Urban Affairs 25*(2), 159–178.

Omi, M., & Winant, H. (1994). *Racial formation in the United States, second edition*. New York, NY: Routledge.

Pratt, M. L. (1992). *Imperial eyes: Travel writing and transculturation*. London: Routledge.

Rose, G. (1993). *Feminism and geography: The limits of geographical knowledge*. Cambridge, UK: Polity Press.

Roy, K. (2003). *Teachers in nomadic spaces: Deleuze and curriculum*. New York, NY: Peter Lang.

Said, E. (1978). *Orientalism*. New York, NY: Vintage.

Sassen, S. (2010). The city: Its return as a lens for social theory. *City, Culture, and Society, 1*(1), 3–11.

Sassen, S. (2011). *The city: Its return as a lens into larger economic and technological histories*. Retrieved from http://www.eera-ecer.de/ecer2011/programme/keynotespeakers/saskia-sassen/

Sassen, S. (2014). *Expulsions: Brutality and complexity in the global economy*. Cambridge, MA: Belknap Press.

Schein, R. H. (1999). Teaching "race" and the cultural landscape. *Journal of Geography, 98*(4), 188–190.

Segall, A., & Helfenbein, R. (2008). Research on K-12 geography education. In L. Levstik & C. Tyson (Eds.), *Handbook of research in social studies education* (pp. 259–283). New York, NY: Routledge.

Shields, R. (2013). *Spatial questions: Cultural topologies and social spatialisations*. Los Angeles, CA: Sage.

Smith, J. S., & Helfenbein, R. (2009). Translational research in education: Collaboration & commitment in urban contexts. In W. S. Gershon (Ed.), *The collaborative turn: Working together in qualitative research* (pp. 89–104). Rotterdam, NL: Sense Publishers.

Soja, E. (1985). Regions in context: Spatiality, periodicity, and the historical geography of the regional question. *Environment and Planning D: Society and Space, 3*(2), 175–190.

Soja, E. (1996). *Thirdspace: Journeys to Los Angeles and other real and imagined places*. Cambridge, MA: Blackwell.

Soja, E. (2010). *Seeking spatial justice*. Minneapolis, MN: University of Minnesota Press.

Tate, W. F. (2008). "Geography of opportunity": Poverty, place and educational outcomes. *Educational Researcher, 37*(9), 397–411.

Tsing, A. L. (2005). *Friction: An ethnography of global connection*. Princeton, NJ: Princeton University Press.

Willinsky, J. (1998). *Learning to divide the world: Education at empire's end*. Minneapolis, MN: University of Minnesota Press.

Robert J. Helfenbein
Loyola University of Maryland

Edward O. Buendía
University of Washington, Bothell

NANCY ARES

3. TUCK AND GUESS' FOUNDATIONAL QUESTION

Whose Places Are We Talking About?

We placed this chapter at the beginning of the book to emphasize the importance of the question, "whose land are we talking about?" Indeed, the very question of ownership is one Tuck and Guess remind us is open to challenge. Beginning with this chapter, we are signaling to readers that the spaces that we are writing about in the book are Indigenous spaces that have been violently overlaid with colonizing practices, actions, images, etc. Further, Tuck and Guess have us consider the reality of Black peoples' history in the US, naming it a "slave estate" (see Tuck & Guess, this volume). Rather than thinking through a Black/White binary, they help us consider the messiness of dangerous encroachment, displacement, violence, and attempts at reconciling troubling inheritances. They point also to the conundrum emerging from involuntary colonization and immigration that challenges peoples' sense of self and place. This framing essay works through some of the historical and epistemological issues undergirding our use of critical geography theories to understand society and institution-building that are being carried out in the aftermath of settler colonialism, a type of colonialism that, through displacement or destruction of Indigenous peoples,

> is a distinct imperial formation…. [that] seeks to replace the original population of the colonized territory with a new society of settlers (usually from the colonial metropole). This new society needs land, and so settler colonialism depends primarily on access to territory. This is achieved by various means, either through treaties with indigenous inhabitants or simply by "taking possession." (Lefevre, 2015, para. 1)

This is not to say that we are in a post-colonial era—not at all, as history lives in the present. As Tuck and Guess note, settler colonialism and its effects are omnipresent. In this book, we hope to illuminate ways it is also evident in present-day social constructions and politics of space.

RACISM AND SETTLER COLONIALISM AS FOUNDATIONS FOR
UNDERSTANDING WHY SPACE IS SO CONTESTED

Tuck and Guess move us into important arenas as they trouble ideas of property, operationalized as land and bodies; relationships among Indigenous peoples, Black

N. Ares et al. (Eds.), Deterritorializing/Reterritorializing, 41–44.

peoples, and white settlers; and relationships to land. Colonialism, especially settler colonialism, rested on notions that Indigenous and Black bodies were, in White society, actually valued as property—inhuman—but still affixed as commodities to be protected and controlled. White settlers saw possessions and objects rather than fellow humans, and protection and control manifested in violent, inhumane, and callous treatment. The focus of a large body of scholarship, policy, and activism, this type of colonialism is endemic to Western societies, as is its role in the kinds of spatial processes and politics that are the focus of this book.

Fanon (1963) wrote about the omnipresent dilemma of spatial and ontological tension that is inherent in the residue of settler colonialism. He noted that, "The zone where the natives live is not complementary to the zone inhabited by the settlers. The two zones are opposed... No conciliation is possible, for of the two terms, one is [treated as] superfluous" (pp. 38–39). Fanon wrote about this in his work on French Algeria as well as South Africa and apartheid. Building on Fanon's work on dichotomous thinking underlying the differential treatment of peoples and spaces, Gordon (1997) situated colonizing spatial moves in neoliberalism's references to rationality/nonrationality: "Blackness...function[s] as the breakdown of reason, which situates black existence, ultimately, in a seemingly nonrational category" (p. 5), while More (2014), also writing about Fanon, stated that, "This apartheid world cut into two, this compartmentalized world inhabited by two different species, is a Manichean world of the good white and the evil black" (p. 8). Appeals to this binary of rational/nonrational give cover to colonialist moves to carve up space under the guise of progress.

Of course, these kinds of spatializing tactics are not confined to Africa or people of the African diaspora. Native Americans' lives, ways of life, and histories are just as fraught, though this is not as visible in scholarship and education as it is for African Americans. In spatial terms, material, bodily, economic, cultural, and social dimensions have been affected:

- The extreme disparity in the number of Native American people living within the United States' borders at the time Columbus arrived, approximately ten million compared to the approximate 2.4 million Indians and Eskimos alive in the United States today, is but one factor that illustrates the success of the government's plan of "Manifest Destiny." (Glauner, 2001, p. 912)
- On September 8, 2000, the head of the Bureau of Indian Affairs (BIA) formally apologized for the agency's participation in the ethnic cleansing of Western tribes (Shelton, 2004, p. 266). From the forced relocation and assimilation of the "sauvage" to the white man's way of life to the forced sterilization of Native Americans, the BIA set out to "destroy all things Indian." (Colwell-Chanthaphonh, 2005, p. 375)
- Whereas government programs such as boarding schools and missions sought to integrate living indigenous communities, the Antiquities Act served to place the Native American past under the explicit control of the American government and

its agents of science. This story of archaeology is vital because it helps explain the contemporary environment in which debates continue about the ownership and management of heritage. (Colwell-Chanthaphonh, 2005, p. 376)

Here again, concepts of people and their histories as property, as commodified objects, form the basis of conquest and genocide. Shared histories of these kinds of oppression and reterritorialization inextricably connect Black and Native American histories and experiences. However, the opening chapter highlights the complexity and messiness of differential experiences of oppression, including relations of power and patterns of resistance.

Importantly, settler colonialism as an institution and society-building process has been and continues to be an organizing strategy for government policy at multiple scales and in all parts of the country. For example, territorial acquisition law in the early 1900s in the US was applied to Puerto Rico:

...in the Insular Cases, decided in 1901, which emanated from tariff disputes about goods entering the United States from newly acquired Puerto Rico, the U.S. Supreme Court ruled that Puerto Rico was not a foreign nation but also determined that the island and its inhabitants were not fully subject to the rights and provisions of the Constitution. ...Puerto Rico was 'foreign to the United States in a domestic sense'. (Thompson, 1989, p. 102; Benton, 2004, p. 837)

The obvious contradiction of being "foreign in a domestic sense" was, one could argue, grounded in another binary—White and Other. Similar othering in colonization of Northern Mexico happened along the Mexico-US border during the Mexican government's repatriation of Mexicans from the U.S. in the 19th century. This example is interesting because it involved Mexican nationals who were "lost" to Mexico when the US annexed Texas in 1845:

...organized attempts to help bring Mexican communities back to the Mexican fold after 1848 ... as Mexican American Colonization place[d] the coerced and recruited movement of Mexicans to Mexico within larger debates over nation-building in the Americas. ... establishment of Mexican communities in northern Mexico should be understood alongside the establishment of Seminole and European religious and ethnic communities in the states of Coahuila, Nuevo León, Chihuahua, Sonora, and Baja California. ... This settlement in this multi-ethnic region made it difficult for competing European and American migrants to establish themselves and helps explain why Mexico managed not to become a popular destination during the peak period of European migration and commercial expansion.... [and] is evidence of successful nation-building, not a failure to whiten or modernize according to American norms. (McKiernan-González, 2014, p. 91)

This time the Mexican government intervened by claiming spaces in Northern Mexico through establishing Mexican communities. In critical geographical terms, this serves as another example of institution-building in light of the colonialist enterprise by the U.S. to encroach on Others' lands. For the U.S., this created a bifurcated landscape (Mexico versus the U.S.), but the social institutions that were assembled were very complex and schizophrenic (e.g., the labor market in Texas that recruited temporary labor from Mexico but was also exclusionary of Blacks). Attempts to reterritorialize parts of Northern Mexico by the Mexican government, relying on Mexican nationals' recolonizing these spaces, were important in rebuffing White and Seminole Indian settlers' attempts to claim space for themselves.

To summarize, accounts of changing demographics of varied spaces across the global landscape are held together by a common logic of conquest whose rationale rests on racist notions of White/Other (everyone who is not white is Other), Black/White (everyone who is not white is Black), and negative exercises of power. The attendant dynamic relationships among and between peoples are rife with competing claims to personhood and notions of possession of land and bodies that are incommensurable. We hope that your reading of Tuck and Guess' chapter helps you retain a sense of historical and present-day context in reading the remainder of the book.

REFERENCES

Benton, L. (2004). "Colonizing Hawai'i" and colonizing elsewhere: Toward a history of U.S. imperial law. *Law & Society Review, 38*(4), 835–842. Retrieved from http://www.jstor.org/stable/1555093

Colwell-Chanthaphonh, C. (2005). The incorporation of the native American past: Cultural extermination, archaeological protection, and the antiquities act of 1906. *International Journal of Cultural Property, 12*(3), 375–391. doi:10.1017/S0940739105050198

Fanon, F. (2004). *The wretched of the Earth* (R. Philcox, Trans.). New York, NY: Grove Press. (Original work published 1961)

Glauner, L. (2001). Need for accountability and reparations: 1830–1976 the United States government's role in the promotion, implementation, and execution of the crime of genocide against native Americans. *The DePaul Law Review, 51*, 911.

Gordon, L. R. (Ed.). (1997). *Existence in Black: An anthology of Black existential philosophy*. New York, NY: Routledge.

Lefevre, T. A. (2015). *Settler colonialism*. Retrieved November 16, 2016, from http://www.oxfordbibliographies.com/view/document/obo-9780199766567/obo-9780199766567-0125.xml

McKiernan-Gonzalez, J. (2014). *Mexican American colonization during the nineteenth century: A history of the US-Mexico borderlands*. Denton, TX: Texas State Historical Association. doi:10.1353/swh.2014.0082

Shelton, D. (2004). World of atonement reparations for historical injuries. *Miskolc Journal of International Law, 1*, 259.

Thompson, W. L. (1989). *The introduction of American law in the Philippines and Puerto Rico 1898-1905*. Fayetteville, AR: University of Arkansas Press.

Nancy Ares
University of Rochester

EVE TUCK AND ALLISON GUESS

4. COLLABORATING ON SELFSAME LAND[1]

If, as David Herman proposes, "storytellers use deictic points and other gestures to map abstract, geometrically describable spaces onto lived, humanly experienced places," then the subjective component of space turns it into an infinite series of authorships—or so it seems—wherein speaking subjects both define it and are defined by it.

(Hortense Spillers, *Topographical Topics: Faulknerian Space,* 2004, p. 535)

Do you remember where we are? No way where we are is here.

(Fred Moten, *Blackness and Nothingness (Mysticism in the Flesh),* 2013, p. 743)

We write to you from the middle of something. It may not really be the middle, but it is not the end and it is not the beginning. We write to you from somewhere, though as we write we are geographically dispersed. We write as collaborators in the truest sense – committed to one another's personal, political, poetical, and professional projects. But our collaboration is contingent (Tuck & Yang, 2012) because of how we are differently implicated and invested, and differently coded, by settler colonialism, Indigenous erasure, and antiblackness.

This chapter is for the most part, a reprint of a blog post we wrote in 2014 for the journal *Decolonization: Indigeneity, Education and Society* (Tuck, Smith, Guess, Benjamin, & Jones, 2014). We share it with readers of this edited volume to bring attention to the tensions of relationships to place and land, especially within settler colonial societies. Settler colonialism is distinct from other forms of colonialism because its main pursuit is land (see Veracini, 2007; Tuck, McKenzie, & McCoy, 2014). In the context of the United States and other settler colonial nation-states, that are also slave estates, the pursuit of land has involved the destruction of Indigenous people and societies and intellectual traditions, and the capture and enslavement of people from Africa to labor on stolen land. The collaboration between Eve Tuck (an Indigenous scholar) and members of the Black/Land Project began as a way to theorize the possibilities for relations between Indigenous and Black peoples living on "selfsame" land without centering settlers, settler colonial knowledge, and their epistemologies.

Eve Tuck and Mistinguette Smith, founder of The Black Land Project, met several years ago at a summer institute hosted by the Public Science Project. When they learned that they were both researching and theorizing relationships to land—Eve as

N. Ares et al. (Eds.), Deterritorializing/Reterritorializing, 45–56.

an Unangax ciswoman scholar and Mistinguette as a Black woman—they agreed to find a future way to be in connection and conversation.

Along with Allison Guess, Tavia Benjamin, and other members of The Black/Land Project, Mistinguette has worked for the past three years to interview and record the narratives of members of many Black communities as they describe their relationships to land *as Black people,* however that identity presents itself in their lives. The formation of the Black/Land Project as an organization was inspired by a central question: "why do Black people talk about their relationships to 'the environment' differently than people in mainstream environmental movements?" (Tuck, Smith, Guess, Benjamin, & Jones, 2015, p. 54).

Eve has theorized decolonization of Indigenous land (Tuck & Yang, 2014), Land education (McKenzie & McCoy, 2014) and the significance of place in social science research (Tuck & McKenzie, 2014). What is important about that first fifteen-minute encounter between Mistinguette and Eve is that they discussed the tripled relationships between Indigenous peoples, Africans-made-into-chattel, and white settlers (see also Byrd, 2011; Tuck & Yang, 2012; Wilderson, 2010). Jodi Byrd (2011) explains these tripled relationships using the concept of "transit" to explore "the multiple subjectivities and subjugations put into motion" through colonization and U.S. imperialism. Indigeneity and discourses of Indian-ness are used by colonizers to maintain control over land, while Black peoples stolen from their own lands have "functioned within and resisted the historical project of the colonization of the 'new world'" (Byrd, 2011, p. xix). We discussed these tripled relationships as antagonisms (Wilderson, 2010), but also spoke of the need for more thought and attention given to the relationships between Indigenous peoples and Black peoples. This is to say that the imbrication of settler colonialism and antiblackness was what sparked our collaboration – but more, our desire has been to supersede the conventions of settler colonialism and antiblackness toward another kind of futurity. Not knowing that futurity is what makes our collaboration contingent, but knowing that there are many futurities available to us brings us to the work. This chapter is meant to be in conversation with other Black writers and Indigenous writers on land, Indigenous dispossession, and antiblackness, but also Indigenous sovereignty and futurity, Black futurity and optimism, and again, land. The focus on land is due to its significance in the tripled relationships between Indigenous peoples, Black peoples, and white settlers. As Patrick Wolfe writes, "contests for land can be – indeed, often are – contests for life" (2006). The settler's quest to acquire territory required the elimination of Indigenous peoples from their land. Conversely, the presence of Africans on the land allowed settlers to increase their wealth through enslaved labour (Wolfe, 2006).

THE BLACK/LAND PROJECT

The Black/Land Project was founded to amplify, re-narrate and regenerate the relationships in which Black people engage with land, including past relationships, present relationships, and future relationships. The Black/Land Project has lovingly crafted interview experiences from members of Black communities in Flint, MI, Las Vegas, NV, Cleveland, OH, and upstate New York, among other places across the US. Interview participants identify racially as Black, as well as a variety of different ethnic and national backgrounds, including African immigrants, Afro-Caribbean, Afro-Latino, African American, and mixed race Black peoples. Interview participants have been diverse in age, gender and gender expression, sexuality, and in the amount of time lived where they live.

The Black/Land Project (BLP) has conducted its work entirely outside the academy and, until recently, completely separate from the codes and discourses that preoccupy academic inquiry. This is not to say that the interview inquiry project has not been conducted in a way that is ethical (it has) or systematic (it has) or antitheoretical (it isn't). Instead, the protocols and theorizing have emerged relationally between The Black/Land interviewers and the interview participants. Rather than bringing (outside) theory to the inquiry, participants and interviewers have engaged in what Allison has come to call a "geotheorizing" of Black relationships to land (see Tuck et al., 2014).

Eve, along with Brian K. Jones and Kondwani Jahan Jackson (SUNY New Paltz), began working formally with The Black/Land Project through an American Studies Association Community Partnership Grant to support BLP in organizing and analyzing their now numerous interviews (see Tuck et al., 2014). Along with this work, Eve also agreed to help bring BLP's work to new audiences. Part of the tension of writing to academic audiences has been how to frame the relevant literature and theory that interfaces so powerfully with what BLP has sought to do; it isn't accurate to say that BLP's work has been informed by the (academic) theorizing of antiblackness, settler colonialism, Black optimism, and futurity; yet, it is useful to presume that from wherever those theories came, Black/Land's work has come too. As a community initiative, BLP does not have roots in academia. Its emergent themes, however, are congruent with academic theories on Black peoples' relationship to land.

So, here and elsewhere, we engage theory not as an origin story, not as a genealogy, but because it may be useful in translating to those who read, or want to read, that theory, the many ways that Blackness persists in making relationships to land.

Empire/Settler Colonialism/Triad/Antagonisms/Fusings

Writing with Marcia McKenzie, Eve has sought to understand how, among other epistemic violences, settler colonialism has attempted to reduce human relationships to land into relationships to property, making property "ownership" the primary vehicle to attaining civil rights in most settler colonial nation-states. In the United States and other "slave estates" (Wilderson, 2010), the remaking of land into property was/is accompanied by the remaking of (African) persons into property, into chattel (Wilderson, 2010; Spillers, 2003; Tuck & Yang, 2012). The remaking of land and bodies into property is necessary for settlement onto other people's land. To be made into property, according to settler colonialism, Black people must be kept landless (see Tuck & McKenzie, 2014) and thus exceptionalized from settler communities.

These manifestations of property suggest multiscalar discourses of ownership (McKittrick, 2006). These include discourses of "having 'things,' owning lands, invading territories, possessing someone," all "narratives of displacement that reward and value particular forms of conquest" (McKittrick, 2006, p. 3). McKittrick suggests that "black geographies, while certainly material and contextual, can be lived in unusual, unexpected ways" (2006, p. 2). Environments and landscapes require the work of imagined possibilities, leaving room for interpretation. Drawing on the work of Edouard Glissant, McKittrick theorizes geographies of settler colonialism as rooted in non-blackness, thus "invalidating the subject's cartographic needs, expressions, and knowledges" (2006, p. 3).

McKittrick (2006) observes,

(This) reward system repetitively returns us to the body, black subjecthood, and the where of blackness, not just as it is owned, but as black subjects participate in ownership. Black diasporic struggles can also be read, then, as geographic contests of discourses of ownership. Ownership of the body, individual and community voices, bus seats, women, "Africa," feminisms, history, homes, record labels, money, cars, these are recurring positionalities, written and articulated through protest, musics, feminist theory, fiction, the everyday. These positionalities and struggles over the meaning of place add geographic dimensions to practices of black reclamation. Yet they also illustrate the ways in which the legacy of racial dispossession underwrites how we have come to know space and place, and that the connections between what are considered "real" or valuable forms of ownership are buttressed through racial codes that mark the body as ungeographic. (pp. 3–4)

Discourses and practices of making-property and ownership are central to the hegemonic relations of settler colonialism and antiblackness. As Wilderson (2010) observes about the United States, there are three structuring positions, antagonisms, which converge to typify relationships of power and place, ultimately remaking land into property. Each of the three structuring positions ("Savage," Slave, and Human in Wilderson's analysis) are "elaborated by a rubric of three demands: the (White) demand for expansion, the (Indian) demand for return of the land, and the (Black) demand for 'flesh' reparation" (Wilderson, 2010, p. 29).

Jodi Byrd's borrowing of the word "arrivants" from African Caribbean poet Kamau Brathwaite in place of "chattel slave," refers broadly to people forced into the Americas "through the violence of European and Anglo-American colonialism and imperialism around the globe," (2011, p. xix). This nomenclature is a recognition of the ways in which arrivants both resist and participate as settlers in the historical project of settler colonialism. The word arrivants helps to highlight the complicity of *all* arrivants [including Black people] in Indigenous erasure and dispossession, because settler colonialism "requires settlers and arrivants to cathect the space of the native as their home," (p. xxxix; see also da Silva, 2013). But arrivants may also conceal the unique positioning of Blackness in settler colonialism and the complicity of white people and nonwhite people (including Native people) in antiblackness.

Thus, settler colonialism fuses a set of (at least) tripled relationships between settlers/settlement, chattel/enslavement, and Indigenous/erasure. Following a discussion between Patrick Wolfe and J. Kehaulani Kauanui, Eve, and various co-authors, has written elsewhere about this set of relationships as a triad, perhaps even a triangle. Yet, as Eve and K. Wayne Yang have argued, this set of relations is tangled, and perhaps even more important for this discussion (though it initially appears as a footnote in Tuck & Yang, 2012):

> [A]lthough the settler-native-slave triad structures settler colonialism, this does not mean that settler, native, and slave are analogs that can be used to describe corresponding identities, structural locations, worldviews, and behaviors. Nor do they mutually constitute one another. For example, Indigenous is an identity independent of the triad, and also an ascribed structural location within the triad. Chattel slave is an ascribed structural position, but not an identity. Settler describes a set of behaviors, as well as a structural location, but is eschewed as an identity. (Tuck & Yang, 2012, p. 7)

Perhaps it is obvious that there is, again, at least a tripled relationship between these nonanalogous locations—but what exactly do these locations comprise? Identities? Structural pigeonholes? Flexible prism points? These questions continue to challenge us. In conversation with Leigh Patel, Eve has constructed some renderings of the triad as groups described by their actions, yet all of these are still actions committed by settlers (grabbing land, "eradicating" Indigenous peoples, bringing in slaves, etc). In K. Wayne Yang's teaching, he describes the triad as a rubber band, bending and stretching to accumulate and not/equivocate. Eve has written with C. Ree about the tripled relations perhaps being analogous to zombies, ghosts, and monsters (Tuck & Ree, 2013). Indeed, decolonization is not a metaphor, but we continue to need compelling metaphors and methods to understand the fusion of relationships generated by settler colonialism's relentless attempts to make Indigenous land and Black bodies into property.

Theorizing Antiblackness and Blackness

Among theorizations of blackness and fugitivity (Moten, 2008), blackness as value + excess (da Silva, 2013), blackness as fungible (King, 2014), and blackness-qua-violence (Douglass & Wilderson, 2013), the work of The Black/Land Project most directly coheres with Spillers's (2004) theorizing of Black spatial practices and McKittrick's (2006) theorizing of Black life as ungeographic. At the same time, the BLP insists on the acumen of Black people's narrations of their relationships to land. Seeking definitions of Blackness beyond accumulation and fungibility (similar to Wilderson, 2010, p. 59; King, 2014), the Black/Land Project has engaged in interviews to co-construct Blackness-as-resistance (James, 2013b, p. 68), and refuse the ever-circulating tropes of Black people as landless.

Fred Moten (2008) lyrically points out these creative im/possibilities of blackness as "thing," being an object without being and without value, whose very value lies in its resistance to the foundations of capitalist value, being, and thingness. Moten (2008) asks:

> What if the thing whose meaning or value has never been found finds things, founds things? What if the thing will have founded something against the very possibility of foundation and against all anti- or post-foundational impossibilities? What if the thing sustains itself in that absence or eclipse of meaning that withholds from the thing the horrific honorific of "object"? At the same time, what if the value of that absence or excess is given to us only in and by way of a kind of failure or inadequacy—or, perhaps more precisely, by way of a history of exclusion, serial expulsion, presence's ongoing taking of leave—so that the non-attainment of meaning or ontology, of source or origin, is the only way to approach the thing in its informal (enformed/enforming, as opposed to formless), material totality? (pp. 181–182)

These questions form a musical fugue of "Black optimism"[2] (Moten, 2013), akin to the grounded theoretical moves that The Black/Land Project (BLP) has made in deciding to attend to the questions that Black people ask and answer about their relationships to land (see also Joy James, 2013a, on Afrarealism). Regarding her participation as an interviewee in the BLP inquiry project, I.B. explains that her interests are in

> … relation to the genealogy piece and not knowing – what people don't know because they don't have access to that knowledge or it hasn't been passed down to them. Moving and transience and separations of families and all that stuff; that makes it hard to track. To know whom your people are and where you really come from and where your history is rooted, that really interests me. I wonder how much that plays a role in other Black peoples' experiences. Finding where they come from and who are their people. Because there is strength in knowing that kind of stuff. (I.B., personal communication)

Like many of the co-participants and co-theorists of the Black Land/Project, I.B. points to the importance of learning from the routes and roots of the presumably rootless, the geographies of those presumed ungeographic, and the genealogies of those presumed kinless.

Theorizing Land

When we say at the outset that we are writing from the middle of something, that something has to do with Black life constructed as landless on stolen Indigenous land, land as epistemology and ontology for Indigenous peoples, and Black narratives which recover relationships to that selfsame land. This is the tangled[3] inspiration for our shared work, and the reason our collaboration must always for now (in this futurity) be contingent. In the following passages, to help describe the something (not the thing [Moten, 2008; da Silva, 2013] but not *not* the thing) we place side by side some of the articulations of land and place—by Indigenous peoples (the first two selections) and by Black peoples (the latter two selections)—that expose the various "wheres" that we are.

This is where our women first planted corn. They have planted it again and again. Each year we have harvested enough to roast and dry and store away. These fields look after us by helping our corn to grow. Our children eat it and become strong. We eat it and continue to live. Our corn draws life from this earth and we draw life from our corn. This earth is part of us! We are of this place ... We should name ourselves for this place! ... You see, their names for themselves are really the names of their places. This is how they were known, to others and to themselves. They were known by their places. This is how they are still known. (Charles Henry [Apache] as quoted in Basso, 1996, p. 21; ellipses inserted)

Land is our mother. *This is not a metaphor*. For the Native Hawaiians speaking of knowledge, land was the central theme that drew forth all others. You came from a place. You grew in a place and you had a relationship with a place. This is an epistemological idea... One does not simply learn about land, we learn best from land. (Manulani Meyer [Kanaka Maoli], 2008, p. 219, italics original; ellipses inserted)

Spatial practice, written on by climate and ideology, as well as history and geography, is so impressed by human bodies *in relations* that it is fair to say that, given the year, one could tell how he or she "felt" about the Mississippi, either vicariously or experientially—the Mississippi of the "Trail of Tears," 1838, the Mississippi of the great floods of 1927 and 1993, the Mississippi of summer 1980, when I crossed the river from the west, en route to Memphis, at the end of a honeymoon, the Mississippi of the Golden Arch of St. Louis, the Mississippi of 2003 and the official opening of the Louis Armstrong Memorial, Algiers Landing, New Orleans. Of the three dimensions of *locatedness*, the *place* of the Mississippi, as of any other topographically representable space, would express its thickest solidity of meaning because it is the scenic apparatus that bristles with "man/woman," "race," "class," "region," and the long arcs of desire in which the sexualities are prolonged and declared; the site of the emblematic and mystic chords of the memorial, place therefore defines what Hannah Arendt calls "the location of human activities" (1958, p. 73), the closest space, the *topos* with an intimate name. (Hortense Spillers, 2004, pp. 558–559)

You know we often don't talk about it. I think that there is a profound relationship between people of African descent and the land because we come from a people that didn't really look on land and ownership as being the way we approach material gains here. I think that the relationship of people to land is a part of who we are. In other words, I think African Americans coming from Africa, we came from a communal relationship among us as people, but also on relating to that which nurtures us and supports us. So the relationship with land was very organic in my opinion. It meant that we had a very personal relationship—almost spiritual—a kind of respect for it and an understanding that there is a relationship between us and land. …[Native peoples] used land like water. It was fluid. Depending on which cultures you look at, whether they are particularly stable people or wanderers what have you, the relationship with land was very important. I think that we see some of that in people who are farmers, who worked the land. But people who live in cities and buy condos and whatnot, we don't see land in that way at all. There isn't that relationship. But I do think that, particularly people of color, and certainly Africans and Native peoples, land is not just simply dirt. It's not just simply space and stuff. It is a part of who we are. I think it is part of how we define ourselves. It really is. (T.G. [speaking on the Black/Land Project,] personal communication)

Multiple meanings of place emerge from the passages above. These meanings include the significance of knowing in relation to place, the manifold nature of names and naming, and identity. Land is seen as a source of knowledge and instruction, and the development of a relationship to land is linked to knowledge production and to self-identity. The names given to places convey their importance as sites of selfhood and understanding, evidenced by fluidity between names of people and names of places.

Blackness as (not) Nowhere: Fantasy in the Hold

Moten (2013), reading Wilderson (2010) explains that the settler and "the savage," unlike the slave, have been afforded cartographic practice. Wilderson notes of the settler and the savage: "although at every scale their maps are radically incompatible, their respective 'mapness' is never in question" (p. 181). The "capacity for cartographic coherence … secures subjectivity for both the Settler and the 'Savage'" (p. 181). Denied a cartographic practice, Moten observes that the interplay between thingliness and nothingness that relates to blackness plays itself out "outside and against the grain of the very idea of self-determination—in the unmapped and unmappable immanence of undercommon sociality" (Moten, 2013, p. 752). Moten calls this playing out "fantasy in the hold" (p. 84). The "hold" is a holding of movement—of "nothing yet and already" objects (Harney & Moten, p. 93) and the hold of the ship (Harney & Moten, p. 94)—suspended in dislocation.

Yet, the participants in the Black/Land interviews press against this suspension, this dislocation. They are inhering a different logic/logistic, one that insists upon the fullness of an exclusive Black geography. T. G. describes the substance of Blackness in place:

The issue is trying to find richness. I mean let's face it, when I'm going to get a haircut, I know where I'm going. I'm not going down to the shopping center. I'm going back to the hood where they cut hair. You get in a barbershop and in the course of two hours in the barbershop, you've solved all the problems of the world because we have all the answers. (T. G., personal communication)

In the interview, T.G. unpacks his decision to continually go back to the *hood* within the context of anti-black development strategies, which, under the guise of increasing the "diversity" of a neighborhood, trick away Black cartographic coherence. Yet, T. G. also suggests that in Blackness, there are endless possibilities. Likewise, Moten asks

Can this sharing of a life in homelessness, this interplay of the refusal of what has been refused and consent, this undercommon appositionality, be a place from which to know, a place out of which emerges neither self-consciousness nor knowledge of the other but an improvisation that proceeds from somewhere on the other side of an unasked question? But not simply to be among one's own; rather, also, to live among one's own in dispossession, to live among the ones who cannot own, the ones who have nothing and who, in having nothing, have everything. (Moten, 2013, p. 756)

Black geographies have been relegated to the hold because of settler constructions of property and scarcity. In this, Black people become viewed by white settlers as place-holders on stolen Indigenous land. The truth is, white settlers have no problem *giving* Indigenous land to Black people, until they want it back. S.P. recalls:

What's also very interesting is that we bought in to this neighborhood where the houses were going for an average of $250,000 before we moved in. When we moved in, they were under $100,000. So you had this influx of people of color buying in and you had this rush of people wanting to sell as the neighborhood began to look different. (S.P., personal communication)

S.P. later explains how the phenomenon of white flight has allowed other people to move in and, as S.P. puts it, "make roots" in a new location.

For The Black/Land Project, land is not just about what is owned. Ownership, according to the storytellers who contribute to the BLP, is not the most important relationship to land. Mistinguette recalls one interviewee who said, "land ownership is a temporary and revokable agreement between you and the government." People often describe their relationship to land "as something that owns them."

Blackness as *not* nowhere means that Black claims to place happen somewhere, on selfsame land. In this regard, struggles against dislocation and gentrification cannot be warranted as the antidote to nowhereness. Not nowhere also evokes the Black doubleconsciousness of unfounded yet found relationships to selfsame land—similar to the afropessimist optimism of Moten, the wisdom of some BLP participants who identify the Black desires to be *not* nowhere without becoming a settler somewhere.

Black dislocation within the settler state is always an unfinished and incomplete project. Policing tactics, gentrification, vigilantism, and political isolation find justification in the settler colonial truism that Black people should not be where white settlers want to be. Yet the struggle to resolve Black dislocation can obscure the fact of Indigenous erasure and resilient, radical relationship to that selfsame land. There isn't something easy to say about this.

In connecting with lived experience through the recording of individual narratives, the Black/Land Project explores the endless possibilities of Blackness. This is part of the work of imagining Black geographies as "a place from which to know" (Moten, 2013, p. 756).

Decolonial Futurity at the Henceforward

Henceforward, the interests of one will be the interests of all, for in concrete fact *everyone* will be discovered by the troops, *everyone* will be massacred— or *everyone* will be saved. (Frantz Fanon, *The Wretched of the Earth*)

Writing about the process of decolonization and the search for a Black cyborg, Joy James meditates on the saliency of the word *henceforward* in these lines from Fanon (1963). Henceforward is "both exhortation and puzzle" (James, 2013b, p. 58) referring to a (later) pinpointable time and space in which the turn toward mass resistance to oppression materializes. Connecting the henceforward with what we have written elsewhere about futurity, it is the future that is made possible in the present, it is the time and space in which we can tumble into something that will be arranged differently, coded differently, so that our locations and labors are more than just who we are to the settler. Henceforward is the start of the future now. James tells us that for Fanon, decolonization, at minimum, means that the colonized will change places with the colonizer. What decolonization can be at maximum remains to be seen, but for it to be more than merely a change in personnel, this requires the colonized to "have visions rather than mere dreams" (James, 2013b, p. 64). For James, it all hinges on the henceforward because, without the henceforward, there is only mutually assured destruction.

We write to you from the middle of the henceforward, from the middle of the rage against the hold.

NOTES

1   Thank you to Deanna Del Vecchio for providing useful editing and language in the reconfiguration of the original blog post into a chapter.

2   Moten writes five years later, "I have thought long and hard, in the wake of their [Wilderson and Sexton's Afro-pessimism] work, in a kind of echo of Bob Marley's question, about whether blackness could be loved; there seems to be a growing consensus that analytic precision does not allow for such a flight of fancy, such romance, but I remain under the impression, and devoted to the impression, that analytic precision is, in fact, a function of such fancy... Like Curtis Mayfield, however, I do plan to

stay a believer. This is to say, again like Mayfield, that I plan to stay a black motherfucker" (Moten, 2013, p. 738; ellipses inserted).

³   This is one of the key differentiations that Wilderson (2010) makes between the Slave and the Savage – The Savage, though a "genocided object" (p. 51) is afforded an ontology (afforded by a genealogy derived from land, presumably, or at least prior occupation of it) whereas the Slave, positioned within a grammar of suffering (p. 11), is denied an ontology so long as she is denied freedom. The Black/Land Project's work takes up an entirely different line of suppositions.

REFERENCES

Basso, K. H. (1996). *Wisdom sits in places: Landscape and language among the western Apache.* Albuquerque, NM: University of New Mexico Press.

Byrd, J. A. (2011). *The transit of empire: Indigenous critiques of colonialism.* Minneapolis, MN: University of Minnesota Press.

Da Silva, D. F. (2013). To be announced: Radical praxis or knowing (at) the limits of justice. *Social Text, 31*(114), 43–62.

Douglass, P., & Wilderson, F. (2013). The violence of presence: Metaphysics in a blackened world. *The Black Scholar, 43*(4), 117–123.

Herman, D. (2004, April 22–25). *Points, spaces, and places: The functions of gesture in everyday storytelling.* Meeting of the Society for the Study of Narrative Literature. University of Vermont, Burlington.

King, T. (2014, June 10). Labor's aphasia: Toward antiblackness as constitutive of settler colonialism. *Decolonization, Indigeneity, and Society.*

James, J. (2013a). Afrarealism and the Black matrix: Maroon philosophy at democracy's border. *The Black Scholar, 43*(4), 124–131.

James, J. (2013b). "Concerning violence": Frantz Fanon's rebel intellectual in search of a Black cyborg. *South Atlantic Quarterly, 112*(1), 57–70.

McKittrick, K. (2006). *Demonic grounds: Black women and the cartographies of struggle.* Minneapolis, MN: University of Minnesota Press.

Meyer, M. A. (2008). Hawaiian epistemology and the triangulation of meaning. In K. Denzin, Y. S. Lincoln, & L. T. Smith (Eds.), *Handbook of critical and indigenous methodologies* (pp. 217–232). Thousand Oaks, CA: Sage.

Moten, F. (2008). The case of blackness. *Criticism, 50*(2), 177–218.

Moten, F. (2013). Blackness and nothingness (mysticism in the flesh). *South Atlantic Quarterly, 112*(4), 737–780. doi:10.1215/00382876-2345261

Spillers, H. (2003). *Black and White in color: Essays on American literature and culture.* Chicago, IL: University of Chicago Press.

Spillers, H. J. (2004). Topographical topics: Faulknerian space. *Mississippi Quarterly, 57*(4), 535–568.

Tuck, E., & McKenzie, M. (2015). *Place in research: Theory, methodology, and methods.* New York, NY: Routledge.

Tuck, E., & Ree, C. (2013). A glossary of haunting. In S. H. Jones, T. E. Adams, & C. Ellis (Eds.), *Handbook of autoethnography* (pp. 639–658). Walnut Creek, CA: Left Coast Press, Inc.

Tuck, E., & Yang, K. W. (2012). Decolonization is not a metaphor. *Decolonization: Indigeneity, Education and Society, 1*(1), 1–40.

Tuck, E., McKenzie, M., & McCoy, K. (2014). Land education: Indigenous, post-colonial, and decolonizing perspectives on place and environmental education research. *Environmental Education Research, 20*(1), 1–23.

Tuck, E., Smith, M., Guess, A. M., Benjamin, T., & Jones, B. K. (2014). Geotheorizing Black/land: Contestations and contingent collaborations. *Departures in Critical Qualitative Research, 3*(1), 52–74.

Veracini, L. (2007). Settler colonialism and decolonisation. *Borderlands e-journal, 6*(3).

Wilderson, F. (2010). *Red, White, and Black: Cinema and the structure of US antagonisms.* Durham, NC: Duke University Press.

Wolfe, P. (2006). Settler colonialism and the elimination of the native. *Journal of Genocide Research, 8*(4), 387–409.

Eve Tuck
Ontario Institute for Studies in Education (OISE)
University of Toronto

Allison Guess
The Graduate Center
The City University of New York

SECTION TWO

CLAIMS TO SPACE

> Borders are set up to define the places that are safe and unsafe, to distinguish us from them. A border is a dividing line, a narrow strip along a steep edge. A borderland is a vague and undetermined place created by the emotional residue of an unnatural boundary. It is in a constant state of transition. The prohibited and forbidden are its inhabitants.
>
> (Gloria E. Anzaldúa, *Borderlands/La Frontera: The New Mestiza*)

As this volume begins with the premise that a Critical Geography is concerned with the conjuncture of space, place, power, and identity, questions of how claims to space are established, limited, or denied holds central position throughout the work presented here. This section however privileges work that emphasizes resistance to structural forces operating to define spaces in particular ways. Grossberg (2002) reminds us that power always has a geography as it is always about access. Indeed, part of the project of a critical geography lies in exposing the ways in which spatial representations often obscure power dynamics. As Gupta and Ferguson (1992) argue, "the presumption that spaces are autonomous has enabled the power of topography to conceal successfully the topography of power" (p. 8). However, a critical approach insists on seeing the spatial "as relational and as the sphere of multiplicity, is both an essential part of the character of, and perpetually reconfigured through, political engagement" (Massey, 2005, p. 183). From participation in a democratic process to political activism to an analysis of the lived experience of spatial production, these chapters all focus on the ways in which claims to space are enacted amidst a reality of political and socio-cultural forces already at work—at work in defining not only spaces but who has access to them.

As the epigraph suggests, borders are socially constructed, rooted in the project of otherness, but borders may be crossed and the borderlands offers a way of understanding claims to space, claims to identity, and a political project. In a traditional geographic study, borders function to highlight a static conception of place. Often treated as *a priori* or in ahistorical, naturalistic ways, the role that borders play in the construction of identity (i.e. who belongs and who doesn't) is obscured. A critical geography troubles, crosses, and complicates borders and the assumptions that underlie their construction. Further, this work acknowledges that the,

> social construction of borders implies that the meanings of both the border and the place defined within are neither guaranteed nor essential. Yet, as real and imagined borders exist in embedded networks of history, politics, and power,

they do indeed have material consequences—real effects on lived experience. (Helfenbein, 2013, p. 152)

In an analysis of claims to space then, the project becomes one of uncovering not only the forces that work to create and sustain spatial constructs but also of exploring the ways in which spatial practices are lived in the hope of identifying and perhaps supporting resistance and resilience.

Robert Helfenbein

NANCY ARES

5. RETERRITORIALIZING AS COMMUNITY ACTIVISM IN AN URBAN COMMUNITY-SCHOOL TRANSFORMATION INITIATIVE

INTRODUCTION

A resident-driven school and community transformation initiative in upstate New York, the Coalition for the Children of Lakeview (CCL), is the site for this chapter's critical geography analysis. A Planning Panel[1] (PP) of approximately 116 individuals representing residents (51%) and social service and governmental agency representatives (non-residents) (49%) was formed in 2005 to make critical decisions regarding the content of the CCL plan (e.g., specific foci such as k-16 education, employment, housing, public safety). The PP was a diverse ethnic/racial and socio-economic group of African American (60%), Caucasian (22%), Latina/o (12%), and Other (6%) individuals. As a critical ethnographer, I found this initiative interesting and important in its positioning of residents as central actors, given organizers' early commitments to resident control of what aspects of the community would be prioritized for transformation. Through numerous meetings, struggles for a definition of "resident," and negotiations around what proportion of people involved in decision-making and planning should be residents, CCL planners finally settled on a majority-rules policy. The "fifty-one percent rule" required that no decisions could be made at PP meetings unless 51% of those in attendance met the definition of 'resident.' The criteria for being identified as a resident included (1) living in the CCL region of the city, or (2) operating a small community-based business or organization in that area (*CCL Community Blueprint*, March 2007). Conversely, 'non-resident' was also a spatial construct identifying those who were outsiders, who lived and worked outside the CCL. The required proportion of residents was dropped to 33% for smaller work groups that were formed to focus on specific topics (e.g., adult education and training, housing). If those proportions were not met, discussion was limited to strategizing how to get more residents to participate. These rules and their consistent enforcement by organizers indicated that this initiative might operate differently from previous forays into urban reform in Lakeview that had left residents out of central roles in planning and implementation. The excerpt from field notes, below, captures some of the tension inherent in this work to privilege residents' experiences, knowledge, and goals while also moving forward in a timely manner.

N. Ares et al. (Eds.), Deterritorializing/Reterritorializing, 61–78.

A group of about 16 people are meeting in a portable trailer that serves as an office on the grounds of an elementary school. They're members of a team working to develop and guide the CCL comprehensive school-community transformation initiative. Their primary charge is to shepherd the process of the reform, leaving the actual content of the initiative to a larger group of residents and other concerned volunteers. Karen is White, and a staff member of a local not-for-profit organization, Alicia is African American, and a resident-community activist, and Norma is a Puerto Riqueña, and an activist-staff member of the local school district.

> Karen: I just want to ask whether anybody here thinks that we are opening ourselves up, again, to the question …that who the heck are we to do this? … I'm just asking everybody for your sensitivity and your read on whether we're vulnerable by doing it this way.
>
>   Alicia agrees that they are vulnerable. Alicia and Norma bring in the voices of people in the community who are concerned with what's happening now in the community. Alicia expresses the frustration of the community with politics, with the idea that other people seem to make decisions for them:
>
> Alicia: They're [the community] talking about people making decisions for people … They're talking about politics, everybody… It's bigger than this, but that's the kind of stuff they're saying: 'Who are you, that's not helping our community, we need help right now at this moment…'
>
> Norma: …What I'm hearing from different people in the community is that we are in crisis mode, and even though we believe that what you're doing is a good thing and you're doing it out of good faith, you're talking about 10 years down the road, we're talking now, immediate, because of all the violence and killings, and so people right now are in the mode of what are we going to do with what we are dealing with now, not talk about 10 years from now.

For this chapter, these tensions around the definition of "resident" and the 51% rule foreground the role that space-as-social-construction played in the CCL, with resident status being tied to a physical place that also embodied assumptions about who residents are, their associations to the initiative, and their relations to people in other parts of Lakeview. Other tensions captured in the excerpts are around immediate vulnerability and real social needs, and commitments to long-term solutions. Thus, though residents were tied to place, what their present and future circumstances could entail were also contested and at times in contradiction.

RECONCEIVING SPACE AND SCALE

The majority of critical geography work has centered on formal planning and policy-making. However, a growing body of work is highlighting community-based efforts to shape place and policy (e.g., Burke, Greene, & McKenna, 2016; Wakefield, 2007). In studying the CCL, I turned to critical geography to disrupt what can be superficial, deficit-based discourses of urban spaces and to center the experiences of residents as they worked to transform and reclaim their communities. Concepts developed by Martin, McMann, and Purcell (2003) that identify three meanings of social space and McCann and others critical geographers' notions of scale as socially constructed were especially important (described in depth, below). The aim of this chapter is to contribute to critical geographical and educational research understandings of the material consequences of shifting policy and practice around economic and urban development to more local entities. Another goal is methodological: to illustrate how this framework guided my analysis of residents' perspectives and participation in the CCL. Thus, the research questions that guided this study are: (1) How do residents' efforts to claim their community spaces manifest in shifting urban economic and development policy and practice to more local entities? (2) How does viewing those efforts as claims to social space help us understand community reform in these neoliberal times?

Setting

The CCL² was a community based collaborative effort to improve the overall quality of life in northeastern Lakeview, a midsized city in upstate New York State. Lakeview, like many manufacturing centers in the northeast US, has experienced drastic job losses as the economy has shifted to more information and service oriented businesses. A former company town with stable jobs, strong unions, and guaranteed pensions, Lakeview is undergoing difficult changes that affect life in general, and race relations and schooling very particularly.

Historical context. The geographical area of focus for the CCL has cultural and linguistic diversity that bring vitality and important resources to the neighborhoods, and a rich history of resilience, including political activism, strong social networks, and community-based advocacy for school and neighborhood improvement. These assets developed in the face of a history of intergenerational poverty, disinvestment by government, school underachievement, violence, and crime. Some seminal events in Lakeview's history include the Great Migration of the 1950s (http://www.blackpast.org/aah/great-migration-1915-1960), when African Americans from the South moved North to find better employment and educational opportunities. At that same time, the third great wave of Puerto Rican migration from the Island to the US mainland was happening as companies recruited Puerto Rican workers as 'cheap labor' (http://palante.org/History.htm). However, many of the major factories that were the core of Lakeview's economic health did not hire non-Whites, creating social and economic hardship in the parts of the City where people of color were concentrated. Tensions rose until, during the Civil Rights and Vietnam War movements of the 1960s, an incident sparked a major conflict in Lakeview. The disturbance was concentrated in the African American and Latinx neighborhoods, as well as downtown, and involved violence, property damage, and police brutality leading to the deaths of four, injury of 350, and arrests of 1000. In the process, more than 200 stores were looted and damaged (Ares, Larson, & O'Connor, 2008). That proved to be a turning point in the City, as white flight ensued, white-owned businesses closed or moved out of the City, and hyper-segregation based on race and socioeconomic status took hold. That history lives in the present. The CCL area of Lakeview includes that conflict zone and adjacent neighborhoods. In addition, activist groups formed in 1964 continue to work in this area to pursue a variety of efforts around school improvement, housing and community development, and youth support.

The CCL Initiative.   The purpose of the CCL was to develop and implement a plan to create an environment for children, families, neighborhoods, and schools to succeed and thrive. The goal was to coordinate, develop, and expand ongoing efforts by schools, community organizations and activists, businesses, community members, and social service agencies that would stimulate more positive, sustainable outcomes in the area. Viewed through a critical geographical lens, aspects of the effort stand out as claims to space and reterritorialization of CCL neighborhoods and communities.

CRITICAL GEOGRAPHY'S APPROACH TO UNDERSTANDING CONSTRUCTION OF SPACE AND SCALE

As the introduction to this book lays out, treating space as a dynamic, relational concept affords us unique insights into human activity and, in this case, resident participation in comprehensive education and community reform. On this view, spaces are not possessed nor filled – they are constructed and negotiated as social relations. People actively build and negotiate environments with political, cultural, economic, and social histories. As a result, CCL residents' claims to community and neighborhood spaces, or what Lefebvre (1991) terms rights to the city, manifested as work to re-territorialize and remake those spaces to meet their goals, desires, needs, and images, and to reposition themselves as active agents and authors of their own lives, neighborhoods, and communities. Lefebvre (2003) described rights to the city as, "not merely a right of access to what the property speculators and state planners define, but an active right to make the city different, to shape it more in accord with [residents'] desire, and to remake [themselves] thereby in a different image" (p. 94). Soja (2010) expanded Lefebvre's definition to include, "...not just as a right to appropriation, participation, and difference but even more broadly as a *right to space,* the right to inhabit space" (p. 108). The focus on the agency residents may wield in their moves to reimagine themselves is certainly germane to this study, especially given the initial positioning of residents as major drivers of the CCL reform. Images are powerful when designing spaces in light of the people, things, and relations that make them up. This can be seen in razing historical buildings for economic development in Lakeview (see Ares, this volume), districts changing school boundaries to change demographics of schools (Ares & Buendía, 2007), and more recent neighborhood schools movements that seek to form an image of a close-knit neighborhood (Tasker, 2008).

Among urban planners, images of who lives where also guide decisions about funding, media representations, and policies. Assumptions about Lakeview's suburbs that inform educational policy and practice, media representations, and land use planning are that they are safer, whiter, and wealthier (this part is true). Assumptions about Lakeview itself that inform educational policy and practice, media representations, and land use planning are that it is dangerous, browner and blacker, and poorer (this part is also true). In terms of cultural geography, Lakeview has a fragmented and hierarchical physical layout, with clear separations of spaces and people. For example, a major river separates people physically, but also divides Lakeview socially. This division has produced and produces an Eastside, a Westside, and within those areas, neighborhoods with specific designations that have local meaning regarding community wealth and ethnic/racial profiles. The Eastside of Lakeview has a neighborhood called Balsamwood that is known as an African American neighborhood, while Acacia Road, in the same geographical area, is known as a Latina/o enclave. Though these neighborhoods share similar educational and economic challenges and are physically close, even abutting each other, they are culturally and linguistically distinct and definitely separate socially and politically, for the most part. However, city planners have treated those neighborhoods as a single place with a homogeneous population as seen through a racialized and social class lens rather than one that acknowledges their multiracial, multiethnic, and mixed income demographic profile. Thus, social constructions of space affecting the CCL are complex, imbued with power relations, historically derived, and dynamic.

Scale is also Socially Constructed

As Martin, McMann, and Purcell (2003) note, "recent work in urban political geography has taken scale as itself an object of inquiry; it has examined how social processes are characterized by particular scalar arrangements" (p. 115). In this work,

> Scale is the geographical organizer and expression of collective social action. … Thus conceived, scale is not a pre-given or fixed platform for social relations, but a socially constructed, politically contested and historically variable dimension of those relationships. (Brenner, 2000, p. 367)

Given capitalism's increasing hold on Western societies, the world's increasingly globalized development, and neoliberal economic and social policies, local entities are having to compete in more and broader economic arenas than in the past, when providing services and supporting citizens were more of their emphasis. Critical geographers are seeking to understand the ways reform initiatives have risen in response to these recent neoliberal State and Federal policies that push responsibility for planning and economic development to more local, i.e., city, county, and district entities.

Scalar fixes: Neoliberal devolution of responsibility to local entities. As noted earlier, work on critical conceptualizations of scale became important to this work because treating scale as a social construction opens up attention to economic and political forces operating and perceived needs to compete in global markets. The spread of free market capitalism has influenced the ways that social spaces are viewed by people and policies operating in various spheres of activity, i.e., state, city, federal, schools, neighborhoods. McCann writes about this in terms of 'scalar fixes" (2003, p. 162):

> a number of scholars ... have conceptualized contemporary restructuring processes in terms of the rescaling of the state and capital. By rescaling, they mean the process in which policies and politics that formerly took place at one scale are shifted to others in ways that reshape the practices themselves, redefine the scales to and from which they are shifted, and reorganize interactions between scales (Brenner, 2000; Jessop, 1994; Swyngedouw, 1997). An associated theme in this literature is the notion of a scalar fix ... (1) fix in terms of stability and order as opposed to flux and fluidity, and (2) fix in terms of problem solving. Scalar fix refers to the social and political process of (re)defining scales to facilitate the accumulation of capital, efficient social redistribution, and effective governance. (p. 163)

The CCL initiative is a telling case of a scalar fix that sought to stabilize a contentious and dynamic region of Lakeview by coordinating the myriad efforts to improve outcomes for its families and children. Importantly, it also opened up space for residents to play a major part in determining to what ends and how resources could be redistributed. The aim of this paper is to contribute to critical geographical research in education and community development through understanding of the material consequences of shifting competition for economic and urban development to, in this case, the CCL as a local entity.

CCL AS CONTESTED SPACE

The CCL, as with any social space, was imbued with meaning and relations of power. It also involved material and ideal dimensions of space, and relations among things both human and non-human. For example, it was demarcated first as a physical space when the Lakeview City School District's superintendent created it to encompass a set of seven under-resourced schools that were similar in academic underperformance and the low socioeconomic status of their students. They were located in a section of the City that was locally infamous for being an "undesirable" place. The CCL originators' rationale for constructing the boundaries they did included school (under)performance, high levels of poverty, high crime statistics, large numbers of abandoned buildings, and troubling health indicators. Thus, this space was marked both physically and perceptually by educators, planners, and media as an area in need of redemption.

For residents of that space, though, the CCL included families, neighbors, friends, small businesses, and schools that were striving to succeed and envisioning a positive future, despite the oppressive conditions and institutional racism that marginalized them. Residents were anxious to improve the physical dimensions (e.g., abandoned homes and other buildings owned by the City, dilapidated buildings, vacant lots) to make their neighborhoods healthy for residents, welcoming to businesses and potential homeowners, and attractive to developers. This transformation of material, social, economic, and cultural dimensions of neighborhoods and communities was at the heart of residents' participation in the CCL and of their struggles to negotiate (or wrest) control of the process and the content of the initiative with social service and other planners. They had a clear-eyed but hopeful vision, even though they had had so many promises made and broken over several decades.

In sum, the CCL space embodied the histories, kinds of assumptions about and within it, the memories and dreams the residents, and those of others connected to their neighborhoods. Our research team was able to witness residents articulate dreams of a future urban space that retained the present assets, attachments, relationships, and traces of historically developed communities while also transforming the precarious social and material dimensions of this part of northeast Lakeview. The analysis presented here will hopefully help us understand how space and scale, as fluid and dynamic dimensions of human activity, were appropriated, transformed, and reproduced as residents sought to advance and implement their dreams and visions.

METHODOLOGY

Again, the research questions guiding this study were: How do residents' efforts to reterritorialize their community manifest in response to shifting urban economic and development policy and practice to more local entities? How does viewing those efforts as claims to social space help us understand community reform in these neoliberal times?

Data Sources

My exploration of these questions drew from a larger ethnographic study of the CCL (Ares, Larson, O'Connor, & Carlisle 2007; Larson, Ares, & O'Connor 2008). The first two years of data document the process through which the CCL participants created future goals and objectives for the area. For this study, I analyzed videos of CCL meetings; field notes; CCL-produced documents; the Civic Blueprint developed as a result of two years of community-based planning and identifying objectives for the initiative; transcripts of individual interviews with four residents; and local newspaper articles.

Analytic Approach: Three Meanings of Space

Residents and other participants' work to transform material and ideal spaces lead me to "analyses that recognize different meanings of space—from its *physical organization in land use planning, human attachments to specific locations, and idealized images*— highlight[ing] areas of contradiction, tension, or difference in the urban sphere" (Martin, McCann, & Purcell, 2003, p. 114). These three meanings are theorized in relation to each other in this paper to embrace the multidimensionality of residents' claims of responsibility and expertise in transformative visioning and action. Further, their relations to residents' rights to the city (Lefebvre, 1991) are explored as a way to link activities at geographic scales that represent residents' lived experiences and the physical and material geographies of the CCL to larger scales of activity in City and State policy and planning.

My analyses were organized around these three meanings of space as *a priori* codes. Table 2, below, presents an example of my coding. This analytic approach supported examination across data sources to explore claims participants made for the spaces of their community. To analyze the interview data, I first read transcripts without coding to get a sense of "what is happening here." The transcripts I analyzed all involved CCL residents so that I could center residents' lives and perspectives. Segments of transcript that related to a particular meaning of space were entered into a data matrix, shown in Table 2. I then conducted focused coding within the three categories, concentrating on references to space, e.g., 'here,' 'there,' 'neighborhood,' street names, etc.

Table 2. Excerpts of interview data coded according to the three meanings of space

Land use planning	Human attachments to specific places	Idealized images
Eastern Development, Inc. invited developers from the Lakeview area to tour the CCL to consider developing housing, business, etc. there. They claimed that, *"there's nothing to develop here"* (field notes, CCL planner meeting, Eastern's Lakeview area director).	"Well I got *the CMC building*, that's through Sector, its *still a sector you know, its right up there*, I want her to see, see she … that would be an awesome building to create into a cultural center … 'cause that'll bring people, *I know it will bring people to Rodham Avenue[3]*."	"My goal is to have that consignment shop on the first floor and be able to have events every week, you know, where this week is *one African American*, the other one is a could be a white one too, you know, *if they live in the neighborhood* you know, and *the other week a Latino*, so every Saturday *something is happening there*."

I analyzed the remaining data sources in a similar way, organizing data initially into the same data matrix seen in the above Table, followed by focused coding within the three categories.

FINDINGS

I organize this section in terms of (1) land use planning, (2) human attachments to specific places, and (3) idealized images. For the analysis, this approach aided in focused coding of the data; for this paper, it helps in organizing findings in ways that make the three meanings and their ties to social, temporal, and physical dimensions of space clear to readers. My analyses show how residents' actions and language functioned as mechanisms for claiming/reclaiming the CCL neighborhoods and exercising power in ways that challenged existing socio-spatial arrangements. That in and of itself is not surprising, but the details involved illuminate the particularities of residents' work to reclaim their community spaces and, almost by extension, their schools. They did not try to build toward a utopian vision but one grounded in physical and social realities.

Three Meanings of Space

Meaning one: Physical organization in land use planning – a mixed bag of hope and pessimism. Urban planners and developers largely viewed this space only in relation to negative physical, economic, and social dimensions. Their vision was limited to seeing CCL neighborhoods as lacking social and material wealth, being devoid of economic and human capital, a lost cause, and imageable only as a wasteland. Supporting this vision was disinvestment by City and state government planners, evident in that a large percentage of vacant, decaying buildings were city-owned; homeownership rates were low; and police surveillance was high (more video cameras on power poles, red light cameras at intersections than other areas of Lakeview) (see Figure 1). Land use planners' meanings of CCL spaces (seen in the press, on TV, in residents' and planners' stories) conjured up images of violence, danger; filth, decay, lawlessness, and failing schools. However, less prominent but still present was the conviction among some (well intentioned but also patronizing) planners who were social activists, good Samaritans, and resident/planners that believed they had a chance to truly make a difference in children's lives. They recognized untapped potential among the residents; strong social/familial networks; schools as spaces of hope as well as despair, danger, and possibility; and persistent, insistent neighborhood activism. Finally, some planners, particularly social service agencies, saw this area as a space in need of physical redemption, including such things as safe corridors between homes and schools, rehabilitation of housing (with the attendant problems of gentrification), *and* fertile ground for collaborative (sort of) work toward more positive developmental outcomes for families.

Residents and others' meanings of the CCL as the focus of urban planning were starkly different but just as mixed. Many participated in the initiative to heighten awareness of the urgency of problems like drug trafficking, poor access to quality health care, and under-resourced schools struggling to educate their students. At the

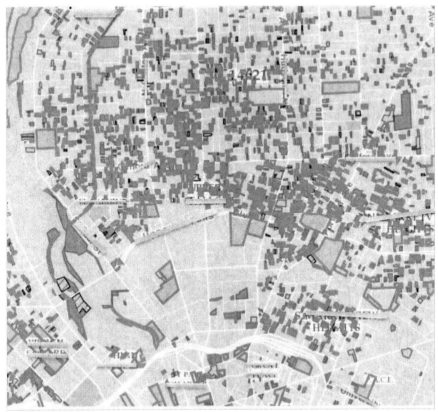

Dark grey=vacant structures   Lighter grey-vacant land

Figure 1. CCL area vacant buildings and vacant land

same time, many residents viewed planners with suspicion, seeing their treatment of the area as a "data plantation" and source of employment. While many CCL planners had good intentions and were truly committed especially to child and youth development, a resident-activist named a dark side to their images of the CCL area:

> Nothing's happening, and then the money, usually the people that get the money *they don't live in the city they live out.* So *here they come,* use our statistics, get all this funding, and *then they leave.* ... there's a lot of poverty pimping in my community. I don't know if you understand what that means, but it is these people that are getting money and *they come here to use our statistics* just so they can get funded to create a job [for themselves], you know, they just want a job. But at the end when you look for the results, *there's no results there*

you know. They play with the numbers and use all the statistics, but *when you come to the community* its still the same, *it's getting worse.* (Eugenio, resident-activist interview, 061016)

This tension and skepticism certainly played into residents' decisions to participate in the CCL, with some opting out, others giving tentative support, and still others committing but remaining watchful and 'carrying the torch' (a term used several times in Planning Panel meetings) for residents' central roles in the initiative's development.

Meaning two: Human attachments to specific places.   This section has three subthemes: Attachments to the CCL as a whole; mixed attachments to schools and community resources; and attachments to streets, street corners, and youth. The residents' attachments to specific locations in the CCL were tied to meanings of home, community, neighborhood, danger, family, school, loss, possibility, activism, violence, as well as of vibrancy and challenge. For example, "Area 57209" was a community-based social service organization, identified by its zip code, and staffed by resident-activists engaged in neighborhood improvement activities (housing, employment, youth support, adult education). Its identification with a particular region of the CCL highlights the social and spatial nature of the region for its inhabitants. Similarly, the CCL represented differential attachments to varied spaces, as references to Lakeview and to the CCL differed in terms of participants' affiliations and commitments. These attachments are described, next.

Attachments to CCL as a whole.   Two members of the CCL, Pacifica (a CCL resident, activist, and director of resources and development for a local not-for-profit) and Derrick (a director of a local center for the study of youth and families) made a public presentation to local higher education and social service staff. Derrick described the CCL using the classic "stone soup" story of travelers entering a small town, carrying only an empty pot. In that story, villagers refuse to give the travelers food, so they gather rocks and water from a nearby stream and begin to heat them up. Villagers eventually become curious and when asked to help spice it up, add scanty portions to the soup, eventually producing and sharing a filling meal. Derrick likened the CCL area to that empty pot, planners to the travelers who added rocks, and residents to the villagers contributing their meager parts. Pacifica followed him as speaker and quickly challenged that representation. Rather than an empty pot, she portrayed the region as rich in varieties of spices, vegetables, and meats. She also presented herself as a professional who is also a resident ("I live there, along with a lot of other professionals"). According to her, that supposedly empty pot was actually a flavorful, hearty stew that retained the integrity of distinct ingredients, and it had been there long before the travelers came along. Her story illustrated her pride in her community, her assumptions of

71

vibrant social ingredients making up the CCL, and fond commitment to the people and places comprising the area.

Mixed attachments to schools and community resources. Danae, a teacher and member of one of the work teams formed from the PP, told of that team's wanting "to know what was happening out there in the CCL." She said that,

> there was talk about in the community, about after school, *parents didn't feel safe to leave their kids out in the neighborhood.* ... there's a *library right in that middle section* now. They don't use it as much as they could. Why are you saying these things *when it is right there*? (frustration) *I'm in the community*, so I don't know ... Getting children *there* is their choice and responsibility. (resident interview, 061006)

Danae's representation of the spaces around the CCL school she worked in was a juxtaposition of wide ranging resources for youth and families (this work team had produced a list of local after school programs and social service organizations) and dangerous paths for students to traverse to and from school. Many parents kept their younger children indoors rather than let them play outside and relied on school buses that dropped students at their homes' doors to avoid their having to walk in through neighborhoods. While there was fear of CCL neighborhoods on parents' parts, Danae focused instead on the safe, supportive spaces available to children and youth. Attachments to neighborhood resources for her and reliance on schools as safe spaces for families illuminate relations among schools and families, showing the common gaps in views found in the data. In addition, the economics of the area meant that people were on the move a lot, highlighting mobility among some families, which may have helped explain parents' sense of risk due to unfamiliarity with their surroundings.

Attachments to streets, street corners, and youth. Both Pacifica and Charice, a resident who was a middle –level administrator at a large local manufacturer, spoke about attachments to youth in the neighborhood. Each of them approached youth hanging out on street corners near their houses to chat. Charice provided meals every Sunday to any who came to her house, following her family's Sunday dinner ritual – an African American tradition of sharing food that she had continued when she moved "up North" from Georgia. Pacifica engaged youth by spending time in spaces they hung out in and claimed by their physical presence. She spent time with them on the corners to provide a caring but insistent sounding board for exploring possible futures. Those corners were considered to belong to the youth, so Pacific and Charice's forays into those spaces were symbolic and material gestures of commitments to them. The social and physical environment shaped the views of all involved, as they wouldn't venture far in recognition of the sometimes contested claims to streets and street corners, and the social/political alliances that marked those spaces as protected territories.

In a spatial analysis, accounting for personal, cultural, political, and place-based commitments to the CCL space is required to capture the nature of Charice and Pacifica's participation in the initiative and in their neighborhoods. As can be seen, their attachments were grounded in this place, contained by sociopolitical relations of place, and characterized by realistic but loving treatment of youth as a way of trying to make place less contested, less difficult, and less lonely.

Meaning three: Idealized images. Charice, Pacifica, and Eugenio all described an idealized image of the CCL as a resident-driven space transformed to be socially and culturally vibrant, safe, communally oriented, and economically robust. Schools were not mentioned so much as families being supported to be economically successful, healthy, well educated, and responsible. This shared ideal of grassroots, culturally grounded, sharing of space is captured in the following excerpt from an individual interview with Eugenio, a resident/activist who served on the Planning Panel:

Nancy: So I'm interested in this mix of Latino and African American cultural groups together in the same building, does that work out pretty well or how do you see …

Eugenio: It's going to work out, yeah, that's the whole idea you know because Latinos are over here and the African Americans are over here and I want to put them together. I've got African blood in me, you know, so do you, you know, so … that's where Puerto Ricans come from, the white and the Black, that's what … and the Indian, the (22:40 unintelligible) you know. So I don't know that's my idea. Then we got to rebuild Lakeview with pride, which is what I want to push through the Coalition for the Children of Lakeview. (resident activist interview, 060616)

Creating a common, multicultural space for residents was important to Eugenio as a way to, as he stressed below, foster pride and independence, as well as developing community resources that could be redirected back into the CCL area.

In talking about a particular region of the CCL that is home to a large Latina/o population, Eugenio stressed the importance of understanding the conditions in the community by being physically present and listening. He also talked about the importance of the cultural vibrancy of the CCL area and the possibilities of pulling African American and Latina/o groups together through art and entrepreneurship:

Nancy: You like to *work on the ground?*

Eugenio: Yeah, I don't like, yeah I don't like, I could right now I could be with those [CCL planners] … I don't want to be with them, *I want to be with my people,* you know. All they do is talk a lot, *I've been there already,* you know, and its hard, its really hard, because *I live in the community, I walk it, I see it every day you know.* I talk to

> the parents, I talk to the kids, you know, and what they tell me is
> not good. ... do something culturally, and you know, we bring *the
> African American artists and Hispanic artists* and we bring them
> *here* you know, and it will be an African American cultural center,
> a Hispanic ... so they went blah, blah, blah, then I started bringing
> all these ideas because we're *building a coffee shop* so I'm thinking
> what about a consignment shop, what about bringing artists who
> have their art and we sell it for them and we make a profit out of it
> too, they do a donation to us because we're now, *it's a 501C3, so its
> not there to make money.* (interview 061606)

The idealized image Eugenio painted crystallized physical, social, cultural, and
economic dimensions of the CCL space into one story. References to keeping profits
in the community while also supporting artists and providing spaces where African
American and Latina/o artists could display their art and share a collective space,
bridging cultural communities, all point to ways that CCL residents and activists
imagined taking responsibility for community development. Residents imagined
and worked toward visions of possible futures that were vibrant, safe, multicultural,
attractive, and economically productive. These visions were in stark contrast to
planners' visions of the CCL as a community that had to be redeemed and rehabilitated
rather than changed based on the rich resources and assets already there.

In summary, in earlier years, such an opportunity for residents to take on
responsibility for their community's development was uncommon. However,
these more recent, neoliberal times in some ways position communities that have
historically been prevented from participating in transformation efforts as central
actors. Still, people who have traditionally held the power to act do not readily, easily,
or willingly share that power. Thus, there was tension among the CCL participants,
as residents were invited to envision and draft change-oriented plans, but they were
also subject to control by dominant forces and people that limited their agency to
implement that change.

DISCUSSION

Governance and Scalar Fixes

Martin, McCann, and Purcell (2003) claim that, "questions of how decisions about
contemporary cities' social and economic futures are made, where they are made,
which institutions or actors are empowered to make them, and in whose interests,
are central to a great deal of contemporary writing in urban, political, and economic
geography" (p. 116). Questions like these were certainly central in Lakeview, where
the CCL was located. Further, in critical urban geography studies examining scale
as socially constructed,

The term governance is used to indicate 'a shift from centralized and bureaucratic forms of decision-making [generally referred to as 'government'] to a plurality of coexisting networks and partnerships that interact as overlapping webs of relationships at diverse spatial scales, from the neighborhood to the globe. (Hubbard, Kitchin, Bartley, & Fuller, 2002, pp. 175–176; Martin, McCann, & Purcell, 2003, pp. 115–116)

This shift was also clearly evident in the CCL, as it brought together social service agencies, schools, not-for-profits, and government entities to pursue community improvement. A consequence of the shift to more local entities as the site of action in pursuing economic development and community improvement was that residents actually took this responsibility (and opportunity) seriously. As a result, central to the development of the initiative were questions about how, where, why and by whom decisions were made. Previous findings from this study show that negotiations between residents and CCL planners around control of the process of developing the comprehensive Civic Blueprint versus control of the actual content of the Plan were a source of tension (Ares, Larson, & O'Connor, 2009).

Here, then, is a site of struggle that can be understood in terms of "rights to the city" (LeFevbre, 1991), this time at the neighborhood scale linked to the CCL scale. Purcell (2002) writes that rights to the city can be understood as

the right to appropriation … a much broader and more structural meaning. … it is also the right to produce urban space so that it meets the needs of inhabitants" …the right to the city stresses the need to restructure the power relations that underlie the production of urban space, fundamentally shifting control away from capital and the state and toward urban inhabitants. (p. 101)

The residents' moves to insert themselves into planning decisions reflected their desires to produce rather than reproduce the CCL space, as their prior experiences, over years and years, showed that they had been excluded or left out.

It's not all Sweetness and Light...

My goal is not to romanticize residents' claims and stories around appropriating urban spaces. As Purcell (2002) notes,

The right to the city offers an approach that at once is exciting and disconcerting. It is exciting because it offers a radical alternative that directly challenges and rethinks the current structure of both capitalism and liberal-democratic citizenship. It is disconcerting because we cannot know what kind of a city these new urban politics will produce. They could play out as a truly democratic challenge to marginalization and oppression, but they could also work to reinscribe new forms of domination. (p. 100)

Reforms may not move toward positive transformation, away from control and production of capital, and toward social justice. This is not inevitable in resident-driven reforms, just like more top-down efforts that maintain power relations favoring uneven distribution of resources and power. In this initiative and important to the focus of this book on educational reform is the resounding silence about schools. The lack of attention to education and schooling represents, perhaps, either a major weakness in residents' views of community transformation or a historical relationship to schools that positions schools as unwelcoming, unresponsive, and educators not understanding their role in oppression in this urban space.

So, What about Education Reform?   Schools were not addressed in the Planning Panel's discourse nor were educators at the table except at the beginning of the CCL initiative. This speaks to potential for unanticipated, unwanted outcomes. As noted elsewhere, "Even though [the CCL] is a rich process by which residents, together with powerful others, are attempting to produce a sustainable community future, schooling practices are not touched (for various reasons, e.g., fossilized practices in the city school district, broader discourses of schooling, standardization, etc.)" (Larson, et al., 2008, p. 4). In that work, we inferred that the silence around schools and schooling was linked to the power of the 'grammar of schooling" (Tyack & Tobin, 1994, p. 453), or practices and policies that normalize such things as age-graded classes, standardized assessments, and Eurocentric curriculum. As a result, the CCL's not questioning "assumptions about what counts as school, literacy, numeracy, and learning … may have [had] adverse consequences on goals of transformation and not doing "business as usual" (Larson et al., 2008, p. 18). Terms such as reading, achievement, and 100% graduation were used, but the meanings behind them were opaque and/or uncontested. The void left in residents' claims to space, in their moves to craft the CCL spaces in ways that served their interests above others', could (re)create schools as islands of deficit thinking and practices and power relations that favor non-residents and external decision making.

CONCLUSION

Understanding localized values, dreams, and historically derived relations of power opens up negotiations among CCL participants to scrutiny in ways that tie varied actors' motivations and histories together. The three meanings of space – human attachments to specific locations, idealized images, physical organization in land use planning – provided a useful framework for making sense of residents' responses to the neoliberal policies of the CCL initiative. Further, this way of examining the CCL foregrounds that these development policies at City and county levels were taken as responsibilities for economic development only and based in capitalism's emphasis on monetary capital to the virtual exclusion of human capital. Most urban planners as well as many (but not all) social service agencies treated the CCL area as a source of jobs for themselves. Thus, physical organization in land use planning treated the space, for the most part, as a very risky small business development zone, not one with particular strengths and resources. In contrast, residents and their allies' (but not all) attachments to specific locations and their idealized but still realistic images of the CCL focused on a variety of forms of capital, including human, relational, and cultural, as well as economic. Responding to the opportunity in neoliberal policies to take responsibility for and control of the CCL space, they fought to exercise their agency to shape the area in their own images and with resources and assets particular to their histories and communities.

NOTES

[1] This is a pseudonym, as are all place and people's names.
[2] For an in depth description of the CCL, see O'Connor, Ares, and Larson (2011).
[3] Rodham Avenue is more than a street and an intersection (Rodham Avenue and D Street). This is considered a Puerto Rican space, Latina/o space to which Eugenio wants to bring people to experience cultural, artistic resources of his community.

REFERENCES

Ares, N., & Buendía, E. (2007). Spatialized and spatializing practices: Commodifying literacy programs. In J. Larson (Ed.), *Literacy as snake oil* (2nd ed.). Germany: Peter Lang.

Ares, N., Larson, J., O'Connor, K. C., & Carlisle, J. (2007, April). *Getting started: First stages of community reform.* Paper presented at the meeting of the American Educational Research Association, San Francisco, CA.

Ares, N., Larson, J., & O'Connor, K. (2008, March). *Rochester children's zone ethnography: Understanding school/community relationships in an urban change initiative.* Paper presented at the Penn Ethnography Forum, Philadelphia, PA.

BlackPast.org. (2016). *The great migration (1915–1960).* Retrieved from http://www.blackpast.org/aah/great-migration-1915-1960

Brenner, N. (1995). Remaking scale: Competition and cooperation in prenational and postnational. In H. Eskelinen & F. Snickars (Eds.), *The limits to scale? Methodological reflections on scalar structuration* (pp. 59–74). Berlin: Springer Verlag.

Burke, K. J., Greene, S., & McKenna, M. K. (2016). A critical geographic approach to youth civic engagement: Reframing educational opportunity zones and the use of public spaces. *Urban Education, 51*(2), 143–169. doi:10.1177/0042085914543670

Hubbard. P., Kitchin, R., Bartley, B., & F'uller, D. (2002). *Thinking geographically: Space, theory and contemporary human geography.* London: Continuum.

Jessop, B. (1994). Post-Fordism and the state. In A. Amin (Ed.), *Post-Fordism: A reader* (pp. 251–259). Cambridge, MA: Blackwell.

Jonas, A. E., & Ward, K. (2002). A world of regionalisms: Towards a US-UJK urban and regional policy framework comparison. *Journal of Urban Affairs, 24*(4), 377–401.

Latino Education Network Service. (2016). *The great migration.* Retrieved from http://palante.org/History.htm

Lefebvre, H. (1991). *The production of space.* Oxford: Blackwell.

Lefebvre, H. (2003). *The urban revolution.* Minneapolis, MN: University of Minnesota Press.

Martin, D., McMann, E., & Purcell, M. (2003). Space, scale, governance, and representation: Contemporary geographical perspectives on urban politics and policy. *Journal of Urban Affairs, 25*(2), 113–121.

McCann, E. J. (2003). Framing space and time in the City: Urban policy and the politics of spatial and temporal scale. *Journal of Urban Affairs, 25*(2), 159–178.

Purcell, M. (2002). Excavating Lefebvre: The right to the city and its urban politics of the inhabitant. *GeoJournal, 58*(2–3), 99–108.

Soja, E. W. (2010). *Seeking spatial justice*. Minneapolis, MN: University of Minneapolis Press.

Swyngedouw, E. (1997). Neither global or local: "Globalization" and the politics of scale. In K. R. Cox (Ed.), *Traces of globalization: Reasserting the power of the local* (pp. 137–166). New York, NY: Guilford.

Tasker, M. (2008). Smaller schools: A conflict of aims and purposes? *FORUM: For Promoting 3–19 Comprehensive Education, 50*(2), 177–184.

Tyack, D., & Tobin, W. (1994). The 'grammar' of schooling: Why has it been so hard to change? *American Educational Research Journal, 31*(3), 453–479.

Wakefield, S. (2007). Reflective action in the academy: Exploring praxis in critical geography using a "food movement" case study. *Antipode, 39*(2), 331–354.

Nancy Ares
University of Rochester

SOPHIA RODRIGUEZ

6. THEY CALLED US THE REVOLUTIONARIES

Immigrant Youth Activism as a Deleuzian Event

*We were arrested. The handcuffs felt tight on our wrists. We claimed that space.
They called us the revolutionaries.*

(Youth Activist, Penny)

INTRODUCTION

Youth activists from marginalized groups and communities across the country have
been fighting educational inequalities. Due to the rise of neoliberal reform agendas,
the world has witnessed a resurgence of youth activism (Kirshner & Pozzoboni,
2011). Specifically, locating productive social spaces for youth to claim, to negotiate,
and to articulate positive social selves are the focus of this chapter as youth engage
in sense-making about educational injustice.

In the face of neoliberal education policies and practices, it is imperative
that education researchers re-think the parameters of reform. To this end, this
chapter begins the process of disrupting the dominant narratives of charter school
proliferation, school choice, and accountability by re-conceptualizing space as
an entry point into excavating an important narrative from key stakeholders in
the educational process—youth. To re-conceptualize space, this chapter draws on
Gilles Deleuze's (1990, 1993, 1995) relational space theory, through the concept of
'event,'[1] and Critical Geography theories of space (Buendía, Ares, Juarez, & Peercy,
2004; Ferguson & Gupta, 2002; Helfenbein & Taylor, 2009; Webb & Gulson, 2013)
in order to understand how "youth cultural practices create social space" (Ares,
2010, p. 67). More specifically, I argue the re-conceptualization of space and youth
identity formation advances our understanding of marginalized youth activism by
revealing the positive and productive ways in which they engage in critical thinking
about issues impacting their communities and schools.

This chapter provides an account of youth activism against the massive school
closures in Chicago during the 2012–2013 school year. The chapter argues that activist
youth in this study re-made white spaces/spaces of power. The lens of Deleuze's
event (1990, 1993, 1995) exhibits the ways in which youth broke themselves/their
identities down, re-made space, and formed new versions of themselves. This means
that youth, labeled as "at risk," and "nothing" by the school district and as "just
regulars"[2] by teachers in their school contested those institutional labels.

N. Ares et al. (Eds.), Deterritorializing/Reterritorializing, 79–97.

The contribution of this discussion to the larger academic literature is that social identities of youth are largely studied through their interaction with race, class, and gender and larger sociological categories that do little to problematize modern identity formation (Davidson, 1996; Eckert, 1989). My research examines the continual remaking of youth culture as a process—an event—of developing a critical consciousness about social reality as well as a process of youth identity transformation from merely a "regular" (my study participants' term) to leaders for their communities; thus, I draw on rich ethnographic data to articulate the symbolic cultural knowledge that "informants" such as the youth in this chapter offer. These youth are the "brokers" of such cultural knowledge and understand their social realities as they work for social change (Foley, Levinson, & Hurtig, 2000, p. 40; Orellena, 2009).

The map of the rest is as follows. First, I conceptualize the process of activist youth identity formation through the notion of event. Second, I prepare the reader for how to read the narrative by outlining key features of Deleuze's notion of event and its connection to critical geographers' concepts of space since Deleuze's work has been gaining currency recently as a part of spatial theory (Rodriguez, forthcoming; Webb & Gulson, 2013). Third, I narrate three critical moments of youth activism. Then I provide discussion, analysis, and implications.

CONCEPTUALIZING SPACE

Social Space

Most recent conceptualizations of space occur through the lens of Critical Geography theories (CG) and often rely upon Edward Soja's work on space (Buendía, Ares, Juarez, & Peercy, 2004; Ferguson & Gupta, 1992; Soja, 2010; Helfenbein & Taylor, 2009). This chapter builds upon the work of Critical Geography approaches by experimenting with the spatial theory of post-structuralist philosopher Gilles Deleuze's (1993, 1994, 1995) and the notion of event to generate a more nuanced, fluid conceptualization of space in which researchers might be able to break down positivist traditions in social research, essentialist dualisms of subjectivity of marginalized groups, and white supremacist logic that governs social spaces of youth from marginalized communities. Bringing together such a conceptual orientation is not a seamless process and it is intentionally doing something new in this endeavor to de-territorialize education reform. In this chapter, I am thinking through what/who governs a space and then the processes that youth undertake to disrupt the logic of spaces that involved educational reform. To this end, this section engages with the conceptual literature on space and its application in education research.

Spatial Theory in Education Policy Studies

Drawing from the educational policy scholarship, Webb and Gulson (2013) argue that "Policy takes and makes place," and thus spatial theory becomes relevant for a study on schools, communities, and cities that are impacted by policies (p. 52). Further, Webb and Gulson (2013), drawing on Deleuze, argue, "Geography matters, not for the simplistic overly used reason that everything happens in space, but because where things happen is critical to knowing how and why they happen" (p. 53). Relational space theory in Deleuze's work (1990, 1993, 1995) is concerned with "situated, indeterminate, contingent concepts, and a positing of enlivened space – space as vital, material, immanent – that provides new spaces for living and new ways of being" (Webb & Gulson, 2013, p. 58). Elsewhere I have argued that space, through a Deleuzian lens, is relationally constituted (Rodriguez, 2013). Similarly, Webb and Gulson (2013), drawing on Doel and Clarke (2001), argue, "To space— that's all. Spacing is an action, an event, and a way of being. Space is immanent. It has only itself. Spacing is what happens and takes place: it is the differential elements within everything that happens" (Webb & Gulson, 2013, p. 59). Space, relationally constituted, becomes a verb in Deleuze's relational space theory, and "Event is the potential immanent within a particular confluence of forces, and events carry no determinate outcome, but only new possibilities, representing a moment at which new forces might be brought to bear" (p. 59).

I consider Deleuze's notion of event and how it connects with and differs from previous Critical Geographers' concepts by scholars such as Edward Soja (1996, 2010). Deleuze's event as a potential lens for spatial analysis understands space as a complex product of social processes. While Soja's (1996, 2010) contributions are important, Deleuze's relational space theory suggests that space can be reconstructed and reconfigured if considered "contingent" rather than the seemingly hierarchical nature of Soja's "firstspace," "secondspace," and "thirdspace" (Soja, 1996). By this, I mean that space needs to be theorized as fluid and malleable so that rich empirical data gathered in spaces can be analyzed without limitations of Soja's "thirdspace," which can only be achieved after the first and second spaces are. While Soja's concept of "thirdspace" is where individuals can give/make meaning, Deleuze's event enables meaning making and transformation without fixed stages (Deleuze, 1994; for an application of Deleuze's spatial and empirical work, see MacLure, 2011; Rodriguez, forthcoming). Instead, social actors' relationships occur in a process. As such, Deleuzian event enables us to witness and experience social identity formation through "ruptures," and "incomplete, always-in-process" tellings of youth desire and actions (Jackson & Mazzei, 2012, p. 750) rather than mapping a space, conceptualizing a space, and then giving meaning to it through representation in the rigid theoretical model of Soja's. To summarize, Deleuze's notion of event offers a nuanced way of thinking about space and how spaces are made and re-made once youth activists transform the space and shed parts of themselves.

Furthermore, Critical Geography theories provide a lens to deconstruct the use of space across a "traveling field" (Clifford, 1997). And, Helfenbein (2010) argues, "Critical geographers are interested in space, place, power, and identity" (p. 304). To elaborate, Buendía (2000) and McDermott (1996) argue that student experiences in schools hinge on "discourses that envelop students to render them institutionally eligible or ineligible for particular educational treatments" and further, that spatial markers tend to fix student identities to particular spaces and often limit them from positive identity development and positive academic experiences (Buendía, Ares, Juarez, & Peercy, 2004, p. 837). The intersection of identity and space is important to consider as youth activists in this study battled institutional labeling as "at risk" or "failures," but still generated activist activities to fight for educational equality. As youth use and negotiate space and generate activist identities, they are able to move outside of school spaces that try to position them in negative ways and transform spaces they occupy such as protests, intersections, or school board meetings.

With a malleable conception of space through the lens of post-structural and critical geography theories, I argue that historically marginalized groups can, and do, reconfigure space. Put another way, space is constructed or produced through power dynamics and social relations. There is a possibility, then, that it can be reproduced by different social actors. For example, the youth activists in my research were able to modify and transform space into one that was productive and demonstrated their power. To be clear, the marginalized youth in this study were in racially marked spaces, e.g. black, poor, ghetto, low-income and other deficit-based words that carry with them negative perceptions of marginalized groups (Blaisdell, 2015), and they sought to reconfigure space and to even resist space with the relationships they built with each other and the new relationships with themselves as youth activists.

STUDY DESIGN

This study was an emergent qualitative research design that was framed through the lens of critical ethnography (Denzin & Lincoln, 2005; Foley, Levinson, & Hurtig, 2000; Levinson, Foley, & Holland, 1996; Madison, 2012; Noblit, 1999; Quantz, 1992; Villenas & Foley, 2011). Denzin (1997) argues, "The ethnographer discovers the multiple 'truths' that operate in the social world, the stories people tell one another about the things that matter to them. These stories move people to action; they rest on a distinction between facts and truth. Truth and facts are socially constructed, and build stories around the meanings of the facts" (Denzin, 1997, p. 355). In this study, I was concerned with the perspectives of youth from low-income immigrant communities, including the processes, procedures, and where truth is produced for, about, and from them.

To conduct research that resists universal truths, critical ethnography as a method is appropriate in order to consider the developing, divergent and potentially contradictory accounts of the real. As such, scholars such as Tamboukou and Ball (2003) argue that ethnography combined with assumptions of post-structuralist approaches to identity and power, subject-formation, and "truth-telling" are "disruptive" and they account for the power-knowledge relations that operate in local and specific settings, enabling the researcher to "focus upon events, spaces which divide those in struggle" (p. 4).

As such, I was attentive to issues of power across social spaces, the ways in which youth attempted to disrupt such spaces, and the ways that they were labeled and managed through "deficit discourses" about their communities (Rodriguez, 2015a). For example, labels such as "regular," and "at risk" were subjectively ascribed to youth from low-income, Latino immigrant backgrounds based on teacher perceptions of abilities of youth from low-income, minority groups. Such labels as "Latino," "immigrant," "low-income" or "minority" were also problematic to youth because these are labels that were placed upon the youth. The practice of labeling students' cultural differences with individual traits such as being "low-income" etc. are part of the institutional, ascription process of identity that allows for hierarchies in schools and society (Gutierrez & Rogoff, 2003) that also set the conditions for positive and negative academic trajectories for youth. This means that youth were often subjectively tracked in the school, with Asian immigrants as the "model minority" placed in higher track, Advanced Placement or International Baccalaureate[3] classes while Latino immigrants were more likely to be placed in the lower track classes as "the regulars" (see for example, Rodriguez, 2015b). The term "regulars" is described in detail below, and is important as it relates to their status in the school as low achieving and "nothing." With a critical approach, I suggest that youth transcended the institutional positioning of identity through deficit discourses to remake youth culture, produce positive social identities, and disrupt white supremacist logic in racialized spaces; thus, this study also explored how youth use and negotiate space to generate positive identities.

Site Selection

I studied a community-school partnership. All names are pseudonyms. Redwood Park Council (RPC) is a community-based, nonprofit organization serving a low-income working class neighborhood in Chicago's southwest side. O'Donnell High School partners with this organization. RPC's main service to O'Donnell students is that they promote youth activism and often supply youth with opportunities and skills to engage in activism. O'Donnell High School is a large, urban high school in the Chicago Public Schools network. As of 2012–2013, there were 2,575 students enrolled at O'Donnell. I learned from the school's website that approximately 50–53% of students drop out of O'Donnell. To connect the site selection to the research design and its frame of critical ethnography, I also considered the current educational policy context that includes the proliferation of charter schools across large urban districts and mayoral policies of privatization here in Chicago.

Data Sources

The data presented in the chapter were collected through participant-observations and interviews with youth from 2012–2014. The data were collected across multiple spaces where youth gathered and engaged in activist work, e.g. school, classrooms, hallways, buses, and streets. The participant-observations also occurred during an RPC-sponsored after-school program as well as other youth organized activities. In addition, I conducted 40 youth interviews. The interview data in this chapter focuses on four youth who were the main youth leaders of student-founded and led groups. Each interview was between 60–90 minutes, audio-recorded and transcribed for accuracy. The four youth in this study were interviewed several times throughout the 2012–2013 school year.

Description of Youth Participants

Youth voice is central in this chapter. Their interpretation of social reality and their increased levels of awareness of educational inequality provide a foundation for the production of youth space. Each youth in the study grappled with and interpreted his or her social reality as a first step toward transforming themselves, transcending the institutional labeling, and hopefully, transforming social spaces that are dominated by white supremacist logic. To draw the reader into the social worlds of the youth, I selected four youth to interpret and help me make sense of activism through the notion of event. Each of the youth discussed his/her perceptions of activism as a process of "bursting their bubble," a theme described later in the chapter, and recognizing segregation and inequality in their city and school system. For instance, Isaiah said to me, "You don't have to be labeled honors, AP or IB to be politically engaged." The four youth described the structural, institutional forces that labeled students and also limited their academic experience as regulars. However, these youth transcend the limitations of what the school thinks it means to be a regular. It was widely noted by students and teachers at the school that the lower tracked classes were called "the regulars" in the school, and the stereotyping attached to the label "regular" was deeply present at the school. The regulars were the students that were perceived to not care about school and were thereby not invested in by school staff and many teachers. Yet the process of activism changed such regulars as those presented in this research, and, as shown in this chapter, they shed parts of themselves in order to transform themselves into positive leaders in the community and city.

In the table below, I summarize youth perceptions of self and policy, and local issues that impacted their community during the course of the study. This table is offered as a way to draw the reader into the social worlds of youth and their interpretation of the social context.

Each of the interviews with the four youth point to reflections upon a rising critical consciousness about inequity and moments when they "shed parts of themselves."

Re-Considering Data Analysis

In this post-structuralist, experimental reading of ethnographic data through the notion of Deleuzian event and relational space theory, I attempted to engage with

Table 1. Summary of youth perceptions of self, policy, and local issues

Youth Participant	Gender	Age (at the time of the study)	Institutional label (self-reported)	Perception of Self in relation to Policy
Isaiah	Male	17	At Risk	My entire life I didn't realize my schools were segregated. We have tiers of education in the same school and systems. Regulars get fewer resources. To realize that is like a bubble bursting.
Penny	Female	17	At Risk	I just opened my eyes to came out of this bubble with the school closings. I care about these communities. Chicago is segregated.
Marley	Male	18	At Risk/ Regular	I just started to realize that kids are being taught to be oppressed. The school closings are happening in black and Latino communities.
Amelia	Female	18	At Risk/ Regular	We did research, and we learned these school closings are impacting people in low-income areas. It is a geographic issue.

the data by "thinking with the theory" (Jackson & Mazzei, 2012, p. 751). Rather than thinking about the subject, and what he/she said or did in the research and what youth action meant I found myself in the middle of the ethnographic space and considered the subject that emerges in events. Masny (2013) argues that events are moments of "rupture, creation," and death (p. 341). This nuanced approach means that researchers orient themselves within a particular concept. In my research, that was the notion of event, rather than building theory from the ground up. To elaborate on how a researcher re-considers data analysis with theoretical concepts, Mazzei (2014) argues:

> This means that in a diffractive process of data analysis, a reading of data with theoretical concepts (and/or multiple theoretical concepts) produces an emergent and unpredictable series of readings as data and theory make themselves intelligible to one another. (p. 743)

This nuanced approach to qualitative ethnographic data analysis enabled me to think with the Deleuzian concept of event in order to produce an experience of reading the

85

youth stories through their words, actions, affectations, images and reflections. To this point, I am trying to "produce a different knowledge" with a different texture that does not lock the researcher/subjects (Mazzei, 2014, p. 743) into a "territorialized place of fixed, recognizable meaning" (Jackson & Mazzei, 2012, p. 12). To produce a different type of knowledge (one outside of the institutional labeling of minority youth and truth-telling practices of social science that perpetuate similar deficit discourses about minority youth),[4] researchers work to disrupt their own epistemological ground from which research is often conceived and to collapse theory/method rather than engage in "normative" knowledge production (Kuntz, 2015). The result of the analysis is a narrative of youth experiences that is messy, reveals moments of "incoherent subjectivity," (p. 12) and does not lead the researcher/participants to a coherent narrative. Rather, the aim is to analyze their experiences and to argue that knowledge is produced in the *process* of youth activism, and to document that messy process. Youth referred to the messy process as a "movement," where they learned about themselves, each other, and slowly began to dismantle the oppression and inequity that exists in Chicago public schools.

Using Event as an Analytic

I offer here an example of how and why it is useful to analyze data through the concept of event. Deleuze's relational space theory offers concepts, such as event, that can speak to an "enlivened space – space as vital, material, immanent –that provides new space for living and new ways of being" (Webb & Gulson, 2015, p. 68). Deleuze (1993) argues that we [researchers] need to describe the process of social relationships when he asks, "What are the conditions that make an event possible?" (p. 86). As such, analyzing data through the lens of event means that one must be attentive to an on-going *process* of youth activism as if one is in the middle of it rather than as if it is a single incident that occurred. For example, youth bodies, words, feet on the pavement during the protests, the smells and energy of 50 youth jammed into a lobby outside of the mayor's office as I stood alongside them are all the "material" of the "enlivened space." The explicit connection to spatial theory here is that Deleuze understands space to be enlivened through the relationships, material, and interactions within a space. The implications of this spatialized view is to see a space as something that is alive and that contains bodies and desires that make meaning and configure a space. I provide examples of how youth activists contribute to this spatialized view.

THINKING WITH DELEUZE'S EVENT

As mentioned in the data analysis section, the process of thinking with theory is threaded throughout the chapter in order to make connections and to "plug into" and make sense of the ethnographic data (Mazzei, 2014). This means that I started with a working definition of event in order to guide the writing of the narrative of youth activism. Deleuze's notion of event reveals that youth identity formation is a process of self-created identities and the restructuring of experience and social space. In this research, I positioned myself within the Deleuzian spatial theory, and thus I offer a few comments below on how one might think with Deleuze's concept of event alongside ethnographic data.

First, Deleuze's event is a process as opposed to a singular, linear moment in time. Deleuze (1995) explains, "Underneath the large noisy events lie the small events of silence. I've tried in all of my books to discover the nature of events: it's a philosophical concept, the only one capable of ousting the verb 'to be' and its attributes" (p. 141). What is gained by ousting the verb "to be," is that subjects in the world are not fixed or positioned by knowledge/power relationships such as the institutional labels of "regular," or "at risk," and can *become* something other than the labels ascribed by institutions, knowledge/power relations.[5] In the next section, I catalogue the small noisy events that youth experienced. Further, Humphrey (2008) argues, "Event is a creative switch. It can be considered itself as a-temporal; it can be an instance or more likely drawn out over a sequence of happenings; in either case, it breaks apart earlier bodies of knowledge by forcing them to be seen in a particular light" (p. 375). Events are the ways that life, desire, and bodies enliven a space, or give space its materiality. To summarize, the narration of event enables the reader to experience event as youth did and as their bodies and desires enlivened the space they occupied.

Second, this chapter documents the voices and bodies of four youth. Their bodies, desires, sensations, and feelings comprise Deleuzian event. For example, I observed the hands of the police officers wrapping handcuffs on the wrists of Marley and Penny and later heard Marley, a youth activist, describe the warm concrete that he felt as they pressed their backs against it during the "die-in" demonstration. I share this brief experience to draw the reader into the sensations that made up event in this research.

Third, Deleuze and Guattari (1987) argue contestation is part of social and political action because often people are struggling over the most accurate description of events. The limit of language to describe an "incorporeal transformation" is common in writing a narrative from ethnographic data. This means it is difficult to capture the sensations, desires, and racing thoughts of both researcher and participant in a given moment. What I aim to do here is to describe and to document youth experience rather than to produce a linear narrative, so at times youth expressions are incoherent and shift in meaning, but they reflect the experience through the notion of event. Thus, seeing the ways in which youth produced space and the activist identities that emerged in the production of youth space are described next.

NARRATING EVENT: "THEY CALLED US THE REVOLUTIONARIES"

In the fall of 2012, the Chicago Board of Education and the mayor released a plan to close a historic number of schools. Each of these school closures disproportionately impacted low-income African American and Latino/a students. Youth from

O'Donnell and other area high schools engaged in conversations during school and after-school programs that responded to the reform by the Board of Education. The youth wanted to understand what exactly the board was undertaking as they targeted low-income communities on the south and south west side of Chicago. The result was a set of youth-conceived and led activist activities. Youth from O'Donnell met with their RPC sponsored after-school program peers and Isaiah, Marley, Penny, and Amelia networked with youth from other south side high schools to form a group called Chicago Youth.

Event: A Walkout and Protest at Chicago Public Schools Headquarters

On April 24, 2013, O'Donnell youth along with youth from other south side high schools were scheduled to take the State of Illinois standardized test. It was a day determined by youth across the city as a day to protest the school closures. Several months of planning went into this day. Students created fliers and held "secret" meetings across the city. Marley noted:

> We conducted research and found that school closures were in low-income communities. We believe those are the communities that need education the most, you know, to get out of the poverty cycle. So, we organize. We did a demonstration to the board of education that we don't want them to close schools. (Field notes, April 24, 2013)

The protest represented a culmination of ideas and desires from months of planning. Despite threats from their high schools that they would fail the state test and fail high school, youth charged ahead. Youth took buses from their respective high schools in time for the protest. I arrived at CPS headquarters at 9:30 a.m. As I stood in the rain, about 100 youth passed me, chanting, "Whose schools? OUR SCHOOLS." Youth wore t-shirts that said, "April 24th Boycott" and "We Demand: (1) No School Closings; (2) Tax Increment Finance Money Back in Our Schools; (3) Elected School Board in CPS." I saw local news reporters lining the sidewalk to capture youth, and one was interviewing a youth from O'Donnell. The message was clear: The youth were there in an attempt to save their schools.

After an hour of protesting, Isaiah yelled, "Mic check! Mic check!," which is a signal that youth learned from the national Occupy Movement that meant those involved in the protest needed to pause and come together in a circle to plan the next steps. As police lined the street alongside the youth, Isaiah told the youth they were going to attempt to enter the CPS headquarters given that the monthly board meeting was in session upstairs. Their plan was to send a few students up to the overflow room, which is a holding cell in the building for those wishing to give public comment to the Chicago Board of Education.

Youth waited for nearly two hours for their turn to go downstairs before the board. We listened to countless parents speak of their concerns about school closures in their communities. We listened to charter organization representatives urge the board to expand their charters in the city and the board smiled and offered praise to these organizations. Youth interpreted the school closures as unjust because the board was allowing charter networks to expand in low-income communities of color.

At about one o'clock in the afternoon Isaiah and other O'Donnell youth approached the podium to execute their plan of getting their voice heard. Despite their initial confidence outside and even as they took the elevators up to the 15th floor of the CPS headquarters building, they seemed reticent. Isaiah said, "Hi my name is…" and he was immediately cut off and told it wasn't his turn to speak by David Vitale, president of the Board of Education. The Chicago Teacher's Union representative at the podium told David Vitale that he was willing to yield his time and "Let the youth have a voice if they want and if the board will allow it." David Vitale immediately said "No." Vitale pointed to the youth and said, "You can't speak."

The youth stood there silently. The entire room was silent despite the 75+ bodies stuffed in there. The youth were ushered out of the room by guards. As youth were ushered out to the hallway, I heard the faint chant of a few youth, "Whose schools? Our schools!"

The stoic board members appeared utterly un-phased by several youth standing before them asking to be heard. The board members refused to even acknowledge the youth action. The repeated comment all over the media has been Barbara Byrd Bennett, CEO of CPS, saying, "The only place students belong today is in school taking their standardized tests."

Event —The "Die-in" Demonstration

After being ignored by the Board of Education, the next steps were set in motion by youth activists. They wanted to plan a demonstration—an act of civil disobedience— to continue to disrupt the oppression of the school closure policy occurring in low-income communities of color. Youth met across the city, in coffee shops after school, to plan what would be called the "die-in," an event that would have them lie down in an intersection on the south side of Chicago. The purpose of lying down in the intersection was to show the possible casualties that could result from school closures. To explain, the youth selected an intersection that also signaled a "gang territory line," Marley said:

> We chose that intersection because that is a dividing line for gang territories. We said that if they close these schools, then children would have to cross a street that would put their lives in jeopardy.

> Penny added: We performed our act of civil disobedience in which we laid down in the streets with white t-shirts with mock blood on the shirts to represent the possible casualties that could result from the careless policy of the board of education and the Mayor. (Field Notes, April 30, 2013)

Marley and Penny were the lead activists. They were arrested, as they had been prepared for with the help of teachers from O'Donnell and youth organizers with RPC, and were taken to a jail on the south side near O'Donnell. They were held at the jail that night when a teacher from O'Donnell was able to be with them. The next day, I was able to reflect on the experience with Marley and Penny. From my field notes:

> Penny said, "We lay down silently, on a red light of course. We were silent but I started chanting when I was arrested." Marley said, "We were protesting, and then a press conference started. And it was all just happening. Penny grabbed the microphone and said, "All my great teachers taught me that if you believe in something, you can make change." The cops told them to get up out of the intersection or they were going to get arrested. "People were chanting. Cars were also beeping at us. We did stop traffic." He said, "We didn't get up, so they put handcuffs on us. It was sorta sharp and tight on my wrists." He continued, "The cops said we were obstructing traffic and it was criminal negligence. We were taken to the police station. I was held there until 1:30 a.m., but Penny got out earlier around 10:30 p.m. Mr. Shepherd was there with us until about 9 o'clock at night." Marley said that of the five students arrested only he and Penny were from O'Donnell. The other two O'Donnell students weren't arrested because they weren't lying in the intersection. Isaiah was among the youth not arrested. He remembered that it was warm that day and he felt the concrete, hot against the thin white t-shirts they had made. They called us, "the revolutionaries," at school when we were walking down the hall today. (Field Notes, May 21, 2013)

These data provide an account of youth activism as it occurred. The youth activists and I reflected upon it together since I am also part of the reflection process and write up. In this excerpt the youth detail the process of being handcuffed, the journey to the police station, and the transition to becoming perceived as "revolutionaries" for their actions. My analysis reveals that youth experienced joy, frustration, confusion, and desire for more change despite the board of education's vote to close schools. Youth, while seemingly facing a loss—a board vote of yes to school closures—still developed a sense of critical consciousness about their community, local policies, and social justice. Throughout the process of developing their sense of self, interpreting their social reality, and enacting their desires for change, youth themselves were part of a "movement," as Marley and Penny expressed to me. The next section offers deeper analysis of the data in relation to the Deleuze's concept of event.

DISCUSSION: EVENT AS A "MOVEMENT," DEATH OF THE SELF, AND THE PRODUCTION OF YOUTH-SPACE

Event as a Movement and the Death of the Self

A phrase that all four youth in this study repeated was, "It's a movement." This phrase reflected the literal movement across spaces such as during the walkout/protest, marches to CPS headquarters, the mayor's office, board meetings, the die-in, and the protest and vigil on the day the board voted to close the historic number of schools. The movement allowed youth to claim and re-make spaces on their terms. The "movement" also reflected the desires that were conjured for youth as they participated in activism, not viewing each move as a singular act but instead viewing their movement of ideas across time and space. This section discusses the ways that Deleuzian event connects to the death of the self and then I discuss the notion of desire in relation to the spaces that youth occupied.

Deleuzian event enables us to witness and experience social identity production, youth voice and desire, and to actually account for the production and enactment of their desire in their brand of activism. From this data, we see youth engaging in a process of self-actualization, or as they stated, "bursting a bubble" from their social reality to the realization that educational inequality existed. Youth recognized themselves as poor and marginalized in particular spaces such as their low-income communities and "failing schools," and not being allowed to speak in white spaces such as those of the board of education meeting.[6] By white space, I mean that the space was governed by white (mostly male) leaders and a school district that was governed by a white racialized logic that viewed minority youth as oppositional, "at risk," and invisible to the educational policy making process.

Furthermore, Lewis (2003) argues that organizing society along racial lines affects peoples' opportunities. The youth in this study were aware of the racialized power dynamics; they knew the school board's actions to close schools disproportionately impacted high-poverty schools with high concentrations of minorities. Social and educational inequality persists along racial lines because "race [and racial meanings in relation structures such as school closure practices] is about inclusion and exclusion" (Lewis, 2003, p. 285). The forces that exclude, Lewis (2003) argues, are seen in the way that social practices operated by dominant groups stratify resources and restrict access and opportunities. Thus, in white spaces such as the board meetings opportunities for access and participation are limited for the minority youth. However, as youth reconfigured spaces and enlivened other spaces in Chicago (the intersection, the streets of Chicago with their protests, the board meeting rooms, etc.), they generated new ideas, new desires, and new acts to engage in as they sought to fight inequity. In this process, this Deleuzian event, they faced new parts of themselves as social space was mapped by youth experience.

To elaborate, moments of self-actualization, emerging in spaces, are critical in Deleuzian events and when youth realize what they are able to do with their activism. For instance, the "die-in" was a performative act in which they laid down in the intersection to represent possible deaths that would be an effect of school closure policy. The youth experienced this as a symbolic death against themselves, saying, "We're not just regular. We're activists." They shed a self that was associated with the schools they attend in the communities in which they live to *become* the activist. Connecting to Deleuzian event and this concept alongside the moments from the data, Deleuze (1990) argues:

> Every event is like a death. With every event, there is indeed the present moment of its actualization [youth's bubble bursts, the school board's policies are "racist," and impact black and Latino communities, youth are arrested, youth are "revolutionaries"], the moment in which the event is embodied in a state of affairs, which we designate as 'here, the moment has come' [April 24th, May 15th, May 22nd as examples of such designation]. But, that which happens before and after is also wrapped up in this event—the movement that is "free of limitations. (p. 151)

Despite the arrest, the policing of school administration to suppress any momentum around youth activism, and being silenced by the board of education, the youth were still able to develop a sense of social justice and a model for change beyond the incidents captured here, describing the space they created out of these experiences. For example, they said:

Marley: I mean I feel like I have learned and developed my view of social justice these last months. I feel like school is a place I at least began to learn and think about these issues, so education became connected to social justice for me. This is a place where you can come and learn, and yet CPS is closing down all these schools and taking that away from kids. That is not justice.

Penny: When we were put in the police car, it was exciting and we had a moment of feeling scared. We're not nothing. We made these acts and changed what that intersection meant.

Marley: Even if the Board votes to close the 50 schools doesn't mean our fight will end. This is a movement.

Penny: As long as there is humanity, there will be people to fight. It's a movement. (Field Notes, May 21, 2013)

Each of the youth experienced themselves through the social processes—the movement of event. The process of experiencing themselves occurs in spaces that function to erase themselves as regulars. Such a moment, for instance, was when they participated in the die-in demonstration, as Penny noted above, youth changed what that space [the intersection] meant to people by enlivening the space with the materiality and vitality of their bodies and desires for social change (Doel & Clarke, 2011; Webb & Gulson, 2013). Youth claimed that intersection and made it mean something on their terms to demonstrate to the city, the community, and the board of education that their policies had/would have negative consequences.

Additionally, the die-in was a symbolic act of violence in the particular youth spaces and "erasure of their ['regular'] subjectivity in the sites of their marginality" (Kaplan, 1998, p. 86). This means that while youth were demonstrating to fight the school board's closure policy, a deeper meaning existed beyond the immediate event. Youth, deemed regulars and failures by the board, engaged in a symbolic act of violence that killed off the identity of regular, or as Amelia said, "I do activist things even though I'm nothing." In effect, youth killed off parts of their marginalized identities (labels such as those mentioned at the outset of the chapter) to become activists in the spaces they occupied. Less important to the youth were institutional labels and more important to youth were the moments that they began to identify as activists on their own terms.

Furthermore, the data analysis and the documentation of the process of activism reveals instances of youth identity formation as a process of committing violence against oneself across racialized spaces. In other words, youth—who are already marginalized through institutional structures and neoliberal accountability mechanisms in public education—find ways to invent new versions of themselves across spaces of power as activists. Deleuze (1995) argues:

> Once one steps outside what's been thought before, once one ventures outside what's familiar and reassuring, once one has to invent new concepts for unknown lands, then methods and moral systems break down and thinking becomes, as Foucault puts it, a 'perilous act", a violence, whose first victim is oneself. (p. 103)

Examples of youth venturing beyond what they know and generating activist activities reveal that they engaged in this 'perilous act' to kill off parts of former selves that were limiting their opportunity to grow and transform.

Further, Deleuzian event connects one's subjectivity to the space in which it emerges. This is a process in which a subject comes into relation with oneself in a particular space, moving toward liberation (Deleuze, 1993, pp. 77–78; Humphrey, 2008). The moments from the data capture how youth "tear" themselves up, but also propel themselves into unknown worlds of social problems (Deleuze, 1994, p. 192). In Deleuzian event, "states of affairs" such as a protest, a march, or an act of civil disobedience reveal the sensation and desire of youth for a more socially just educational policy and experience (Colwell, 1997). Using Deleuze's notion of the event, accounting for desire, movement, and liberation, we can begin to break the reproduction of social spaces and theorize youth space on the terms of unheard groups such as the youth activists. It is the desire for knowledge, for "more," and that sustains them. Isaiah claimed, "I just came to realize how valuable youth are when it comes to injustice" (Interview, June 3, 2013). It was the unsteady and uncertain desires these youth experienced that enabled them to experiment socially, culturally and politically with their social identities and to produce youth cultural organizing. It's a movement.

The theoretical tools engendered in Deleuze's event, such as the death of the self and the new subjectivities that emerge in various spaces, open up possible ways of seeing youth identity formation in material, enlivened spaces of activism. These spaces reflect a process of self-making and re-making as youth desire manifests in action.

IMPLICATIONS

The meditations I have offered contribute to the literature on youth activism by engaging with new conceptualizations of space through Deleuze's relational space theory and new ways of experimenting with ethnographic data analysis by "thinking with theory" (Jackson & Mazzei, 2012). This is an important step in opening up spaces to study youth identity formation and its connection to spatial analysis. Much of the previous research, as has already been argued, views youth culture, experiences, space, or identity within dualistic paradigms that fail to see the productive ways in which youth re-create and re-claim space to make possible and to render visible stronger, politically conscious versions of themselves.

The data in this research study challenged this view of youth identity across social spaces because youth in the study—while certainly Latino immigrants and some undocumented—preferred to distance themselves from a racial or ethnic marker such as Latino, the political status of immigrant, or the instructional status of 'at risk regular". Instead, through the Deleuzian event, what emerged was a complex set of social relations and experiences for youth as they interpret their unequal socio-economic conditions and seek to enact social change. Specifically the social identity formation and the production of space in the study adds to a non-essentialist, discursive and complex view of relational space and the ways in which youth remake and produce space through their activism. It is challenging in our current neoliberal era of reform to generate lines of inquiry on spaces of education reform to initiate non-essentialist models that render identity of marginalized youth as "unresolved" (Ngo, 2010).

The significance of this study addresses in particular how youth activism moving through spaces can help them re-claim and re-invent new versions of themselves, escaping institutional marginalization and offers new ways of conceptualizing spatialized identities that are productive. By this I mean in order to escape the institutional marginalization of identity, youth had to leave the school spaces and also experience symbolic deaths of themselves. Youth were able to emerge and produce new selves as activists across spaces. In addition, youth organizing and the transition toward the activist-identity was a process youth reflected upon the educational inequalities they observed in order to determine the most appropriate approach for daily interactions in the spaces of education. Youth activists sought to ameliorate the conditions of existence that limited their experience and positioning in the world while also attempting to maintain a certain degree of autonomy within their identity transformations. What matters here is that these processes are youth organized and experienced, and this chapter sought to capture these youth perceptions and experiences despite the painful struggle that comes with shedding one's connection to institutions, ideologies, and histories of oppression.

NOTES

[1] Hereafter, anytime the word event is used it refers to a Deleuzian event.

[2] The phrase "just regulars" became important for understanding youth perceptions of themselves and how the school perceived them. I describe the term "regular" and its meaning for youth and how they contested it later in the chapter.

[3] At the school in this study, the students were tracked. The youth activists explained this to me as the lowest track being "just regulars," the middle track was the Honors/Advanced Placement, and then the International Baccalaureate (IB) track was the highest track. At O'Donnell a very low percentage of students were in IB, approximately 50 students out of the 2,575 students, so there was a perception in the school that the IB track had the best students. Additionally, the "regulars," perceived the IB students to be getting a better education given that IB students had a small cohort that took all their classes together and were isolated from the rest of O'Donnell students. The IB program is a prestigious, critical thinking-oriented curriculum that aligns with international standards, see, http://www.ibo.org/

[4] For this budding area of scholarship on disrupting research methodology and critiquing social science paradigms and practices, see, Kuntz (2015); Rodriguez (forthcoming).

[5] The movement from being to becoming is significant to understanding Deleuze and others' philosophies and understandings of subjectivity, power, and knowledge production. The notion of becoming is also a cornerstone of Deleuze's (1993, 1994, 1995) work and others' problematizations of subjective and power as it relates to methodology (see for example, Kuntz, 2015; Lather, 1991, 2001; MacLure, 2011, 2013; Masny, 2013; Rodriguez, forthcoming).

[6] Leonardo (2002) argues, 'Whiteness' is a racial discourse, whereas the category 'white people' represents a socially constructed identity, usually based on skin color. For practical purposes, we are born with certain bodies that are inscripted with social meaning (2002, p. 31; 2000). I am invoking "whiteness" here because the white spaces of the school board intersection with issues of race and power. In the white space of the board, youth are faced with exclusion and rejection. Youth were silenced literally, but also symbolically as members of a non-white racial group and as members of lower class status. Leonardo (2002) goes onto argue that whiteness is supported by material practices in institutions. That said, Leonardo argues that whiteness is collection of everyday strategies that are characterized by the unwillingness to name the contours of racism, the avoidance of identifying with a racial experience or group, the minimization of racist legacy, and other similar evasions (2002, p. 32). When the board refused to let youth speak and had them ushered out, it demonstrated the ways that issues of racial injustice are avoided and rejected in white spaces. But, youth complicated this by bringing their black and brown bodies into white spaces.

REFERENCES

Ares, N. (2010). *Youth-full productions: Cultural practices and constructions of content and social spaces.* New York, NY: Peter Lang.

Buendía, E. (2000). Power and possibility: The construction of a pedagogical practice. *Teaching and Teacher Education, 16*(2), 147–163.

Buendía, E., Ares, N., Juarez, B. G., & Peercy, M. (2004, March 8). The geographies of difference: The production of the East Side, West Side, and Central City School. *American Educational Research Journal, 41*(4), 833–863.

Blaisdell, B. (2016). Schools as racial spaces: Understanding and resisting structural racism. *International Journal of Qualitative Studies in Education, 29*(2), 248–272.

Clifford, J. (1997). *Routes: Travel and translation in the late twentieth century.* Cambridge, MA: Harvard University Press.

Colwell, C. (1997). Deleuze and Foucault: Series, event, genealogy. *Theory and Event,* 1(2). Retrieved from http://muse.jhu.edu/journals/theory_and_event/v001/1.2colwell.html

Davidson, A. L. (1996). *Making and molding identity in schools: Student narratives on race, gender, and academic engagement.* Albany, NY: State University of New York Press.

Deleuze, G. (1990). *The logic of sense.* New York, NY: Columbia University Press.

Deleuze, G. (1993). *The fold: Leibniz and the Baroque.* Minneapolis, MN: University of Minnesota Press.

Deleuze, G. (1994). *Difference and repetition.* New York, NY: Columbia University Press.

Deleuze, G. (1995). *Negotiations 1972–1990* (M. Joughin, Trans.). New York, NY: Columbia University Press.

Deleuze, G., & Guattari, F. (1987). *A thousand plateaus: Capitalism and schizophrenia.* London: Athlone Press.

Denzin, N. K. (1997). *Interpretive ethnography: Ethnographic practices for the 21st century.* Thousand Oaks, CA: Sage Publications.

Denzin, N. K., & Lincoln, Y. S. (2005). *The Sage handbook of qualitative research.* Thousand Oaks, CA: Sage Publications

Doel, M. A., & Clarke, B. (2011). Gilles Deleuze. In P. Hubbard & R. Kitchen (Eds.), *Key thinkers on space and place.* London: Sage.

Eckert, P. (1989). *Jocks and burnouts: Social categories and identity in the high school.* New York, NY: Teachers College, Columbia University.

Ferguson, J., & Gupta, A. (2002). Spatializing states: Toward an ethnography of neoliberal governmentality. *American Ethnologist, 29*(4), 981–1002.

Foley, D. A., Levinson, B. A., & Hurtig, J. (2000). Chapter 2: Anthropology goes inside: The new educational ethnography of ethnicity and gender. *Review of Research in Education, 25*(1), 37–98.

Helfenbein, R. (2010). Thinking through scale: Critical geography and curriculum spaces. In E. Malewski (Ed.), *Curriculum studies handbook: The next moment* (pp. 304–317). New York, NY: Routledge.

Helfenbein, R. J., & Taylor, L. H. (2009). Critical geographies in/of education: Introduction. *Educational Studies, 45*(3), 236–239.

Humphrey, C. (2008). Reassembling individual subjects. *Anthropological Theory, 8*(4), 357–380.

Jackson, A. Y., & Mazzei, L. A. (2012). *Thinking with theory in qualitative research: Viewing data across multiple perspectives.* London: Routledge.

Kaplan, C. (1996). *Questions of travel: Postmodern discourses of displacement.* Durham, NC: Duke University Press.

Kirshner, B., Gaertner, M., & Pozzoboni, K. (2010). Tracing transitions: Effect of high school closure on displaced students. *Educational Evaluation and Policy Analysis, 32*(3), 407–429.

Kuntz, A. M. (2015). *The responsible methodologist: inquiry, truth-telling, and social justice.* Walnut Creek, CA: Left Coast Press.

Lather, P. (1991). *Getting smart: Feminist research and pedagogy with/in the postmodern.* New York, NY: Routledge.

Lather, P. (2001). Postbook: Working the ruins of feminist ethnography. *Signs, 27*(1), 199–227.

Leonardo, Z. (2003). *Ideology, discourse, and school reform.* Westport, CT: Praeger.

Levinson, B. A., Foley, D. E., & Holland, D. C. (1996). *The cultural production of the educated person: Critical ethnographies of schooling and local practice.* Albany, NY: State University of New York Press.

Lewis, A. (2003). Everyday race-making: Navigating racial boundaries in schools. *American Behavioral Scientist, 47*(3), 283–305.

MacLure, M. (2011). Qualitative inquiry: Where are the ruins? *Qualitative Inquiry, 17*(10), 997–1005.

MacLure, M. (2013). The wonder of data. *Cultural Studies, Critical Methodologies, 13*(4), 228–232.

Madison, D. S. (2012). *Critical ethnography: Method, ethnics, and performance.* London: Sage.

Masny, D. (2013). Rhizoanalytic pathways in qualitative research. *Qualitative Inquiry, 20*(5), 339–348.

Mazzei, L. A. (2014). Beyond an easy sense: A diffractive analysis. *Qualitative Inquiry, 20*(6), 742–746.

McDermott, R. (1993). The acquisition of a child by a learning disability. In S. Chaiklin & J. Lave (Eds.), *Understanding practice: Perspectives on activity and context* (pp. 269–305). Cambridge, UK: Cambridge University Press.

Ngo, B. (2010). *Unresolved identities: Discourse, ambivalence, and urban immigrant students.* Albany, NY: State University of New York Press.

Noblit, G. W. (1999). *Particularities: Collected essays on ethnography and education*. New York, NY: Peter Lang.

Orellana, M. F. (2009). *Translating childhoods: Immigrant youth, language, and culture* (Rutgers series in childhood studies). New Brunswick, NJ: Rutgers University Press.

Quantz, R. A. (1992). On critical ethnography (with some postmodern considerations). In M. D. LeCompte, W. L. Millroy, & J. Preissle (Eds.), *The handbook of qualitative research in education* (pp. 447–506). San Diego, CA: Academic Press.

Rodriguez, S. (2013). "Can't we just get rid of the classroom?": Thinking space, relationally. *Taboo: The Journal of Culture and Education, 13*(1), 97–122.

Rodriguez, S. (2015a). The dangers of compassion: The positioning of refugee students in policy and education research and implications for teacher education. *Knowledge Cultures, 3*(2), 112–126.

Rodriguez, S. (2015b). "I hate my own race; the teachers just always think we are smart": Re-conceptualizing the model minority stereotype as a racial epithet. In N. Hartlep (Ed.), *Modern societal impacts of the model minority stereotype* (pp. 205–230). Hershey, PA: IGI Global.

Rodriguez, S. (2016). Toward a methodology of death: Deleuze's "event" as method for critical ethnography. *Critical Questions in Education, 7*(3), 232–238.

Soja, E. (1996). *Thirdspace : Journeys to Los Angeles and other real-and-imagined places*. Cambridge, MA: Blackwell.

Soja, E. W. (2010). *Seeking spatial justice*. Minneapolis, MN: University of Minnesota Press.

Tamboukou, M., & Ball, S. J. (2003). *Dangerous encounters: Genealogy and ethnography*. New York, NY: Peter Lang.

Villenas, S. A., & Foley, D. F. (2011). Critical ethnographies of education in the Latino/a diaspora. In R. Valencia (Ed.), *Chicano school failure and success: Past, present and future* (3rd ed.). New York, NY & London: Routledge and Falmer.

Webb, P. T., & Gulson, K. N. (2013). Policy intensions and the folds of the self. *Educational Theory, 63*(1), 51–68.

Webb, P. T., & Gulson, K. N. (2015). *Policy, geophilosophy and education*. Rotterdam: Sense Publishers.

Sophia Rodriguez
College of Charleston

MIKE GULLIVER

7. SEEKING LEFEBVRE'S VÉCU IN A "DEAF SPACE" CLASSROOM

In this chapter, tools drawn from Lefebvre's work on space are used to explore the spaces produced by a mixed hearing and deaf class within a series of nested departmental and university spaces. Before setting out those spaces, it is key to briefly return to Lefebvre's spatial triad of *perçu*, *conçu* and *vécu*,[1] and to explore how those "moments" of spatial production intersect with senses, language, culture and politics to produce Deaf spaces.

LEFEBVRE'S SPATIAL TRIAD

Lefebvre's spatial triad is well-known to geographers, and increasingly understood beyond the Field for me not to labour their description. Emerging from Lefebvre's quest for *Totalité*—a quest that he posited in spatial terms as the pursuit of a moment in which, rather than finding itself squeezed into ill-fitting and ill-constructed spaces, we might integrate ourselves and our environments in ways that allow complete integrity and freedom—Lefebvre's spatial triad manifested as the building blocks of encounter, three spatial moments that are innocently devoid of any over-authoring. Raw engagement with life, with others, and with ourselves.

The first are *espaces perçus* [trans. perceived/apprehended/sensed/intuited] where the question of perception can be both an encounter with the new and previously unacknowledged, or/and the habitual manipulation by body and movement. The *perçu* is the commonsensical stuff of life lived; traces upon reality that the individual or society, through their everyday "competence" "Secretes… propounds and presupposes" (Lefebvre, 1973, p. 38). They are spaces encountered, inhabited, and in-habit-ed until they are eventually banal. At least, until they are not, at which point they become the striking, flummoxing, awkwardness of sudden encounter. They are, according to Rob Shields, "Ignored one minute and over-fetishised the next" (Shields, 1998, p. 160).

Shaping those traces both through description and measure as well as prescription and ordering is the second moment; *espaces conçu* [trans. conceived, begotten, abstractly conceptualised/understood/theorised/imagined]. The *conçu* is space planned, described and understood, constructed and "ordered" (Lefebvre, 1973, p. 33): "the space of scientists, planners, urbanists, technocratic subdividers and social engineers" (Lefebvre, 1973, p. 38). It is a space that identifies space. *Perçu*,

N. Ares et al. (Eds.), Deterritorializing/Reterritorializing, 99–107.

describes it, knows it and discourses on it (Shields, 1998, p. 161). It is a space that is symbolised, known, codified, and objectified (Merrifield, 2000, p. 174), finding its "objective expression" (Lefebvre, 1973, p. 49) in the fixity of structures both concrete—buildings, roads, schools—and in "bureaucratic and political authoritarianism immanent to a repressive space" (Lefebvre, 1973, p. 49).

Finally, offering hope and release to the tension that must inevitably arise from the entrapment of *perçu* spaces: irreducibly multiple, organic, manifestations of life lived, within crystalised, measured, ordered, prescribed *conçu* cages, are moments that Lefebvre terms *vécu* [trans. alive, animate, transformative, uncompromising, full]. *Vécu*, for Lefebvre, is not the simulacra of life-support, the artificial maintenance of a *perçu* by a repressive and unrelenting *conçu*. Rather it is a "space which the imagination seeks to change and appropriate" (Lefebvre, 1973, p. 39); the explosive and transformative "joie de vivre"; "moments of presence... that shock one into a new conception of the spatialisation of social life" (Shields, 1998, p. 161).

For Lefebvre, the key to understanding the three—*perçu, conçu* and *vécu*—is to see that although they can be analysed separately, their reality is that they are never entirely discrete. Thus, although they might appear as independent elements, (cleanly distinct, hermetic, static, observable) they are in fact entangled and intertwined as a landscape; one that is eternally irresolvable, always in motion. For Lefebvre, the lack of resolution of this landscape is unimportant. Rather, it is in that constant motion of spatial play that the importance rests—forces twisting and pulling, bursting out, tamping down, and spilling over in de- and re-territorialisation. As Rob Shields describes it, what is important is how this roiling spatial challenge represents the quest for *totalité*; the bursting-forth of a "dis-alienated moment of the embodied 'total person' at one with their context... localised 'reappropriations' of space that may furnish examples... by which certain sites are removed or severed from [a] governing spatialisation..." (Shields, 1998, pp. 161, 165).

Deaf Space and Its Place Within the U of B

One of those governing spatialisations is the University of Bristol, an internationally-renowned, research-intensive university in the UK, which was recently Lefebvre, positioned within the top ten for UK research intensity. Its spaces, as might be expected for an institution of that nature, are produced by and perform the culture of the academic élite; by *perçu* hearing—instinctively, and unthinkingly perceiving, apprehending, sensing and intuiting reality from bodies equipped with a sensorium that includes and foregrounds hearing and speech; and by *conçu* élite—conceiving and abstractly conceptualising, understanding, theorising and imagining standards for acceptability in terms of both social and academic Establishment.

Upon this hearing-established UofB landscape, one of Shield's localised "reappropriations" of space that was created was the Centre for Deaf Studies (CDS). Established in the 1970s, the CDS was initially a research centre in education before quickly establishing its own identity, in no small part because of its distinctive mission and cultural profile. Collocated with, and housed within, the same physical spaces as the UoB, CDS was not only dedicated to studying Deaf culture, but also carried a political aim to achieve visibility and recognition for Deaf knowledges within mainstream academia. Internationally, it achieved this through its work.

Locally, however, its impact was achieved in a far more humble way. Whereas outside of CDS, Deaf people found themselves faced with the challenge of how to access what was, in effect, a "hearing-institution," within the CDS there was no reason not to simply use sign language. Furthermore, as Deaf people signed, it became normal for hearing people there to sign as well. Sign language gradually displaced hearing language and signing space gradually took over; office furniture was moved to cater to sight rather than sound, doors were propped open, windows became portals for conversation; the default clothing worn to work became friendlier to sign-reading eyes. And as the *perçu* within CDS shifted, so did the *conçu*: Business meetings gradually became sign-only, were chaired to allow for visual turn-taking, and allocated time to let the minute-taker (who couldn't watch and write at the same time) catch up, and it became considered normal to sign and "rude" to speak because, even if no deaf people were immediately present, they might happen along during the conversation.

Another barely registered rudeness was knocking on a door and using sound to gain attention rather than using the light-generating doorbells or a wave. The bell at reception, therefore, was only really used by visitors. Some of those visits demonstrated just how different the space that CDS had become. One event in particular remains firmly etched in my memory—a meeting called by one of the university management with the staff from the centre, who was keen to ensure that an interpreter would be present so that the Deaf staff "would be able to understand." It was only as I sat in the meeting and looked around that I realised that the only one present that didn't sign was the manager himself. While he viewed all of the Deaf staff as "disabled" within the *conçu* of the wider university for their lack of a sense, within CDS itself, his hearing was irrelevant; it was he who was the one who needed the interpreter.

That "reversal" of norms within the CDS space was something that gradually soaked into the perception of those more often in contact with CDS and may represent, in their most advanced form, something of a *vécu* moment. It was revealing to watch one manager, whose time overseeing CDS began with a staunch declaration that he was going to "sort out the failure of Deaf staff to publish." He gradually came to understand how ill-fitted the *conçus* of an elite hearing university's individualistic publishing culture were for a department employing staff who, although working for the "Academic Industrial Complex," drew both their skills and priorities directly from Deaf spaces outside of that Complex. He was faced with academics who were brilliant teachers, and who communicated their work regularly and richly to the Deaf community in ways and forms that the community could access and understand, but who had "weak" English, and who were "failing" in terms of their prestige publication record and their grant writing. Over time in that Deaf space, with its particular arrangements of people and things suited to people using sign languages, as well as its privileging of embodied communication, the manager came to understand how the previous systemic disempowerment of those Deaf academics by the poor-quality education that they had received as deaf children and young people also extended into the way that their performance was now being assessed. The simple positioning of CDS as only one subsection within the university and its administrative structures, however, made any more widespread participation in such *vécu* moments very rare. Thus, although some longer-term managers did gradually become more adept at navigating CDS' alternative spaces, they always did so more like tourists who delight in the exotic of the foreign than those who are driven by reverse culture shock to challenge their own native spaces. In the case of the manager mentioned above, he found his role not as a transformer of the wider university, but as a human buffer between it and CDS. CDS, therefore, never really succeeded in achieving what Deaf people have long envisaged from their spaces:

> Those strangers who come in 'chez nous' will take away an enduring memory of their time in our midst and will return to occupy themselves in remedying all that is left lacking in the situation of Deaf people. (Gaillard & Jeanvoine, 1900, p. 278)

The CDS Deaf Studies Masters

An additional reason for why encounters between the university and CDS provoked so few *vécu* moments was perhaps because, even though on the surface it appeared staunchly different, the individual agency of students and staff to find ways to deal with the cultural fracture between CDS and the wider university effectively diluted its all or nothing "intransigence." This can be seen through a closer look at the main focus from the point of view for this chapter; the postgraduate Masters degree in Deaf Studies (MScDS) offered by CDS, and its course on Deaf History (DH).

At the time of my involvement, the MScDS had been running for a number of years. Taught by a mixed faculty of CDS' deaf and hearing academics, it attracted an equally mixed cohort of between eight and twelve deaf and hearing students from both the UK and overseas. Within each years' intake, Deaf and hearing, signing and non-signing, lecturers and students all mixed, producing a space that was neither Deaf nor hearing, nor static, but that ebbed, and flowed, and shifted based on who was there and how they communicated. It was a space that, in many ways, did more than the academic content of the course could ever do to challenge assumptions, and to produce new ways to be,

As the Centre's own practices began to dovetail with those of the *conçu* space of the UoB more formally, things became more limited. Teaching, for example, could be done in either speech or sign. The choice, however, was not entirely free, but depended on whether interpreters would need to be present and how to pay them. In a bizarre form of policy ballet, while deaf faculty could teach a mixed signing and non-signing class in BSL because they were officially "disabled," (and so qualified for a voice-over interpreter for those who needed it), and hearing faculty could teach the same mixed class in spoken English because any deaf *students'* deafness qualified *them* for a signing interpreter, hearing faculty could not teach a mixed class in sign if non-signing students were present, there being no funding for a voice-over interpreter because the lecturer's choice of language then was exactly that; a "choice," and because although non-signing students couldn't understand the lecturer directly, they were not officially "disabled."

I had experienced this odd, improvised semi-CDS/semi-UoB space for myself as a student on the MScDS in 2002, and so it was very familiar when I was asked to teach the DH unit while its regular faculty lead was on study leave. My situation was rendered even more complicated by the delightful presence alongside me of a co-teacher who was deaf herself. Together, we wrote and delivered the entire semester's teaching; I in spoken English with a signing interpreter for formal teaching (and in either sign or English without interpreter for less formal interactions), and she in sign at all times with a voice-over interpreter if required. The following figure necessarily simplifies this,[2] but gives some idea of the different linguistic "entanglements" that were present in front led teaching. (see Figure 1)

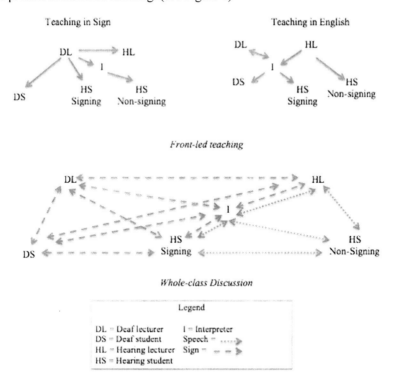

Figure 1. Flow of communication in front-led teaching and whole-class discussion

To attempt to simplify the to-ing and fro-ing of interpreters, and to reduce confusion from students, rather than teach with both of us at the front of the class, we took turns. I noticed very quickly that our change-overs at the front were not simply seamless turn-taking, but that something more substantial was happening at the same time. Class after class, I would take my turn at the front, flip my slides up onto the overhead, give out hand-outs, and then teach through 20 or 30 minutes of pretty dense material, only to then find that when my colleague stepped up to the front, her teaching seemed to consist of little more than chat… "How are you? How are we doing? Wasn't that interesting? You know, when I was a girl… has anyone here had the same experience?" I would then take over, and try to make up lost time. She would then come back to the front and carry on as before. It got so bad after a few weeks that I sat down with her and asked her, quite crossly, what she was playing at. She simply said:

"Deaf classroom"
"But what does that mean?"
"I'm teaching how Deaf people teach—how Deaf people learn."
"But you're not teaching anything—you're just chatting."
"That's how Deaf people learn, little by little, all together."
"But we've got so much material to cover, we'll never get through it."
"Better learn a bit, all together, than a few students know everything and some nothing."

The last phrase speaks volumes of the collective nature of Deaf learning,[3] and the tension between success in learning defined by my colleague and the individualistic learning criteria that my university would have preferred. We were, however, within that individualistic setting and I was curious to learn how the students perceived what was going on.

"We connect to her," one of them, a Deaf EU student (A) told me. "She signs, we sign, it's all visual—we don't have to work through the interpreter, and so we learn directly; her experience, is our experience."

"She's terrible," said another, a hearing student (B) who signed his own national sign language well, but who hadn't mastered BSL in the time he'd been in the UK. "I don't get anything out of her teaching. I do all my work in the library afterwards."

"She's not terrible," said another hearing student (C) who *had* transferred her signing to BSL. "It's great to be able to work through things with the Deaf students and a teacher all together, in sign. And yes, I can always go to the library afterwards if I need more reading."

"We don't spend so much time in the library" said A. "That's where hearing people go to learn… they don't really learn in class. They spend, like 20% of time learning with others, and 80% reading. Deaf people, it's the other way around. We learn best face to face."

"But how do you do that" I asked, "When there's no provision in the timetable?"

"We meet up a lot outside of the class… lots of coffee conversations, and then we go to the library to check things."

"We might as well be teaching ourselves," said B.

It was that last comment that made me think the most. If hearing students believed that they were essentially teaching themselves through what A had referred to as their '80% library time', and Deaf students believed that they were spending a great deal of their time also teaching themselves but in small 'coffee conversation' groups, then what was the classroom time really for? I began to pay attention to what was happening in the classroom itself, and what I saw profoundly impressed me; for what was going on was little less than a shift in the very space produced in the room. As I stood to speak, the room would become a hearing academic space with hearing codes; the hearing students would face me, and adopt hearing ways of learning – taking notes, asking questions directly in speech, looking at the slides while listening in the background, etc. The Deaf students, on the other hand, watched the interpreter, waiting for their opportunity to get out of the classroom to spend time discussing and digesting material with each other. It was, in effect, a hearing classroom—the same hearing classroom in which those Deaf students had learned to cope as they had come up through a predominantly hearing educational system.

As my Deaf colleague stood to teach, however, an almost tangible shift would occur in the room. Deaf students, engaging directly with the teacher, were delighted at being guided in some of their 80% conversation-learning time by an expert who not only taught them through deaf experience, but had direct feedback on how well they were following and who could therefore monitor their reaction to new ideas and introduce new thinking at an appropriate speed. Hearing students, similarly, could watch her even if they couldn't understand her signing because of the voice-over provided by the interpreter. With their 80% library learning time secure in the back of their minds, they could spend this 20% classroom time simply playing with ideas.

In fact, the only people in the class who were unhappy were student B—who was particularly resistant to the idea that anything that wasn't painfully front-led was "real learning"—and me. I was quickly able to resolve my own worries by describing to the students what I thought was going on, and allowing them to define how they thought we should conduct the class so that it would work best. Thankfully, since nearly all were deeply engaged in the subject, and we could rely on the interpreters' goodwill to support communication in whatever form, whether I or the hearing students who signed decided to speak or sign, our solution was to largely abandon formal teaching, to provide all of the teaching material in advance, and to simply to use class time to discuss their own reading and thinking and to introduce and challenge ideas.

When a Vécu Is Not a Vécu

Our final solution was effective, but it relied as much on the closed space of the classroom as it did on a real definitive resolution to the issues that the case study above really surfaces. Had we been at the mercy of inflexible interpreters or their funding, a less than equal deaf/hearing student ratio, less-than-ideal self-study resources, or even a particularly belligerent response from dissatisfied students, we would have had far less room for manoeuvre. Indeed, it was only when the final essays were handed in, and I was able to see that not only had the students performed well, but that they had cooperated in the essay-writing as they had in the classroom; sharing skills and expertise to ensure that not only was the content sufficiently strong, but that the formal expectations of referencing and bibliography had been correctly polished and delivered, that I was able to breathe a sigh of relief. I thanked my colleague (who had now, through battle perhaps, become a close friend), packed up my teaching materials, and vowed that I would never do anything as irresponsible as agree to teach that course again.

As relieved as I was to successfully reach the end of the course, I was still frustrated by what I had observed. Hearing students had largely adapted to the changes that we had brought but, with their self-directed learning still intact, had experienced the changes in the classroom more as an innovative pedagogical method than as a change that fundamentally transformed their learning landscape. Given that the transformed classroom, then, had only really changed things for the deaf students, surely they would be the first to lose by returning to the status quo. What would be needed to ensure that that didn't happen? How could we achieve a more wholesale change? What did the evidence of what we had done mean to the validity of fusty, elitist *conçu* structures? Had the MScDS DH classroom not ended up becoming a new space, one that demonstrated a "new conception of the spatialisation of social [and academic] life" (Shields, 1998, p. 165)? Was there not, as the result of a moment of encounter, a collision, between the *perçus* and *conçus* of hearing and deaf Higher Educational learning; between the structures, expectations, criteria for success, pedagogies, and understandings of deaf and hearing academia? Had our classroom not been a *vécu*?

Perhaps it had. And yet, because it had satisfied acceptable criteria for its successful completion—essays that were marked and approved, student satisfaction grades that were positive, and a body of administrative material that was filed in the prescribed manila envelopes—it was... acceptable. Somewhere between the reality of that classroom and its lived experience of radically challenging the taken-for-granted nature of Higher Educational learning and teaching and the potential that it had to re-author the very nature of learning and teaching, the DH course, and all its learning was somehow translated into a set of benign markers of normalcy. Utterly unnoticed by the university at large, the *vécu* of the DH classroom was lost.

Perhaps it will now have an impact through this chapter. Perhaps, since the *vécu* still lives in my own knowledge of what a classroom is, or could be, it will have an impact on reshaping what I do in the future. Were I, for example, to run a similar course in a similar way, what other directions might that *vécu* take me in? In the end, I may never know. Only a few years after the experience I have described, the University of Bristol closed down the Centre for Deaf Studies completely. By doing so, it may have robbed itself of the opportunity for a Deaf space *vécu*, forever.

NOTES

[1] I maintain use of the French terms throughout this chapter. In part, this is to avoid any confusion between the common English translations of the concepts (often given as 'perçu' = Spatial Practices, 'conçu' = Representations of space, 'vécu' = Spaces of representation) and other mentions of 'practices' or 'representation'.

[2] For example, it removes any question of variation in the quality of communication assuming an either/or situation – either two individuals could communicate effectively, or couldn't. This has been done instrumentally to clarify questions of medium and space below.

[3] See Ladd (forthcoming) for more information about this.

REFERENCES

Gaillard, H., & Jeanvoine, H. (1900). *Congrès international pour l'étude des questions d'assistance et d'éducation des sourds-muets: Compte rendu des débats et relations diverses/par henri gaillard,. henri jeanvoine,. ; exposition universelle de 1900* Impr. d'ouvriers sourds-muets (Paris).

Lefebvre, H. (1973). *The production of space.* Oxford: Blackwell.

Merrifield, A. (2000). Levebvre, anti-logos, and Nietzsche: An alternative reading of "The Production of Space." *Antipode, 27*, 294–303.

Shields, R. (1999). *Lefebvre, love, and struggle: Spatial dialectics.* London: Routledge. doi:10.4324/9780203983959

Mike Gulliver
University of Bristol

NANCY ARES

8. STORY MAPS AS CONVINCING REPRESENTATIONS OF CLAIMS TO SPACE

INTRODUCTION

The goal in this chapter is to illustrate how a critical geography framework guided my analysis of one resident/activist's perspectives and participation in the Coalition for the Children of Lakeview (CCL; for an in-depth description, see O'Connor, Ares, & Larson, 2011), a resident-driven community-transformation initiative in upstate New York. As such, it is both a methodological piece and a report of research findings. I was part of a team of critical ethnographers that conducted a 4-year ethnography of the CCL. This initiative was a community based collaborative effort to improve the overall quality of life in northeastern Lakeview, a region with a rich history of resilience, including political activism, community-based advocacy, and cultural and linguistic diversity that bring vitality and important resources to its neighborhoods. The region also has a history of poverty, student underachievement, violence, and crime, which is why the CCL was formed. The purpose of the CCL was to develop and implement a plan in which children, families, and neighborhoods in this area of Lakeview could succeed academically, economically, and in terms of their wellbeing. The goal was to coordinate, develop, and expand ongoing efforts by schools, community organizations, activist organizations, businesses, community members, and social service agencies that would stimulate more positive, sustainable outcomes in the area.

THEORETICAL FRAMEWORK

Flores (2000) cites de Certeau in writing about "personal narratives [that] perform the 'everyday' acts of resistance that are often characteristic of groups with limited access to traditional forms of power" (p. 691). Residents in the CCL were positioned in such a way at the outset of the initiative. A major discovery of the larger ethnography was the ongoing struggle between residents and planners over control of the CCL process (designing, planning, implementing) versus control of the content (aspects of the community that should be the CCL's focus, e.g., k12 education, public safety, youth supports, adult training and employment) (Ares, 2014). At the heart of these struggles were competing conceptions of the CCL space in Lakeview as residents sought to claim central roles within the initiative as people responsible for authoring and shepherding substantive reform. Our research team

N. Ares et al. (Eds.), Deterritorializing/Reterritorializing, 109–120.

was able to witness them narrate dreams of a future urban space that retained the assets, attachments, relationships, and traces of historically developed communities while simultaneously transforming the precarious social and material dimensions of this part of northeast Lakeview. A critical geography perspective provided a powerful explanatory framework for what residents were saying and how they were "performing" as resident/activists in the CCL space. Caquard's (2013) work on maps and narratives proved to be helpful in my making sense of the data with an eye to relations of power:

> Overall, the critical turn in cartography has dramatically modified the relations between maps and narratives in two ways: by deconstructing and exposing the meta-narratives embedded in maps, and by envisioning maps as a compelling form of storytelling ... MacFarlane (2007) introduces the concept of 'story maps' to describe forms of spatial expressions that embody our personal experiences of the environment and contribute to creating a deep understanding of places. The idea that a story map is defined by its experiential dimension echoes other researchers' acknowledgement of the importance of developing emotionally charged maps and geo-visualization in order to better understand places and to mobilize for action. (Caquard, 2001, p. 136)

Connections among emotions and place, narrative and place, and rights and place are made clear through using maps as artifacts that can be annotated and narrated (Aitken & Crane, 2006; Dodge, Perkins, & Kitchin, 2009; Kwan, 2008; Nold, 2009). This methodological approach aligns well with the goals of a study exploring spaces as social constructions. In this study, Pacifica (the participant/co-researcher) and I traversed two- and three-dimensional spaces so that she could narrate her embodied experiences in the CCL space and initiative.

CRITICAL GEOGRAPHY-DRIVEN METHODOLOGY

This study was designed to ground data collection and analysis in movement through and attachments to space—in short, it was designed to illuminate the socio-spatial dimensions of residents' experiences with the CCL reform.

The Setting: The Coalition for the Children of Lakeview

The CCL was very clearly demarcated as a physical space (see Figure 1), bounded by three streets and a river, enclosing seven under-performing schools that served as the anchors of the reform. However, that space also embodies the histories, the kinds of spatialized assumptions about and within it, and the memories and dreams that the residents connected to their neighborhoods and told us about in our ethnographic work with them. DeCerteau (1984) writes about stories as "spatial trajectories" (p. 115), capturing images of both movement and space: "[stories] regulate changes in space (or moves from one place to another) made by stories in the form of places put in linear or interlaced series: from here (Paris), one goes there (Montargis); (a room) includes another (a dream or a memory)" (p. 115). The reference to dreams and memories being evoked in a room speaks to the ways that residents narrated their perspectives on, and experiences with, their neighborhood and community spaces as well as ideas of moving from one place to another, as the stories involved tracing paths in, through, and around the CCL area (i.e., the northwest along the river was where the Puerto Ricans lived; a particular block was where Puerto Rican neighborhoods changed to African American neighborhoods until they reached the river, across from where European Americans had moved).

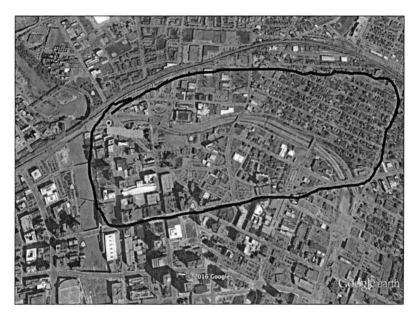

Figure 1. The CCL space, outlined in black.

Pacifica, Resident/Activist and Research Partner

This chapter focuses on one key participant, Pacifica. I had known Pacifica through the ethnography, as she was an active participant in some of the early efforts by residents to claim ownership of the CCL effort. She describes herself as a:

Hard-working professional, just about a year and a half shy of earning a bachelor's degree. Divorced single mother of two, grandmother of two. Oldest of four kids, and always an overachiever. Earned a scholarship to Lakeview University at graduation… Left school instead to marry… Worst decision I could ever have made. I need that degree now. Desires to earn a doctorate and travel the world teaching people like me how to advocate for themselves. Wishes she had kept the Urban League Black Scholar Award and stayed in college instead.

I know Pacifica as a committed professional whose dedication to advocacy for, as she says, "people like me" (African American, among the working poor) comes through in both talk and action. She held a leadership position as the CCL moved to become independent of the Lakeview School District and served on the CCL speaker's bureau, giving presentations to the public and potential funders. She positioned herself in an asset-based position rather than one grounded in deficit notions of the CCL residents and neighborhoods, as was evident in a panel presentation she was part of at Lakeview University. Derrick, a member of the original design team, and she were invited to the University to update staff about the progress the CCL was making and to inform them about opportunities to volunteer. The following is taken from field notes written at that event:

> The hall is filled with tables – about 50 people are in attendance. Most are staff from the hospital, though there are some administrators. The vast majority is white and female. The speakers are at a table at one end of the long room, with audience members seated at round tables. This is a lunch meeting. The menu is based on Southern food traditions (collard greens, grilled chicken, white rice, green beans, dessert – I think it is bread pudding). Derrick, a member of the original design team and a non-resident, is the first speaker. He tells the story of stone soup,[1] describing the CCL space as the empty pot three travelers in the story were carrying. The travelers stopped in a small village, hungry and tired, putting the empty pot in plain sight and adding stones and water. The townspeople in the village gradually came out and added vegetables and meats to the stones and water, producing a tasty soup that all shared. In Derrick's telling of the story, the townspeople represented participants contributing their time, resources, and money to the CCL. Pacifica is next. She introduces herself as a professional and a resident. Then she responds to Derrick's stone soup story. She says that the image of an empty pot doesn't capture her experience of the CCL, because the pot is full already. It is a rich stew, full of a variety of things – broth, broccoli, peppers, grains, meats, tamales, empanadas, rice, greens, spices, and on and on. She leaves the metaphor and talks about accountants, doctors, lawyers, teachers, business owners, and other professionals that live in the CCL area. She stresses the multicultural mix of cultures, races/ethnicities, and linguistic groups as a source of strength and resources. (Field Notes, 2004)

Her clear and confident rebuttal of the negative portrayal of the CCL space was a powerful example of how she viewed the area and the people living there. She presented herself as an advocate and a representative member of the CCL. Her willingness to participate in this study was a gift to the project, given her insider status and commitment to resource-rich renderings of her community.

DATA COLLECTION

I took advantage of the creativity afforded to researchers in interpretive methodologies to develop data collection strategies that were responsive to the setting, acknowledged the social nature of space, and to address power relations between researcher and participant. I chose to use both traditional interviewing with a map of the CCL as a focal artifact and a walking interview with Pacifica (described in more depth, below). In examining "sedentary" and "walking" interview, Evans and Jones (2011), noted that,

> Walking interviewees liked talking about specific buildings and environmental features and their use (57% of stories told), whereas the sedentary interviews tended to produce narratives that, although prompted by places, focused on people (58% of stories told). … walking interviews produce data about the way in which people relate specifically to place, … [and] produce a decidedly spatial and locational discourse of place, which is structured geographically rather than historically. Mapping these interviews produces a narrative that unfolds through place, organising experiences spatially rather than temporally. (p. 856)

The combination of map-focused and walking interviews afforded me the opportunity to understand Pacifica's experience in a multi-modal way that accounted in some ways for the multi-dimensional nature of social space. Further, this methodological move acknowledged power relations between Pacifica-as-participant and me-as-researcher. Jones, Bunce, Evans, Gibbs, & Hein (2008) note,

> Movement brings an additional dimension to these messy issues relating to power. … Consider the issues that arise when thinking about the location in which an interview takes place. Even before one gets into the room, the whole act of *travelling to* an interview sets up these power issues. (n.p.)

Pacifica was the expert in this case and I was the learner. It made sense to meet in spaces that paid attention to those power dynamics. Meeting at my home for the map-focused interview was a move that recognized our relationship as friends and as advocates; Pacifica was familiar with all parts of Lakeview, so getting to my house was comfortable and, given our prior relationship, my home was a space of warmth and welcoming. Meeting in her former neighborhood for the walking interview recognized that she was the guide and narrator, and that I was the listener and learner. I am also familiar with the CCL area and comfortable getting to the site she chose; Pacifica's former neighborhood was a space of inquiry and storytelling.

Following Seidman's (2006) phenomenological approach to interviewing, the protocol below was developed to incorporate a map of the CCL area as a focal artifact and a participant-led walking interview (Jones et al., 2008) to take advantage of "walking as a way of addressing the performative nature of mapping (Vaughan, 2009)" (Caquard, 2011, p. 139). Phenomenological interviewing relies on "textual evidence as a way of getting at the essence" of an experience (Seidman, 2006, p. 18). In the approach used here, language was accompanied by maps/cartographic representations of space and embodied in the participant-led videotaped tour of an area in the CCL that she wanted me to understand differently than possible with words alone.

Table 1. Phenomenological interview protocol, modified

- Initial interview – include a map with the CCL highlighted as a shared artifact to refer to and to write on
  - We're interested in your experience with the CCL area. How would you describe your life and/or work here over time?
  - How do you see the CCL effort in light of your history and experience in the area?
- Follow-up interview – Conduct a walking interview that invites participants to take us on a stroll (videotaped) in a part of the CCL that they want to talk to us about and to show us. Questions to guide the walk:
  - What is it that you want us to see and understand?
  - How do these places represent/capture your experience with the CCL area? The CCL initiative?

Map-focused Interview

MacFarlane (2007) coined the term, "story maps" to characterize "forms of spatial expressions that embody our personal experiences of the environment and contribute to creating a deep understanding of places" (as cited in Jones et al., 2008, p. 136). The map-focused interview was of this type: Pacifica drew on the map while narrating her story of coming to the CCL area and joining in the CCL effort. The two broad questions, stated above, framed the interview to allow Pacifica to tell her story as she saw fit while also grounding it within the CCL space. Given that framing, her story included her travels to, and life in, that region of Lakeview as well as her experiences with the CCL initiative.

Walking Interview

In this interview, I was interested in exploring the processes of tying space to experience and making richer connections to Pacifica's experience of space than were possible with more traditional approaches to interviewing. The emotional and spatial dimensions of experience are more accessible in this technique. According to Evans and Jones (2011),

> Walking has long been considered a more intimate way to engage with landscape that can offer privileged insights into both place and self (Solnit, 2001). Ingold

and Lee (2008) suggest that walking with interviewees encourages a sense of connection with the environment, which allows researchers to understand how, for example, places are created by the routes people take. (p. 850)

Jones et al.'s (2011) Rescue Geography and Ferrándiz and Baer's (2008) Recovery of Historical Memory projects used walking interviews to record and analyze participants' experiences with space and place. As part of their study of a comprehensive redevelopment effort in the Digbeth region of Birmingham, England, Jones et al.'s purpose was to document residents' desires to have their perspectives and values included in the planning phase of the effort so that the implementation would reflect their histories and social network of relationships and resources. Residents volunteered to take the researchers on a guided tour of the area; the researchers also used GIS mapping to gather quantitative geographical data to accompany the walking interview data. Ferrándiz and Baer recorded witnesses and survivors' travels to and observation of exhumation of victims of Spain's President Ferdinand Franco's regime as they "(1) locat[ed] graves and exhume[ed] corpses of the victims of Franco's repressive policies, both during the Civil War (1936–1939) and after Franco's victory, and (2) recording oral testimony from victims and relatives, mostly in digital video format" (2008, paragraph 1). In both studies, visual, audio, and interview data tied to specific spaces and times were gathered to understand space as multidimensional and to inform action on the parts of urban planners or members of a social movement.

Data Analysis

The map-focused conversation produced biographical information (where she lived before Lakeside, the three places where she lived in Lakeview once she and her mother arrived) as well as information about what led her to become involved in the CCL. This analysis took the form of memos and jottings (Saldaña, 2012). In elaborating on my field notes and analyzing the audiotaped interview, I noted significant events that she highlighted as important to her as well as those that spoke to her commitment to her neighborhood, wider community, and the CCL.

I created a Google Earth tour of our route and wrote an accompanying storyline based on Pacifica's narration as we walked (the Google Earth tour is not included to protect the anonymity of participants in the CCL study). I noted her accounts of specific places where we stopped for a bit and where she made specific mention of people, relationships, buildings, and movement of people along the blocks we traversed.

In writing the final narrative, I used the aforementioned narrative as the primary source and incorporated memos and jottings from the map-focused interview to elaborate on and make the broader CCL context and the walking interview easier for readers to visualize. Weaving together the data and analysis from both types of interviews with visual artifacts (Google Earth tour, map of CCL) allowed me to tap into the affective, visual, and cognitive dimensions of Pacifica's story mapping.

Finally, Pacific read the narrative and provided feedback that it captured her story as she told it very well. Her "member checking" supports the credibility of our findings.

PACIFICA'S STORY MAP

Pacifica had envisioned the CCL as a "guided missile," but "… instead of a guided missile, people are off doing individual things (the image of individual vectors comes to mind) …. I still see um a possibility that it could still happen, because I just feel that, honestly, we didn't make the right choices with reference to leadership." Her own vision for the community was a virtual organization, using community centers as hubs connecting residents, businesses, activist/social service organizations, and schools in a web of relationships. Her concepts centered on supporting families, children, and youth in physical and ideal spaces, reclaiming the CCL area materially, socially, economically, and politically. At a 2012 city planning commission meeting that concerned the expansion of a local brewery wanting, which would have required the razing of a historic building in the area, Pacifica spoke out in favor of the brewery. Her speech included the phrase, "History lives through the people," and this caught my attention because of its reference to what she sees as most important—people and social/economic relations rather than the physical or built environment. She is still tied to the physical location, but her most salient attachments are to the social dimensions of that place that, for her, make it the CCL.

In our initial interview, Pacifica used the map I gave her with the CCL boundaries to talk about her early life. Browsing the map, she told me of when she came here and looked at "all the skycrapers—coming from 3 paved roads, 3 stoplights …" (she paused, shook her head, rolled her eyes, smiling, and resumed speaking). She and her mother moved to Lakeview when she was 13, leaving their family behind in a small town in Mississippi. They lived in three different houses in Lakeview, the third one being on Rodham Avenue in the CCL area (she points to them on the map as she speaks. She showed movement with her finger, pointing the houses out on the map, traveling down Rodham to find her intersection at Santos Street. This is where she would take us to film.). It was "A great melting pot…all ethnicities, a little bit of everything. Clean neighborhood, clean…everyone knew everyone." Her activism began with the Lakeview 2010 Project that sought to develop a 10-year plan for the City—she sat in on that one. CCL was a second round of advocacy for her. When I asked her about trying again, she responded, "Anyone who believes in their community" must persevere. She had been determined, working to help neighbors and other residents maintain optimism despite fears in the community about talk and no action. In fact, Pacifica was asked to "carry the torch for residents" at a meeting where she subbed for Jeanne, an upper-level administrator in the Lakeview City School District and one of the primary CCL planners.

Two weeks later, we met at the intersection of Rodham and Santos. Barbara (a doctoral student) and I arrived in my car, camera in tow; Pacifica arrived in a large four-door car, dressed for church as it was a Sunday and she is a pastor. We parked on Santos Street, facing Rodham. On our right, there were new houses, under construction and development by Latinidad funding. On our left were houses of various ages and levels of upkeep. In front of us, across Rodham, was where her childhood home had been. It is now an empty lot, with green grass, houses on two sides and another open spot at the back of the lot. She asked Barbara to point the camera at the empty lot and told us about how it was when she was growing up as a teenager there. The house on the right, a large yellow rangy colonial with white trim, was where a woman who always kept an eye on the block's kids. It is in pretty good shape. The back part of the house has a room with windows that open to the back and to the side where Pacifica's old house was. Pacifica talked about how Misses B would sit at a table looking out of the window and into Pacifica's house and yard. Misses B knew when they were home, when they were outside in the yard, or when they were in the room she could view from her house. She knew when they should be in school and at church. Pacifica didn't feel that she and her siblings were under surveillance as much as that they had a caring, watchful, stern set of eyes trained on them. She noted that being from Mississippi made the concept of a village raising children something she was familiar with, and expected. As we walked down Rodham toward Boulevard M, she asked us to train the camera on the houses we were passing on her side of the street, naming the former and remaining homeowners from her era. She knew great detail about them: where they had moved to, what kind of work they did, how many children they had. One man who was still living there had a boat in his yard—this made her laugh, as he had had that boat for years and years and had never taken it out of the yard. She spoke fondly of that memory and of the man. Another story about neighbors keeping tabs on her and other youth living on that block of Rodham launched her into talking about how close knit the mini neighborhood was, how safe she felt walking and playing there, and how her routine of going to and from school was comfortable and enjoyable (for the most part). Neighbors even knew her grades sometimes, she said with awe and a bubbly giggle. By the time she got home from school, her mother would have heard about a bad or good grade, greeting her with either a "now tell me about that C" or a hug and "Sweetie, I knew you could!"

As we got to the end of her street, passing houses in a progression of good, to moderately good, to definitely bad shape, we stopped in front of a corner store. Like a lot of the corner stores nearby, it was difficult to see inside, as there were posters advertising products covering the windows. Pacifica declined to go inside, fearing that the shop owner would object to the camera. She mentioned shyly, giggling again, that she and her boyfriend would meet at this store and ride the bus together to school or go to his mother's house. She showed us her ex-mother-in-law's house and yard, a shaded yard with a garden that produced many vegetables in the summer. She is still in touch with her, though she has been divorced for many years. The stories she told evoked images of a pastoral scene on a tree-lined street. The emotional attachment to place, people, ambience, and community was a mixture of nostalgia, sadness, and hope. The physical realities of where we were walking that day are in direct contrast to the memories she spoke of. We saw nobody on the street; there were unkempt yards interspersed with well kept ones. Some houses had boarded up windows and aging paint. She declined to walk anywhere else, stating that she didn't know other blocks/streets well anymore and didn't feel comfortable. Walking around with a video camera and filming could intimidate or anger people.

Returning to and paraphrasing de Certeau (1984): "From here (Montgaris) one goes to there (Paris)"—from her old house you go to the corner store. Similarly, "(a room) includes another (a dream or a memory)"—the two-block area includes, for her, a vision of a lively, safe neighborhood (the dream) and a village/neighborhood raising its children in difficult economic and social times (a memory as well as a reality of the present). Her experience with the neighborhood-as-village resonated with her perception of the CCL, as she felt an "ignition of hope at her first meeting with the CCL," because its goals were to provide a safety net for families, youth, and children in need of support in the face of intergenerational poverty, underachievement, and hopelessness (the CCL's founders' initial vision). That safety net, as Pacifica perceived it, would be made from social connections and resources among residents first, bolstered by relationships with others working to overcome racism, classism, and disinvestment in CCL communities.

DISCUSSION

Pacifica's story can be viewed as a mix of nostalgia, realism, and optimism about her childhood street and the CCL initiative. Her reference to the physical or built environment of her former neighborhood as a "clean neighborhood, really clean" was linked to the social dimensions of "a village raising the children," and close-knit social relations among neighbors. This is the nostalgia—a somewhat stereotypical vision of a cohesive and warm community. Like many stereotypes, there was truth to her memories, just as there were problems of poverty that also affected that neighborhood and community at that time. Those problems continue to this day. Pacifica wanted us to understand the evolution of her neighborhood, or at least the few blocks that she identified as her neighborhood, on the day of our walking interview. She pointed to empty lots that once had houses with people she knew by name and who knew her, recalling a past with a different physical arrangement but an enduring image and meaning. At the same time, she pointed to buildings and objects that remained somewhat the same—the boat and the man that had not moved in years. She related the story of it changing from a place where everyone knew everyone else, where neighbors cared enough to watch over children, and where it was accepted that neighbors report to parents on their children's good and bad behavior. That change resulted in a place where neighbors stayed to themselves, building maintenance was inconsistent or non-existent, and children's walks to the corner store or bus stop were seen as dangerous. This is the realism in her present-day story map. Things had changed in the material and social dimensions of that space in ways that fractured the networks among neighbors. Still, she was optimistic that, given the right mix of people, access to resources, and opportunities for residents and activists to exercise agency in fomenting change, the CCL initiative could make positive strides in transforming the spatial politics and realities of that part of Lakeview.

CONCLUSION

Story mapping helped make several dimensions of social space visible in this study. Pacifica spoke about the significance of the CCL in terms of it being a relational space, imbued with friendships, family ties among neighbors, and mutual responsibility for each others' well being. She also spoke about it as a network of relationships, with a close neighbor serving as the guardian of her and her sister's safety and proper behavior, and others relaying information about grades to her mother. Related to the physical environment, as shown earlier in this chapter, Pacifica privileged people over tradition. She placed the social over the physical in talking about the prospect of razing an historic building, favoring job creation for residents over the physical-though-socially-valued building. Taken together, these multiple dimensions of the CCL, "… appears[sic] as both matter and meaning, i.e., as simultaneously tangible and intangible, as a set of social circumstances and physical landscapes and as a constellation of discourses that simultaneously reflected, constituted, and at times undermined, the hegemonic social order" (Arias, 2010, p. 29). The undermining in the CCL case was seen through residents' claims to being experts and authors of their own lives and communities, and in Pacifica's embodiment of their collective claims to rights to their community spaces, histories, and futures.

Finally, in terms of methodology, story mapping as a research design flows well from a critical geography framework, as the emphasis on multiple spheres of activity, e.g., socially constructed space and scale, and on the material and ideal realms of human experience, can inform research and practice aimed at clarifying processes of education reform. Policy and practice are linked through analyses that treat policy formation, implementation, and translation into practice, spread over time and space, as mutually constituted and constituting. Further, as Arias (2010) notes, to account for the critical in critical geography studies:

> Bluntly, it has become increasingly apparent that space shapes not simply what we know, but how we know it. In this light, spatiality enters into our understanding of how the world works, our individual and collective identity, and our means for producing and interpreting knowledge. Elevating space in this sense from the ontological to the epistemological poses significant challenges to how scholarly information is constructed, claims to "truth" (whatever that may be) are interpreted, and the priorities of academic work. (p. 40)

NOTE

[1] For a version of this story, see http://www.michaelppowers.com/prosperity/stonesoup.html. There are numerous versions and adaptations.

119

REFERENCES

Aitken, S., & Crane, J. (2006, February). Guest editorial: Affective geovisualizations. *Directions Magazine*. Retrieved from http://www.directionsmag.com/articles/guest-editorial-affective-geovisualizations/123211

Ares, N. (2014, April). *Resident claims to space: Linking rights to the city and meanings of space*. Paper presented at the American Educational Research Association meeting, Philadelphia, PA.

Arias, S. (2010). Rethinking space: An outsider's view of the spatial turn. *GeoJournal, 75*(1), 29–41.

Caquard, S. (2013). Cartography I Mapping narrative cartography. *Progress in Human Geography, 37*(1), 135–144.

de Certeau, M. (1984). *The practice of everyday life*. Berkeley, CA: University of California Press.

Dodge, M., Perkins, C., & Kitchin, R. (2009). Mapping modes, methods and moments: A manifesto for map studies. In M. Dodge, R. Kitchin, & C. Perkins (Eds.), *Rethinking maps: New frontiers of cartographic theory* (pp. 220–243). Abingdon: Routledge.

Ferrándiz, F., & Baer, A. (2008). Digital memory: The visual recording of mass grave exhumations in contemporary Spain. *Forum: Qualitative Social Research, 9*(3). Retrieved from http://www.qualitative-research.net/fqs/

Flores, L. A. (2000). Reclaiming the "Other": Toward a Chicana feminist critical perspective. *International Journal of Intercultural Relations, 24*(5), 687–705. doi:10.1016/S0147-1767(00)00022-5

Jones, P., & Evans, J. (2011). The walking interview: Methodology, mobility and place. *Applied Geography, 31*(2), 849–858.

Jones, P., Bunce, G., Evans, J., Gibbs, H., & Hein, J. R. (2008). Exploring space and place with walking interviews. *Journal of Research Practice, 4*(2), 2. Retrieved from http://jrp.icaap.org/index.php/jrp/article/viewArticle/150/161

Kwan, M. -P. (2008). From oral histories to visual narratives: Re-presenting the post-September 11 experiences of the Muslim women in the USA. *Social and Cultural Geography, 9*(6), 653–669.

Larson, J., Ares, N., & O'Connor, K. (2011). Introduction: Power and positioning in concerted community change. *Anthropology & Education Quarterly, 42*(2).

Macfarlane, R. (2007). *The wild places*. London: Granta Books and Penguin Books.

Nold, C. (2009). *Emotional cartography: Technologies of the self*. Retrieved from www.emotionalcartography.net

Saldaña, J. (2012). *The coding manual for qualitative researchers*. New York, NY: Sage.

Seidman, I. (2006). *Interviewing as qualitative research: A guide for researchers in education and the social sciences*. New York, NY: Teachers College Press.

Vaughan, L. (2009). Walking the line: Affectively understanding and communicating the complexity of place. *The Cartographic Journal, 46*(4), 316–322.

Nancy Ares
University of Rochester

SECTION THREE

SPATIAL POLITICS

We (the indivisible divinity that works in us) have dreamed the world. We have dreamed it resistant, mysterious, visible, ubiquitous in space and firm in time, but we have allowed slight, and eternal, bits of the irrational to form part of its architecture so as to know that it is false.

(Jorge Luis Borges, *Avatars of the Tortoise*)

The essays that follow examine the spatial politics of education. Spatial politics is a focus on the struggle over the meanings and valuations of bodies and objects constituting and entering spatial fields. The writings of Henri Lefebvre, Michel Foucault, David Harvey, and Gloria Anzaldúa have argued that space is politicized. They, and the empirical work propelled by their theorizing, have collectively asserted that bodies and objects are entangled in the nexus of power and resistance that imbues spaces, with theorists placing different points of emphasis on one pole of the dyad of power and resistance.

The conceptual units of power, practice, and representation have been central to understanding the myriad processes involved in spatial politics. Theorists have moved between modernist and post-modernist frameworks to theorize relations constituting the political, with the former foregrounding materialist and sovereign concepts of force and marginalization, and the latter centering theories of discourse and distributive power. Spatial theorists have asked a range of questions that explore how margin and center, community, and nation are spatialized constructions as effects of power, practice, and representation. Key constructs such as Anzaldúa's 'borderlands', hooks' 'margins', and Soja's 'thirdspace' all acknowledge the processes of differentiation and difference that are central to examining the politics of space.

Educational research has begun to utilize the units associated with spatial politics in its work. The genesis of this focus on spatial politics in education can be found in the lines of Marxian and post-Marxian informed scholarship conducted in the 80s and 90s focused on urban education—such as that of Harvey Kantor, Michael Katz, Pauline Lipman, and Thomas Popkewitz. They interjected ecological sketches of educational institutions and processes that showed the cross-fertilization between themes taken up in Critical Geography, the field of Cultural Studies, and that of critical educational research. While researchers pursued different questions and applied a variety of methods, a common theme of this earlier work was on understanding how students' racialized, gendered, and social-class subjectivities were produced and given meaning through relationships found in schools and communities. Researchers brought the field closer to spatial analyses in noting that educational policy, school structure, educational knowledge, and the curriculum were all entwined mechanisms shaped by society.

The essays that follow make the spatial politics motif an explicit focus. They explicate how difference is constructed spatially through educational apparatuses and institutions. The chapters denote different contexts and scales of analysis. Some approach spatial politics, such as Gerschon's chapter, from the macro-context of the American educational enterprise. Others, such as Huddleston's and Buendía and Fisk's, respectively, examine different municipal regions and the effects of borders. The micro-contexts of school sites also become focal points in processes of differentiation, such as the analyses found in Schmidt's and Tefera's individual chapters.

Edward Buendía

WALTER S. GERSHON

9. SAME AS IT EVER WAS

U.S. Schools as Jim Crow Spaces

There has been much recent attention to understandings of our contemporary moment as what is being called "the new Jim Crow" (e.g., Alexander, 2012; Forman, 2012). This talk has primarily centered around discussions of ongoing practices in law and the criminal "justice" system that continue to lead to the overwhelmingly disproportionate incarceration of African American, Latinx and other people (often males) of color. While there continues to be some debate over whether or not such practices actually constitute a new Jim Crow,[1] many are in agreement that contemporary practices are generally aligned with such arguments—if it is not Jim Crow, the consequences are often at least as dire for many people of color.

This chapter is another examination of such understandings, this time at the intersection of schooling, neoliberal policies and practices, and critical geography. It is a braided, messy, interrelated argument that schooling in the United States has always been a neoliberal, Jim Crow space. What makes this argument difficult is that this particularly toxic combination is as much a result of sociocultural contexts that inform education as the norms and values educators and policy makers continue to reify.

Such an argument is also difficult because the ways in which contemporary schooling functions in the United States are also strongly informed by both a resurgence in Jim Crow era practices, particularly those that regard disenfranchisement around voting rights, and a doubling-down of neoliberalism in public education. Instead of a both/and construction, this argument sits at what Lyotard (1984) referred to as the neither/nor: at once neither education-as-usual nor altogether uncommon education.

Looked at askance, neoliberalism and Jim Crow are different articulations of the same racist, classist educational tendencies toward educational inequity. Where Jim Crow is a representation of expressly separate but unequal rights, neoliberalisms claim universality in ways that present a veneer of sameness-as-equity that simultaneously masks and reifies these very same injustices. In spite of their apparent obviousness, both trajectories towards disenfranchisement nonetheless are enacted in ways that serve to obfuscate their respective ideologies, rhetoric, and practices.

In order to express the interrelated, nuanced layers of the neither/nor, this chapter is comprised of three discursive moves. It begins with a definition of fields and

N. Ares et al. (Eds.), Deterritorializing/Reterritorializing, 125–150.

constructs central to this argument: critical geography, neoliberalism, Jim Crow, and resonance. The second section attends to key resonances through the lens of critical geography, first between Jim Crow and contemporary education, then between neoliberalism and education. A final section places these resonances in relation, documenting how contemporary education in the United States is simultaneously pressed into new neoliberal, Jim Crow spaces and has always been so—material consequences of conceptual resonances, squeaky, leaky spaces (Helfenbein, 2009) that are often hidden by large scale data-driven constructions of inequity.

CRITICAL GEOGRAPHY, JIM CROW, NEOLIBERALISM, AND RESONANCE

Critical geography is distinguished from traditional (or landscape) geography in that its focus is not solely on such aspects as land, water, and mountains. Instead, critical geography tends to focus primarily on people and their relationships to one another, the ways in which they create spaces and places both physical and imagined, and the interactions between people and the ecological (see, for example, Harvey, 2001; Massey, 2005; Soja, 1989). At its core, critical geography and its twin sister human geography conceive of space and place as simultaneously constructed and irrevocably material—their being entirely made up does not make them any less real. Unlike many discussions in education in which theoretical space and/or place is falsely split from physical ecologies (for more on this critique, see Nespor, 2008), such is not the case in critical or human geographies.

As but one paradigm-shifting example, Doreen Massey (2005) argues that space is "a product of interrelations," that can be understood "as the sphere of the possibility of the existence of multiplicity in the sense of contemporaneous plurality; as the sphere in which distinct trajectories coexist" and is "always under construction" (p. 9). Instead of a physical area carved out by equally physical boundaries, Massey conceptualizes space as a node of interactions, histories, and ecologies, each of which are themselves moving in myriad ways.

Massey's definitional articulation of place, like space, contends that it is constantly in flux: "[t]hen 'here' is no more (and no less) than our encounter, and what is made of it. It is, irretrievably, here and now. It won't be the same 'here' when it is no longer now" (p. 139). It is a "throwntogetherness" of history, norms and values, ecologies and their constituent parts; place is an ever-changing "constellation of processes" (p. 14). One can never truly go home again, as the physical place and its surrounding ecologies and trajectories, as well as one's own, have necessarily changed between the time one leaves and the time one returns.

If one takes Massey's position seriously, then the continuing multiplicity of plural trajectories that is Jim Crow can be understood as a space. This conceptualization of space and place-as-event removes concerns about whether this new Jim Crow is the same as previous Jim Crows, for such a congruence is literally impossible, and also removes any need for a space or place to have some kind of implicit or explicit quantifiable congruence before it can be labeled as "Jim Crow."

If, like all spaces, Jim Crow is comprised of multiple moving and evolving trajectories, events, and ecologies, then neoliberalism too is a space and/or place. Parallel to the above argument about Jim Crow, neoliberalism cannot exist as a singular expression that is "neoliberalism," but is instead a nexus of interactions, histories, and ecologies. From this perspective, although there cannot be a singular neoliberalism, there certainly are neoliberalisms and, in the same way, there is not the Jim Crow but are instead a multitude of possible Jim Crows. Precisely what "counts" as either Jim Crows or neoliberalisms, the possible sociocultural markers of each s/pl/ace, is taken up directly below this section on critical geography. However, if they are both recognized as spaces, then they can be mapped.

As in many fields, the "critical" in critical geography is linked with Marxism and discussions of politics on one hand and on understandings that are critical in their attention to questions of power on the other. Where Massey's discussions of space and place can be understood as attending more to questions of power and possibility, David Harvey's arguments about the relationships between neoliberalism and the city (2007a) and his *Brief History of Neoliberalism* (2007b) are both unabashedly Marxist. Yet, for the contexts of this chapter, although central aspects of their scholarship are unaligned at best, their understandings about the relations between power, people, place, and space are often congruent. Social sciences scholars such as Anna Lowenhawpt Tsing's (2005) discussion of the relations between people, politics, and place (while yet another conceptualization of critical geographies writ large) is another prominent example of this shared node of understanding.

Robert Helfenbein has been particularly helpful in bringing the language and possibilities of critical geography in general and in the fields of social studies education and curriculum studies specifically (see, for example, Helfenbein, 2004, 2006, 2009). What Helfenbein rightly notes is that schools can be constructed as spaces and/or places and that such readings are subject to understandings across questions of scale (Helfenbein, 2009). As I have argued elsewhere (Gershon, 2013b), there is much congruence between notions of scale and how social scientists often conceptualize schooling as sitting in nested and layered norms and values that run from the immediately local through increasingly less local contexts. For example, how an African American fourth grader is treated and perceived is at least as much about her and her relationship with classroom peers, her teacher, and students throughout her school as it is about how girls and children of color are understood in her district, state, and nation.

Critical geography, then, is most central to at least the following two points I seek to make in this chapter. First, there is now a history of scholars in education applying and utilizing the theories and language of critical geographers in the examination of schools and schooling (e.g., Buendía & Ares, 2006; Gershon, 2013b; Helfenbein, 2004, 2009; Tuck & McKenzie, 2014). Second, because schools and schooling can be explored through the lens of critical geography as spaces and places, and both Jim Crows and neoliberalisms can be conceptualized as spaces, it is possible to evaluate the extent to which contemporary education in the United States might or might not be either Jim Crow or neoliberal spaces.

How then might one be able to empirically document the kinds of things that might be considered Jim Crow or neoliberal spaces in contemporary United States education? One answer to this question is a term that Massey uses to describe how notions of place are central to neoliberal conversations in ways that fetishize (my framing) the significance of the local, "totemic resonance" (2005, p. 5). By this she means totemic in both senses of the word: as a marker for a given set of understandings and the consistent and constant evocation of a given locale within a broader chain of ranked importance.

Critical cartographies of resonance have also been used to great effect in mapping neoliberal projects of globalization. One such example is the artistic-works-as-maps and essays in Alexis Bhagat and Lisa Mogel's (2008) collection, An Atlas of Radical Cartography – the end product of artists, activists, and scholars who turned to various forms of cartography to literally map injustices. As the authors note in their brief introduction to the textual portion of their edited work, "this slow, cumulative, and constant work across many scales of action is what creates social change" (p. 11). This provides another set of understandings of how resonance functions, as vibrations that operate across many scales of action and possibility. This chapter, then, can be understood as mapping the resonances of Jim Crows and neoliberalisms.

JIM CROW AND ITS MANIFESTATION IN VOTING RIGHTS

Because the United States is a representational democracy, elected officials are supposed to represent the views of the people in particular spaces and places that voted them into office. Both who gets to cast a vote and who is elected to office have strong consequences, locally and more broadly. Laws are therefore significant not only because they set the parameters of legality for actions and interactions but also because they express the norms and values of particular spaces and places. Ongoing tendencies in the United States can therefore be seen in the kinds of federal and state laws that have been passed in general and in the laws that govern voting rights in specific.

As is detailed here, the United States has a long, troubling history of racialized, if not distinctly racist, laws and practices that have governed voting rights.[2] Further, laws and voting rights not only express but also set norms and values, and in so doing, change what those spaces and places might mean as well as the contours of those impacted ecologies, both theoretically and physically. These racist practices, then, are also a map of Jim Crow spaces.

Richard Wormser (2003), in his book, *The Rise and Fall of Jim Crow*, states: "In 1828, Jim Crow was born. He began his strange career as a minstrel caricature of a black [sic] man created by a white man, Thomas "Daddy" Rice, to amuse white audiences" (p. xi). The website for the Jim Crow Museum (www.ferris.edu/jimcrow/origins.htm) further describes the minstrel character as follows: "Rice darkened his face, acted like a buffoon, and spoke with an exaggerated and distorted imitation of African American Vernacular English. In his Jim Crow persona, he also sang 'Negro ditties' such as 'Jump Jim Crow'" ("The Original Jim Crow," para. 1). Rephrased more directly, Jim Crow was a minstrel character that a white man performed in blackface while making racist jokes and singing racist songs to the delight of other white folks for the better part of two decades in the 1830s and 1840s.

The Jim Crow era is generally understood to be a period of time from 1890, when Louisiana law determined that resources, services, and good could be split along racial lines as "separate but equal," to 1896 when a set of practices was made national law through the Supreme Court case, *Plessy vs Ferguson*. These racist practices were, further codification of so-called Black Codes that legalized racial discrimination following the Civil War in the late 1860s. Stepping back a layer of scale, it is not enough to say that the United States enabled and engendered the racist practices that made the birth of the Jim Crow era possible, for that discussion misconstrues racism and Jim Crow practices as a particularly Southern series of recursive events. Instead, as *Plessy v. Ferguson* shouted from the legal rooftops, Jim Crow may have in many ways lived largest in the South but was, at the very least, supported by the US as a whole. Whether these were for economic, political, personal, or other reasons is not as consequential as the combined impact on schooling was segregation across the nation. Period. Similarly, although there were indeed abolitionist and anti-racist resistance and practices that marked specific places in the United States, when taken at a country-wide layer of scale, the United States was a racist, Jim Crow space.

Further underscoring Massey's points that spaces are constructed based on never-ending trajectories, the literacy tests and other racist polling practices outlawed by the 1965 Civil Rights Act are still present today. For example, in 1999, "a group known as Citizens for a Better Hamtramck" challenged voters' citizenship prior to them casting a vote because they "had dark skin and distinctly Arabic names, such as Mohamed, Ahmed, and Ali;" in addition to this, local "election inspectors required them to take a citizenship oath as a prerequisite for voting" (Weinberg & Utrecht, 2002, p. 410). The law of the land had changed, but the kinds of places that are available to be understood as American-as-racist, not so much.

This complex intersection of voting rights and Jim Crow speaks to the relationships between agency, policy, and race, particularly in light of the Fourteenth and Fifteenth Amendments. As a brief reminder, the Fourteenth Amendment to the US Constitution was adopted in 1868 and claims that all US citizens have equal protection under the law. The Fifteenth Amendment was adopted a year and a half later on February 3, 1870 and states that "The right of citizens of the United States to vote shall not be denied or abridged by the United States or by any State on account of race, color or previous condition of servitude," this last phrase in deference to service in the Civil War.

It is in the context of these two laws that aspects of voting rights laws and practices can be seen as a clear antecedent to contemporary neoliberal rhetorical practices. Now a cornerstone of many social justice practices, "voter registration procedures were first instituted to erect hurdles that made it difficult for people to become voters. Most famously, voter registration requirements adopted after the Civil War kept thousands of African-American [sic] people from registering to vote" (Weinberg & Utrecht, 2002, p. 403). Here "voter registration," a term that appears to speak to increasing equity and access had been coined to mean the practice of creating previously nonexistent rules and procedures in order to gain access to a legal right guaranteed under the constitution. Voter registration is therefore also an example of how spaces keep their contours but change their meanings over time. Voter registration space has flipped back on itself so much so that the very practices that were once intentionally racist and promoted as such have become a tool for equity and access that are now in many ways blocked by the very forces that were behind its inception. It is a history of a racist policy meant to block Black and Brown voters, that was subverted to become a central tool for voting rights. And, in an unpleasantly ironic twist, is again being used as a tool to block Black and Brown voters from the polls, this time by blocking access to voter registration, a move that reinscribes the original purpose of voter registration: to keep voting as Anglo (and male) a process as possible.

Their original intent is clear as voter registration was coupled with other laws that were also explicitly discriminatory. When those laws were found to be unconstitutional for violating the 15th Amendment, groups enacted new discriminatory, racist laws that navigated around recent rulings that declared the previous laws unconstitutional. These groups also enacted practices that served as de facto laws without the need for their explicit expression as law. Laws and procedures in Oklahoma and Texas serve as strong examples of such practices (Weinberg & Utrecht, pp. 403–404).

In Oklahoma, for example, an amendment to the state constitution in 1910 "required literacy tests of all applicants for voter registration, but exempted everyone who was eligible to vote on January 1, 1866, and all their lineal descendants" (p. 403). Because this was prior to the 15th Amendment, this meant that whereas white voters and their children were exempt from literacy tests, African Americans were required to take them. Given the amazing effectiveness of literacy tests for declaring African Americans ineligible to vote (describe below), this was a legal step keeping Blacks from voting "called grandfather laws" (p. 403). The legal root of what are now common practices in law and commonplace understandings of exceptions to the rule are grounded in explicitly racist practices—"[l]aws that insulate persons from a new requirement based on preexisiting characteristics, which those persons have or get from the antecedents" (p. 403). This, then, can be understood as yet another example of how the creation of the potential for exceptions and individuality, central aspects of US individualism and rights to many Americans, continues a history of the United States-as-raced or racist.

The Supreme Court declared this grandfather clause to be unconstitutional in 1915 in the case *Guinn v. United States*. However, the legislature of Oklahoma then created another statue that, as Weinberg and Utrecht note, "disallowed voter registration to everyone qualified to vote in 1916, but who neither voted in 1914, nor registered to vote during a two-week period in 1916" (p. 403). Again, because this time period was after 1910 and before 1915, when African Americans could not register to vote due to the application of literacy tests in the state, African Americans were again subject to the same racist practices in the administration of literacy tests, a statue that was not struck down until 1939. In these ways, Oklahoma enacted intentionally discriminatory, racist laws that disenfranchised African Americans who were legally kept from voting from 1915–1939 through voting registration practices that included passing literacy tests, an act that simultaneously changed the theoretical and practical geographies of voting rights, racial politics and policies, and statewide policies that continue to disproportionately disenfranchise people of color.

Legislators in Texas also worked to enact new laws that kept Blacks from voting and created practices that functioned in a similar fashion when existing laws were declared unconstitutional. For example, in 1927, the case *Nixon v. Herndon* caused Texas "to abandon its white-only law for general elections but attempted to remove the state from involvement in political party selection" (p. 403). In short, when the state of Texas was legally blocked from holding whites-only general elections, state legislators then argued that it was political parties, not the state of Texas that were involved in elections. When this too was ruled unconstitutional in 1944,

> the Texas Democratic Party delegated its authority for candidate selection to a 'whites-only' club, arguing that an election to nominate a political party's candidate for office is private action, not state action, and therefore the party can legally include or exclude whoever it wants from voting in the election. (p. 403)

Although eventually found unconstitutional in 1953, "the pendency of these cases state laws effectively kept African-Americans from voting in Texas for decades" (p. 404).

There is also another tendril of the roots for contemporary neoliberal arguments and policies, both about schooling and more generally, in this brief history of Texas voting laws. Where Oklahoma utilized egalitarian-sounding practices to bar access to guaranteed rights (voting registration), Texas first created laws that were explicitly and intentionally racist. When those laws were declared unconstitutional, they either (a) created new, similarly worded and racist laws in the loopholes from the laws that were previously struck down or (b) argued that public, federally protected and state-sponsored processes were in fact private enterprises that lay outside of both federal and state laws. It is a clear antecedent of neoliberal practices in and outside of schooling, an understanding that the law of the land is indeed the law except for private spaces, business and schools for example, that are exempt from those universalities.

The idea that such policies are somehow part of Texas' past is also not the case. In 2013, the Texas state legislature obtained the successful repeal of Section 4, and, incidentally, Section 5, of the Voting Rights Act (VRA) in the Supreme Court (*Shelby County, Alabama v. Holder, Attorney General, et al.*). Section 4 is the provision that grants extra attention to nine primarily Southern states that were traditionally discriminatory in their voting practices as well as many counties and municipalities in states not specifically named in Section 4 (Alabama, Alaska, Arizona, Georgia, Louisiana, Mississippi, South Carolina, Texas, and Virginia). As Adam Liptak (2013) summarized in his New York Times article about the decision, Section 4 is, "[t]he section [that] determined which states must receive clearance from the Justice Department or a federal court in Washington before they made minor changes to voting procedures, like moving a polling place, or major ones, like redrawing electoral districts" (Supreme Court Invalidates Key Part of Voting Rights Act).

Section 4(b) of the VRA was the formula through which states, counties, and municipalities became subject to the policies of Section 5 of the VRA that required them to undergo federal review for any changes to laws or policies regarding voting (rights). Because the purpose of Section 5 was to require federal preclearance for any changes to voting (rights) laws and policies from those states, counties and municipalities named in Section 4, it too was essentially also repealed when the Court struck down Section 4 in a 5–4 vote along party/ideological lines – a change that is starkly evident on the webpage dedicated to Section 5 of the VRA on Department of Justice's website (http://www.justice.gov/crt/about-section-5-voting-rights-act). The results of this ruling can be seen in a wide-ranging set of recent challenges that center around voting rights, from so-called Voter I.D. laws to an uptick in gerrymandering (covered briefly below). While they serve their stated purposes, they also enact their not-so-hidden intentions towards re/further/continuing-disenfranchisement of voters of color. This is a reflection of neoliberalisms expressed above in which private spaces, because they are composed of individuals acting outside of the public in a private fashion, are rendered exempt from public policies (for more on this point, see Harvey, 2007b).

Texas is now pressing for a repeal of Section 2 of the VRA that is designed to provide equal *access* to polling/voting for traditionally disenfranchised populations. Texas has moved in this direction in an effort to enact voter ID laws that have been shown to most often impact poor voters (who are also disproportionately people of color, immigrants, and the elderly) as they are less likely to hold the requisite state-sponsored identification cards. While not as insidious as literacy tests or literal poll taxes described below, voter ID laws do place another barrier to voting that disproportionately impacts traditionally marginalized populations who have historically faced impediments to voting and polls and reinscribe the notion that the US does harbor racist possibilities among its citizenry.

LITERACY TESTS, POLL TAXES, AND GERRYMANDERING

Literacy tests, poll taxes, and gerrymandering were key tools in racial discrimination around voting rights during the Jim Crow era. Where literacy tests and poll taxes are specific to racial discrimination, practices of gerrymandering, the redrawing of districts to favor particular groups or political parties, are more longstanding voting-related practices that were adopted as yet another means for racially profiling and discriminating against people of color during Jim Crow. To be clear, gerrymandering is alive and well across the United States and often still functions to disenfranchise African American and other traditionally marginalized voting populations (e.g., Indigenous peoples, Latinxs).

As detailed below in this section, its continuation does not mean either that such practices were not altered during the Jim Crow era or that contemporary gerrymandering practices somehow are absolved of their racialized and racist histories. To these ends, this section first addresses literacy tests and poll taxes and then considers gerrymandering due to its historical differences. Finally, as the purpose of this section is to document that literacy tests, poll taxes, and gerrymandering were key components of Jim Crow era voting disenfranchisement for traditionally marginalized voting populations, this history is not meant to overly detail the long history of these events but instead to articulate how they functioned in practice during the Jim Crow era.

Literacy tests were first used in the 1890s to keep African Americans from the polls and continued in use, in spite of various pieces of legislation, until the passing of the VRA in 1965. As with the case in Oklahoma described above, the first two to three decades of literacy tests saw conditions where Anglo voters were provided a grandfather clause through which they were exempt from taking the tests. Once those laws were ruled unconstitutional and literacy laws applied to all citizens regardless of race, and after the passing of the 19th Amendment in 1920, which gave women the right to vote, literacy tests again morphed into two overarching possibilities, both of which were extremely effective at disenfranchising Black voters.

On one hand, decisions regarding who was required to take literacy tests were unequally applied. Statements declaring literacy could lead to exemptions from literacy tests. It was not unusual for statements by white voters to have but a single signature from. On the other hand, the kinds of questions asked of poor and illiterate Anglos during literacy tests were also applied unequally, also as determined by the Registrar, creating a context in which white voters were much more likely to pass the tests than traditionally disenfranchised voters. Literacy tests also tended to fall into one of two categories: those that asked rather obscure questions to which any voter would be highly unlikely to know the answers and literacy tests, like those given in Louisiana, that had little or nothing to do with civics or democracy.

Most typical were questions like those found on the "B" section of an Alabama literacy test circa 1965 that asked intentionally obscure questions about laws, governmental decisions, and roles of various branches and services of local and federal governance as in the following two questions.

1. Has the following part of the U. S. Constitution been changed?
   "Representatives shall be apportioned among the several states according to their respective numbers, counting the whole number of persons in each state, excluding Indians not taxed." _____

4. Law requires that "In God we trust" be laced on all money issued in the United States.

_____.

(retrieved from http://www.crmvet.org/info/litques.pdf)

Further, registrars were always white and understood their role as a, if not *the*, gatekeeper for voting. As such, registrars functioned as voting rights bouncers, actively working to keep disenfranchised voters continually disenfranchised. More bluntly, white voters always passed literacy tests and voters of color always failed them. As African American voters entered the middle class in increasing numbers post-World War II, movement often bolstered by their service and participation in GI bills designed to provide education and housing for veterans, literacy tests increasingly functioned to maintain disenfranchisement in ways that poll taxes could not.

Following the passing of the Voting Rights Act, literacy tests again morphed in ways that were equally discriminating yet subtler. For example, ballots were written only in English, a move that effectively disenfranchised voters whose first or home language was not English. To rectify this Section 4 of the VRA was "amended and expanded in 1975" (Weinberg & Utrecht, p. 410) so that all aspects of the voting process and related materials be offered in languages other than English when "more than five percent of the citizens of voting age residing in such State or political subdivision are members of a single language minority" and that the state "shall provide them [language minorities] in the language of the applicable minority group as well as in the English language" (amended Voting Rights Act, as cited in Weinberg & Utrecht, p. 411). This is a wonderfully clear example of how changes in the people voting, in both demographic and number, changed the political and social landscapes of the nation. These were changes that, in turn, further altered how places called "polling places" and "voting booths" theoretically and physically operated. This is also an example of how changes in the kinds of places available at a local level impact how broader spaces can function, not that there are not still ongoing concerns about voting rights but that who is present and has a voice alters what is possible, as the continuing debate over voting rights for immigrants documents.

It is important to note that with the repeal of Section 4 of the VRA, the language requiring voting materials, information about polling, accessibility to and at polls, and the ballots themselves have also been stricken from the Voting Rights Act. However, it is equally significant to emphasize that the language(s) in which voting materials and information remains protected under Section 203 of the Voting Rights Act: "Whenever any State or political subdivision [covered by the section] provides registration or voting notices, forms, instructions, assistance, or other materials or information relating to the electoral process, including ballots, it shall provide them in the language of the applicable minority group as well as in the English language." Yet, overall, states are now in many ways responsible to police themselves towards such aspects of voting equity and access, something that many states have a long history of using to disenfranchise voters of color and voters whose home language is not English, as documented above.

Its removal is at once a regression in rights and, at the same time, a continuation of the kinds of norms and values that can be considered as "American." Such moves can also be conceptualized as yet another brick in a foundation of understanding the United States as, at the very least, a space that condones and continues racist practices, those that simultaneously disenfranchise people of color while making the voices of Anglos more prevalent and powerful in the face of rapidly changing demographics in which people of color are predicted to outnumber outnumbering Anglos. Said another way, regarding laws enacted to (at least) interrupt Jim Crow era practices and policies as unconstitutional in spite of overwhelming evidence to the contrary—especially those that regard voting rights that, in many ways, created the foundation for the Civil Rights act of 1968—speaks to a regressive politics that explicitly seeks to make Jim Crow era voting practices the law of the land, again.

Poll Taxes and Gerrymandering

Poll taxes were another direct way to disenfranchise poor to working class, primarily African American voters. As their name suggests, these were taxes one needed to pay in order to vote. While such taxes were in many ways nominal, they were more than sharecroppers and other poor African Americans, and some poor whites, could afford. Often, such taxes created a context in which poor citizens needed to choose between their ability to put food on the table and pay rent or to pay the tax that granted access to the polls.

As shown below, gerrymandering has long been a tool for those in power to create jurisdictions that favor one group or political party over another. In the Jim Crow era, these practices became a tool to a tool to marginalize people who were not white by either drawing voting by either drawing voting jurisdictions where African Americans were always in the minority or by creating fewer spaces where African Americans were in the majority. The former guaranteed that Blacks could not win the vote in their area, should they manage to somehow get to the polls, and the latter tactic created a few Black-majority districts that would always lose to the white districts that were in the majority. Gerrymandering is still alive and well in contemporary voting practices, moves that tend to use political parties rather than race as the rationale for redrawing and redistricting. However, because such lines often serve to not-so-incidentally create contexts in which traditionally marginalized voting populations again become voting minorities, it is often difficult to argue that the racialized contexts of gerrymandering are somehow a thing of the past.

As but one example, the 2010 census showed that enough people left Ohio over the previous decade to reduce the state from 18 to 16 delegates in the US House of Representatives. The Republican-led statehouse and governorship built upon gerrymandering that worked well in the previous decade (Eaton, 2012; Exner, 2010; Hungeski, 2012) to redraw the Ohio 9th District in the northern part of the state.

That new district covers but a sliver along the lake and splits Cuyahoga County, a move that just happened to pit two longstanding Democratic representatives against one another. The 9th now runs from Toledo to Cleveland, carefully weaving its way around in ways that at once (a) creates a Democratic majority that then cannot interrupt previously split counties (that themselves were previously split) and (b) forms a long, lean 11th District as the state's only "majority minority" district while dividing voters of color from the rest of their counties. The gerrymander of the Ohio 9th is so partisan and explicit that it is often refered to as "the mistake on the lake" and used as an example of egregious gerrymandering nationwide (Toeplitz, 2011).

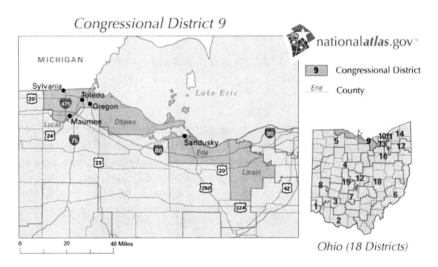

Figure 1. Ohio 9th District, 112th Congress (Pre-Mistake)

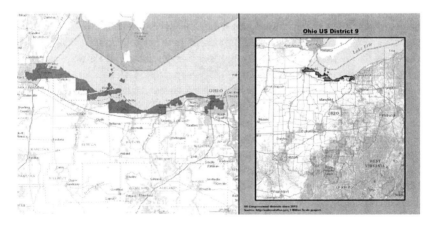

Figure 2. Ohio 9th District, 113th Congress (Mistake on the Lake)

Along similar lines, consider how Democrats faired in the 2014 midterm elections in neighboring Pennsylvania. Due to the ways that Republicans have redistricted the state, "Democratic candidates collected 44 percent of the vote, yet Democratic candidates won only 5 House seats out of 18. In other words, Democrats secured only 27 percent of Pennsylvania's congressional seats despite winning nearly half the votes" (Fang, 2014).

Gerrymandering is also an abject lesson in racial geographies of the United States. At the outset, gerrymandering began as the manipulation of districts to favor one party over another that was, simultaneously, a continuation of understandings that voting was for Anglo men only. Men of color were a null set of voters, noticeable only through their absence and through the lens of history. Then, when all people of color were given the right to vote, gerrymandering operated in ways that guaranteed their disenfranchisement in one of two ways: redrawing district lines so that a few spaces are included a majority of people of color and most districts were majority Anglo or breaking up districts that had a majority of people of color and creating majority Anglo districts, or, most often, a combination of both.

In our contemporary moment, gerrymandering primarily operates in a systemically racist fashion, most evident in redistricting at the state level. Harkening back to the origins of gerrymandering, redistricting is now often most often done along party lines by the party in power. However, in a two-party system where one party most often has the largest voting block of people of color, redistricting along party lines is also redistricting along racial lines, creating de facto disenfranchisement of people of color under the veneer of partisan politics. By removing one layer of scale, one can readily observe how gerrymandering has managed to retain its political and racial roots, a combination that not only disenfranchises voters but also significantly alters what counts as normal and the ideas and ideals that are valued.[3]

Were literacy tests, poll taxes, and gerrymandering not enough, African American voters were often strongly pressured and threatened not to vote, not to register to vote, and not to register others to vote. There are countless stories of voter intimidation, physical and verbal abuse, and other undisguised expressions of voter suppression. For example, it was not unusual for those who helped others to register to vote to lose their jobs. Mr. Weinberg relayed a story about this in an interview about the history of voting rights conducted as part of the research for this piece. As a young lawyer interviewing African Americans on behalf of the Department of Justice in the early 1960s, he spoke with a woman who had a job as a maid. One day, she went to clean the house and the back door through which she was required to enter was locked. After some time, the woman who owned the house came to the door and told the maid she no longer worked there because she voted (Personal Communication, April 28, 2015). While awful, this story does not involve any of the physically violent tactics that were not unusual for groups such as the Klu Klux Klan and other hate groups that actively worked to terrorize people of color so that they were not involved in any aspect of the voting process. Exercising one's right in the voting process, while legal, was often still a very dangerous action for people of color both prior to and after the passing of the Voting Rights Act in 1965.

One possible way to begin conceptualizing Jim Crow as a space is to note that the Jim Crow era bridged centuries, lasted approximately eighty-five years, impacted multiple generations, and was carried out across multiple states. From this perspective, anything described as a Jim Crow era is certainly not singular, uniform, or universally applied. And yet, it had characteristics that were similar enough in kind to be understood as somehow not only interrelated but varying expressions of the same kinds of intentions and events. In light of this multiplicity of expressions, a focus on voting rights provides a means to examine these kinds of intentions and events as well as their expression in policy and practice. Here, I have chosen to build on events described above along questions of scale.

At a macro level, laws and policies enacted by state legislators are expressions of intent to systematically disenfranchise people of color, primarily African Americans. The reason for such intent is a combination of racism and understandings about the centrality of voting to the construction of policies and laws as well as the relationship to access for employment at both state and local levels. A continuum of racism in United States history is found to be evident, beginning with the decision to legally allow Africans as slaves, to the denial of basic rights post-slavery, to the many contemporary instances of the murder of unarmed people of color. The micro level, the ways in which racist and raced voting policies and practices are enacted on individuals and communities is equally evident and stark. As but one example of how such inequities and disenfranchisement resonates across scales, Fulton County, Georgia "admitted to illegally disenfranchising and misleading voters in the 2008 and 2012 elections" (Ollstein, 2015), a county that includes the city of Atlanta.

Regardless of all other contexts—a bi-racial president who is held up as the nations first "Black" for example—it is difficult to categorize continuing violence (physical, verbal, emotional, etc.) against people of color across all levels of scale as anything other than racism. Even if an entire community perceives itself not to be racist or have lives informed by understandings of race, that such aggressions, both macro and micro, continue against people of color is an indicator of persistent racism at a cultural and individual level. The point here is not that everyone is racist but rather that the persistent and consistent nature of such aggressive interactions across all levels of scale, as shown above, is a strong indicator that racist beliefs are one way that Americans can understand themselves in relation to others.

In sum, from a voting rights perspective, key indicators of a Jim Crow space are literacy tests, poll taxes, gerrymandering, and pressure from groups that operated officially and unofficially to suppress voting, as well as an understanding that people of color should be kept from voting by any means possible. For the purposes of this chapter, these are the resonances of a Jim Crow space. Yet, as noted briefly above, another set of forces are alive and well, those of neoliberalism. In light of the often-intertwined nature of Jim Crow and neoliberal spaces, the following section concerns constructions of neoliberalism before placing both forces alongside one another to detail how contemporary schooling in the United States resonates with their imbricated understandings.

NEOLIBERALISM, US EDUCATION, AND SOCIAL EFFICIENCY

Discussions of neoliberalism often contend that neoliberal tendencies are the central forces towards privatization and accountability. However, here neoliberal ideas and ideals are placed along side longstanding educational practices and the notion that neoliberalism, like Jim Crow, can be conceptualized as a space.

Neoliberalism is so named because of its relation to economic liberalism, a rational theory in that it does not attend to questions of context or content—these are theories that operate with an understanding of a universality of construction and application. As Wendy Brown (2005) notes in her essay, "Neoliberalism and the End of Liberal Democracy," liberalism can be split into economic and political expressions. Where economic liberalism, in "its classical version refers to a maximization of free trade and competition achieved by minimum interference from political institutions," in "*political* thought, while individual liberty remains a touchstone, liberalism signifies an order in which the state exists to secure the freedom of individuals on a formally egalitarian basis" (Brown, 2005, p. 39, emphasis in original). Further, political liberalism can:

> harbor liberal or Keynesian economic policies—it may lean in the direction of maximizing liberty (its politically "conservative" tilt) or of maximizing equality (its politically "liberal" tilt), but in contemporary political parlance, it is no more or less a liberal democracy because of one leaning or the other. (Brown, 2005, p. 39)

Yet, "what is crucial is that *the liberalism in what has come to be called neoliberalism refers to liberalism's economic variant*" (Brown, p. 39, emphasis in original).

The neo, the new, in neoliberalism, Brown contends, is the multiple ways in which all aspects of life have been turned into markets with quantifiable data that can be used to simultaneously track and hold those now-markets accountable, both literally and figuratively. Morally, neoliberalism functions with the same rationality as economic liberalism, irrespective of contexts including race, class, gender, social class, geography, and the like. Practically, neoliberalism, unlike its economic foundation, involves actively constructing and maintaining what was previously only an economic rationality in such a way that it "reaches individual conduct" so that it "perceives the citizen-subject of a neoliberal order" (Brown, 2005, p. 42).

> In making the individual fully responsible for her- or himself, neoliberalism equates Moral responsibility with rational action; it erases the discrepancy between economic and moral behavioral by configuring morality entirely as a matter of rational deliberation about costs, benefits, and consequences. But in so doing, it carries responsibility for the self to new heights: the rationally

calculating individual bears full responsibility for the consequences of her or his action no matter how severe the constraints on this action. (Brown, 2005, p. 42)

In sum, from a neoliberal perspective, individuals are now not only responsible for all choices, as these choices are constructed as fully free choices from an unlimited set of possibilities regardless of context, experiences, or history; they are also constructed as being framed by the quantifiable (and often economic) success of those decisions. Instead of governments, institutions, and services being responsible to the people, the people are now responsible for their choices as they negotiate aspects of the state, institution, services, and other daily experiences as "free" actors or, as Brown frames it: "Neoliberal subjects are controlled *through* their freedom" (p. 44, emphasis in original).

As noted in the introduction and is the case with Jim Crow, neoliberalism is also a space. It is a space that actively engenders neoliberalization through the consistent and constant re/construction of the myriad interrelated trajectories and interactions that combine to form particularized ecologies. Insofar as education promotes neoliberalism, education, then, is a neoliberal space.

Neoliberalism and Education

One reading of contemporary education policy in the United States is that it is a project fully rooted in neoliberalism. Educational policies from No Child Left Behind to the newly minted Every Student Succeeds Act (both reauthorizations of the Elementary and Secondary Education Act) have reduced schools to markets, administrators to managers, teachers to workers, and students to data points. The rational/liberal aspects of neoliberalism mean that schools, administrators, teachers, and students can be measured against one another if provided reasonable and equally applied regulations and information, standards and curricula. The need for each to be properly measured requires turning the product of those regulations and information into that which can be rationally and objectively measured—numbers. This then requires a means of standardized assessment through which the product (students) can be measured.

Because the product reflects both the rules under which they were formed and the information they received, the measurement of the product (students) then stands not only for the strength of the product but also the degree to which the regulations and information were applied. In an economic sense, the strength of a factory, its management and its workers can all be measured by the success of the product produced. In schools, students become the products against which labor (teachers) and management (local administrators) and the institution/factory (school) is measured.

Yet, this reading of neoliberalism and education ironically miss the sociocultural, and socioeconomic educational tendencies in the United States. It is certainly the case that, following a move in critical geography (e.g., Springer, 2010) what might be called the neoliberalization of education in US education has markedly changed the ways in which policies and practices have evolved and continue to evolve. US education has become commodified, quantified, and measured in ways that have allowed unprecedented understandings of schools-as-markets and people-as-products (Hill, 2011; Lipman, 2011). It is a neoliberal space both in its norms and values and in the ways in which it redefines education from the gaining of knowledge to the measurement of products.

However, the majority of readings of the many connections between neoliberalism and US education in policy and practice overlook a central trajectory of education in the United States—a longstanding history of neoliberal-like tendencies in educational policies and practices related to desires for efficiency, effectiveness, and accountability. Because these central aspects of education tend to be overlooked, I describe in the next section how neoliberalism is in many ways a commensense extension of education policy; everyday schooling practices in the United States have been similarly overlooked in discussions of the relationship between neoliberalism and education. In short, as education in the United States may have always been a neoliberal space, one that engenders the creation and maintenance of US education as a Jim Crow space.

SOCIAL EFFICIENCY, NEOLIBERALISM, AND US EDUCATION

Historical narratives (e.g., Jackson, 1992; Kliebard, 2004; Schubert, 1986) from across the field of curriculum studies have documented what the late Herbert Kliebard (2004) named "the social efficiency group." This group can be understood as a lineage that begins with Franklin Bobbitt's (1918) *The Curriculum*, continuing through Ralph Tyler's (1949) *Basic Principles of Curriculum and Instruction*, and expressed today in myriad ways such as standards, learning objectives, and standardized assessments. Irrespective of how it is named, this curricular trajectory has the following tendencies that are also, as often as not, the dominant strain of educational ideologies that stretch from the beginning of the previous century into this millennium.

Perhaps the most defining characteristic of the social efficiency group is its conceptualization of educational processes as smoothly running production lines. At its historical roots, the central metaphor for education is as a factory model in which the more efficient the process (teaching), the better and more uniform the products (students). This model has certainly morphed over the years, as a shopping mall metaphor (Powell, Ferrar, & Cohen, 1985) that understands students-as-consumers who pick from a wide variety of possibilities that fit their personal tastes, for example. In its current incarnation, social efficiency metaphors have again morphed to a service industry in which students-as-consumers are catered to by faculty and administration, particularly in higher education (Brookes, 2003; Lusch & Wu, 2012). Yet, at the core of all of these understandings is an understanding about the importance of efficiency and that effectiveness—not care, thought, or wonder, for example—is inexorably central to teaching.

Ends-means interactions in teaching and learning from lesson plans to curricular maps to standards are another hallmark of the social efficiency group. Here what is to be learned in prescribed prior to the lesson and information is what Hugh Mehan (1979) famously called "known information questions," those that have correct answers known prior to the teacher asking students to consider a given idea. This way of approaching classroom lessons is so widely held that genuine inquiry, when students explore questions to which there are not singular correct answers is designated as "inquiry based learning" and assessment according to such openness is deemed to be "authentic assessment."

The social efficiency group also has a tendency to conflate teaching and learning. Rather than seeing them as separate acts in which teachers teach and students learn, they are understood as inexorably related, as if every time a teacher provides new information students should be able to grasp it immediately or that learning requires a classroom teacher. The difficulty with this position is that knowledge takes time, learning requires a willingness to engage and consider, and teaching is not simply a matter of delivering the correct material in the correct manner to arrive at an often-singular correct answer.

Finally, there is the continuing notion that teaching and learning can be quantifiably measured. Aspects of teaching and learning can be quantified—scores on assessments, self-reporting on Likert scales, the number of times a student is called on, and the like. This is to say that in order for educational processes to be measured requires both a steady, exacting baseline and a limiting of variables, something that is next to impossible in people. While multiple people can take the same assessment in the same space at the same time, their very human-ness gets in the way of both internal and external validity. It is rather difficult to document the exact moment one learns something, that such learning is a result of a given teaching, and that what students grasp is what teachers in fact intended to deliver. For example, a student might have different versions of the same information delivered to them over the course of the week but only have it make sense in the middle of the night between Saturday and Sunday.

What is often not stated in discussions of the social efficiency perspective of education is that it is a universalist, rational perspective devoid of context and complications. Take Herbert Kliebard's (1975) critique of Ralph Tyler's (1949) "rationale," the cornerstone of his work, *Basic Principles in Curriculum and Instruction*, the work that codifies and further theorizes Franklin Bobbit's (1918) *The Curriculum*. It is from this work that we get measureable educational objectives and their assessment as cornerstones of teaching and curriculum. According to Tyler, there are four central aspects to well-structured educational objectives and curricula: students' perspectives, contemporary life, subject matter specialists, and the philosophical screen. As Kliebard rightly argued, one can find students who agree with one's perspectives, subject matter specialists whose understandings match one's own, and an understanding of contemporary life that agrees with one's own. This leaves the philosophical screen, another filter that is ultimately one's own perspectives, creating a context in which the curriculum is primarily a person's understandings combined with what they find to be normal and of value, rather than what might be significant knowledge outside one's sphere of experience and opinions. This combination provides a rationale for the study of only that with which is familiar and comfortable.

While social efficiency understandings of education have a strongly codified set of procedures, it is a perspective that speaks out of both sides of its metaphorical mouth, calling for objective, rational understandings while simultaneously enforcing dominant, status quo biases that actively maintain the success of students at the expense of others.

Standardized measurement in education has a longstanding history of marginalization through assessment that functions in much the same way—the application of assessments that mask bias through a sameness of procedure. For example, the SAT test was first designed to keep immigrants, primarily Jews, from entering Harvard (Weschler, 2007), and current standardized assessments are more an indicator of zip code and social class than of academic understandings (Boaler, 2003). When placed in combination, the symbolic space of exclusion and disenfranchisement of testing that fed (feeds) a physical space of exclusion and disenfranchisement at Harvard, in turn, feeds the symbolic space of testing in a feedback loop of exclusion that echoes across scales from the personal to the policy and back again.

In other words, such decisions are intentional. US education, then, has long contained central aspects of neoliberalism: a rational, universalist theoretical foundation, the quantification of complex interactions through measurement, and the reduction of individuals to scores in both numerical form and letter grades. Even those who agree with the possibility of measuring student success critique contemporary educational measurement practices (e.g., Popham, 2001), and, in a perhaps unintended fashion, critique educational measurement practices in general. Education in the United States also often shares an additional assumption about education: that it occurs almost solely in schools and needs to follow particular, measurable pathways for teaching and learning to be either successful or regarded as such.

From this perspective, neoliberalism in US education was always already there. This may help account for why many educators saw few differences or had difficulty in expressing the changes in tenor and tone they felt as neoliberal educational practices have become the norm since the late 1990s. For the purposes of my argument here, and as I detail in the following section, this also means that US education has always been not only a neoliberal space but also a Jim Crow space.

UNITED STATES EDUCATION AS A JIM CROW SPACE

Both historically and in our contemporary moment, education in the United States is a Jim Crow space. Returning to the aspects of Jim Crow through the lens of voting rights provided above, this section articulates how education policies and practices of literacy tests, de facto poll taxes, gerrymandering, and recent forms of teacher intimidation clearly mark US education as a Jim Crow space. In order to make this argument, I begin by drawing parallels between Jim Crow and educational practices. Then, although neoliberalism has brought longstanding educaitonal inequities to a particularly pernicious point, I show how these tendencies are part and parcel of the Jim Crow spaces that are the educational history of the United States.

Contemporary standardized assessments function in many ways exactly like a literacy test. They are administered only in English, given to students who are designated as part of special education regardless of either the cause or the solutions in place to help them mitigate their educational needs as prescribed by the Americans with Disabilities Act, and also given to immigrants who have been in the United States for six months or longer (Macswan & Rolstad, 2006). In an ironic twist, high schoolers who are eligible to vote can request a ballot in their home language but are given tests that will determine their future lives only in English. This is also the case for the standardized assessments many universities still require as part of application packages for admission. Not surprisingly, such testing often has particularly negative consequences for students of color whose first language is not English, not only in generally scoring less well than their peers whose home language is English but also resulting in the increased likelihood that their scores will place them in special education.

Another factor in how students score is what I have come to think of as educational gerrymandering. This form of gerrymandering, like its voting counterpart, has both explicit and implicit designs and consequences. Explicitly, schools in the United States are linked through public policies to neighborhoods that are in turn linked to social class and, yet again, to race in a never-ending feedback loop across all levels of scale. Public schools in the US serve the communities in which they are situated. Neighborhoods are inexorably linked to social class—the kind and cost of housing in a community is perhaps the strongest determinant of its members—and housing in the United States has a long history of connections not only to class but also to race (see, for example, Harvey, 2001, 2007b).[4] Because schools serve their local communities, how a district draws the boundaries for all schools and the pathway it determines for students to negotiate multiple middle and secondary schools in larger districts, is also a determinant by both race and class.

It is not uncommon for urban school districts with fairly diverse populations to have a large discrepancy by race in the services students receive, the courses available to students, and in the condition of their schools. For example, the population of a local large urban area and its associated school district is split nearly evenly in its populations of Anglos and African Americans. However, as often is the case in city schools, an elementary school in this district has a population that is approximately 87% African American students, has 90% of its students receiving federally provided free meals and 8% of those remaining receiving reduced-rate meals. This school was largely torn down and rebuilt so that when it reopened five years ago, it was one of the most aesthetically pleasing and technologically advanced buildings in the district and across much of Northeast Ohio. The school then began a transition to a STEM focus. The trajectory for students from the school used to be routed through two average middle schools to two average to lower performing high schools, students are now routed to the two middle schools that are regarded as the best in the district to the district's premier high school. Indeed, although students in the school now benefit from gerrymandering that places their elementary school on a path to the best scoring and most affluent junior high and high schools in the district. *However*, in spite of possible material gains, students are still negatively impacted by gerrymandering of their school community because changes in their pathway to high school do not impact negative perceptions of race and class differences, especially when compared to the wealthy Anglo students who still overwhelmingly attend a school just a mile or so down the road.

Then there are the "educational poll taxes" school fees for various services, events, and, often, sports. It is not unusual for schools to require fees for each high school student and, in some areas, for elementary and middle schools to also pay such fees, for beautification or needed improvements for example. These fees are then further compounded by those often associated with extracurricular activities like sports or band as well as for advanced placement courses. A teacher at a local suburban high school informed me that students have to pay fees for their regular classes, a $200 fee for science for example, and then it is "pay to play" for all extracurricular activites to boot. Because it is a public school, administrators cannot enforce any consequences for students' not paying "regular" fees (though they do apply pressure by sending letters from school). However, students who cannot afford to pay are not eligible for the advanced placement classes, athletics, or band. The rules disproportionately impact the school's small population of students of color, who happen also to be less wealthy.

Adding further insult to injury, what is measured and considered are only for public schools (see, for example, Dreier & Kahlenberg, 2014). Private schools, (places that, not-so-incidentally, many politicians from the President to local school board members send their children), are required to be measured by standardized assessments. Their curricula are not subject to the same state standards nor are they required to keep academic content by the same grade-level limitations. All this adds to the open secret of the ways in which admissions officers at universities give preference to students in private schools. Such understandings are not hyperbole, as George W. Bush and other elites have benefitted from a kind of affermitve action of their own, "legacy" admissions where poor grades were not a barrier to his admission to Yale.

Then there are personal moments of intimidation for teachers and parents. Across the country, teachers and parents are regularly pressured through both implicit and explicit means not to have their students/children opt out of annual standardized assessments, even though it is their legal right to do so. In some states, such as Ohio, the legislature has only recently passed legislation protecting students who opt out of testing. More common are instances such as this one in which a parent was banned from entering school grounds where his nine year old daughter attends elementary school for opting her out of testing, not even one month prior to the Ohio legislature's passing a bill protecting parents from situations like this one (Knapp, 2015). These are examples of individual harassment for acting upon legally guaranteed rights.

Although the relatively recent neoliberalization of schooling has brought these conditions into stark relief, as discussed in the previous section, education in the United States has always been a neoliberal space in a number of key ways. It has also always been a Jim Crow space. There is a long history of discrimination and disenfranchisement of students of color and poor students that similarly mirrors these transgressions. For example, eight years after the passing of the Civil Rights Act of 1965, Ray Rist (1973) was writing about city schools for (poor) students of color as "factories of failure," conditions that echoed Carter G. Woodson's (1933) concerns about education for people of African descent in the Jim Crow era, a work that, in turn, similarly resonates with conditions and concerns Anna Julia Cooper (1892) raises four decades earlier.

Ultimately, US educational policies and practices have worked hard to maintain public schooling as Jim Crow spaces, first during the Jim Crow era and then through the continuing decisions in policy and practice that continue to disenfranchise students of color and poor students. Were the evidence presented to this point not convincing enough, charter schools, the front line of educational privatization in this era of neoliberalization, began as a response to *Brown v. Board* in segregated whites only schools paid for with public tax dollars (Bonastia, 2015). Just as voter registration began as a hurdle to intentionally cause disenfranchisement, school choice has its roots in intentionally racist segregation of schools with public funds.

CONCLUSION

Contemporary education in the US was in many ways born in the Jim Crow era and, as I have argued here, has never left. Jim Crow era education gave way to understandings of education as Jim Crow spaces in ways that have become normalized to a point that the continuing inequities and injustices are not only commonplace but also, for many, commonsense. Aiding and abetting such understandings is a parallel history of US education as a neoliberal space, through an evolving history of the social efficiency camp of US education and educators that manifest in the contemporary neoliberalization of education. What makes this conception of education so damaging, and difficult to swallow, is that we continue to build more efficient and effective means for the constant re-creation and maintenance of schools, schooling, and education as neoliberal Jim Crow spaces.

Recent calls for changes in educational policy towards testing have resulted not in the repeal of tests but in the changing of what assessments are used and to what end. Rejections of common core standards are not rejections of ends-means educational objectives and measurement, tools that require the continuing mismeasurement of some so that others might be understood as successful or superior. The coupling of a rationalist educational history and a refinement of those universalist understandings through neoliberal lenses creates a public education system in which students of color and poor students, who are often one and the same, are subject to intentional practices that are designed to measure them as lesser. For, if these practices were unintentional, they would not be so continually and willingly reproduced—their ongoing, apparent omnipresences serves as a signal, both implicit and explicit, that such raced and racist practices are part of "how we do things" in the United States.

If one breaks down racism according to questions of scale, it can be categorized as individual/interpersonal, institutional, and systemic. What makes education as a Jim Crow space so abusive is that it operates on all levels of scales simultaneously in ways that continually reassert its normalcy. In this way, the violence done to young people of color is an artifact of an intentional alignment of practices and policies across all levels of scale that allows an ever-shrinking Anglo majority to continue asserting its socio-cultural-economic-historical dominance, in spite of a multitude of better alternatives.

Finally, if US education is both a neoliberal and a Jim Crow space, it can be mapped. Following possibilities set forth in critical, artistic, and narrative cartographies (e.g., Bhagat & Mogel, 2008; Harmon, 2009; Wood, 2010), such mapping can not only help us better understand how educational places and spaces operate in practice, but also to can help document the discursive and material consequences of these top-down, universalist educational policies and practices on traditionally marginalized student populations.

Critical geographies, then, provide a means for attending to often-elusive resonances across multiple layers of scales that tend to further obscure both the patterns they make and the ripple effect that occurs in their wake. It is the language of critical geographies that allows Jim Crow and neoliberalisms to be seen not only as practices but also as ideas, ideals, and interactions that combine to create physical and discursive spaces. And it is their ability to be conceptualized spatially that allows such spaces to be mapped like blips and echoes across a critical screen.

NOTES

[1] For those less familiar with racial/racist histories in and of the United States, as I describe in greater detail below, Jim Crow refers to an era of specifically racist US laws, policies, and practices most often associated with the Southern United States that lasted the better part of the century between the end of the Civil War and the mid-1950s. However, as will also be detailed throughout this chapter, these forms of institutional, systemic, and personal racism are, in many ways, alive and well in contemporary United States education.

[2] This section closely attends to *Temple Political & Civil Rights Review* (2002, v11n2), "Problems in America's Polling Places: How they can be Stopped," by Barry H. Weinberg and Lyn Utrecht; and in personal communication with Barry Weinberg who also happens to be my father. Their account is also reflected and supported in most online resources on voting rights including those posted at the Department of Justice; Alexander M. Bickel's (1966) review of voting rights cases for The

Supreme Court Review; and Chandler Davidson's (1992) introduction titled "The Voting Rights Act: A Brief History", to the Brookings Institution's Publication, *Controversies in Minority Voting: The Voting Rights Act In Perspective.* It also relies on sections of a few recent works about Jim Crow: Jerrald M. Packard's (2003), *American Nightmare: The History of Jim Crow*; William H. Chafe, Raymond Gavins, and Robert Korstad, and the staff of the Behind the Veil Project's (2001) edited work, *Remembering Jim Crow: African Americans Tell About Life in the Segregated South.* It should similarly be noted that this chapter focuses on the historical discussions of Jim Crow and voting rights rather than on either Mr. Weinberg or Ms. Utrecht's perspectives about contemporary voting rights or their suggestions on how continuing inequities might be alleviated.

³ For further review of how gerrymandering functions nationwide, check Shira Toeplitz's (2011) piece, Top 5 Ugliest Districts: Partisan Gerrymandering at rollcall.com.

⁴ For a longer discussion of connections between housing, discrimination and race, see Title XIII, the Fair Housing Act of the Civil Rights Act, 1968, the addition of disability and family status in 1988, and again for disabilities as part of the Americans with Disabilities Act of 1990.

REFERENCES

Alexander, M. (2012). *The new Jim Crow: Mass incarceration in the age of colorblindness.* New York, NY: The New Press.

Bhagat, L., & Mogel, L. (Eds.). (2008). *An atlas of radical cartography.* Los Angeles, CA: The Journal of Aesthetics and Protest Press.

Bobbitt, F. (1918). *The curriculum.* New York, NY: Houghton Mifflin.

Boaler, J. (2003). When learning no longer matters: Standardized testing and the creation of inequality. *The Phi Delta Kappan, 84*(7), 502–506. doi:10.1177/003172170308400706

Bonastia, C. (2015, January 6). *The racist history of the charter school movement.* Retrieved from http://www.alternet.org/education/racist-history-charter-school-movement

Brookes, M. (2003). Higher education: Marketing in quasi-commercial service industry. *International Journal of Nonprofit and Voluntary Sector Marketing, 8*(2), 134–142.

Buendia, E., & Ares, N. (2006). *Geographies of difference: The social production of the east side, west side, and central city school.* New York, NY: Peter Lang.

Brown, W. (2005). Neoliberalism and the end of liberal democracy. In W. Brown (Ed.), *Edgework: Critical essays on knowledge and politics* (pp. 27–59). Princeton, NJ: Princeton University Press.

Cooper, A. J. (1892). *A voice from the South (by a Black woman from the South).* Xenia, OH: Aldine Printing House.

Dreier, P., & Kahlenberg, R. D. (2014, September 12). Making top colleges less aristocratic and more meritocratic. *The New York Times.* Retrieved from https://www.nytimes.com/2014/09/13/upshot/making-top-colleges-less-aristocratic-and-more-meritocratic.html

Eaton, S. (2012, November 11). In evenly split Ohio, redistricting gives GOP 12-4 edge in congressional seats. *Cleveland.com.* Retrieved from http://www.cleveland.com/open/index.ssf/2012/11/in_evenly_split_ohio_redistric.html

Exner, R. (2010, November 16). Ohio GOP made 2002 congressional redistricting work to its advantage through 2010 election. *Cleveland.com.* Retrieved from http://www.cleveland.com/datacentral/index.ssf/2010/11/ohio_gop_made_2002_congression.html

Fang, L. (2014, November 5). Gerrymandering rigged the 2014 elections for GOP advantage. *Moyers & Company.* Retrieved from http://billmoyers.com/2014/11/05/gerrymandering-rigged-2014-elections-republican-advantage/

Forman, J. (2012). Racial critiques of mass incarceration: Beyond the new Jim Crow. *New York University Law Review, 87*, 101–146.

Gershon, W. S. (2013b). Sonic Cartography: Mapping space, place, race and identity in an urban middle school. *Taboo: The Journal of Culture and Education, 13*(1), 21–45. Retrieved from http://freireproject.org/wp-content/journals/taboo/vol13_files/07gershon.pdf

Harmon, K. A. (Ed.). (2009). *The map as art: Contemporary artists explore cartography* (essays by G. Clemans). New York, NY: Princeton Architectural Press.

Harvey, D. (2001). *Spaces of capital: Towards a critical geography*. New York, NY: Routledge.

Harvey, D. (2007a). Neoliberalism and the city. *Studies in Social Justice, 1*(1), 2–13.

Harvey, D. (2007b). *A brief history of neoliberalism*. Oxford, UK: Oxford University Press.

Helfenbein, R. J. (2004). A radical geography: Curriculum theory, performance, and landscape. *Journal of Curriculum Theorizing, 20*(3), 67–76.

Helfenbein, R. J. (2006). Space, place, and identity in the teaching of history: Using critical geography to teach teachers in the American South. In A. Segall, E. Heilman, & C. Cherryomes (Eds.), *Social studies—The next generation: Re-searching in the postmodern* (pp. 111–124). New York, NY: Peter Lang.

Helfenbein, R. J. (2010). Thinking through scale: Critical geography and curriculum spaces. In E. Malewski (Ed.), *Curriculum studies handbook: The next moment* (pp. 304–317). New York, NY: Routledge.

Hill, D. (Ed.). (2011). *Contesting neoliberal education: Public resistance and collective advance*. New York, NY: Routledge.

Hungenski, Q. (2012, August 6). Ohio fights grotesque gerrymanders. *The Paragraph*. Retrieved from https://theparagraph.com/2012/08/ohio-fights-grotesque-gerrymanders/

Jackson, P. W. (1992). Conceptions of curriculum and curriculum specialists. In P. W. Jackson (Ed.), *Handbook of research on curriculum: A project of the American Educational Research Association*. New York, NY: MacMillan Library Reference.

Kliebard, H. M. (2004). *The struggle for the American curriculum* (3rd ed.). New York, NY: Routledge.

Knapp, A. (2015, February 21). Dad banned from school buildings after opting daughter out of state tests. *CantonRep.com*. Retrieved from http://www.cantonrep.com/article/20150220/News/150229895

Lipman, P. (2011). Neoliberal education restructuring dangers and opportunities of the present crisis. *Monthly Review, 63*(3), 114–127.

Liptak, A. (2013, June 25). Supreme court invalidates key part of Voting Rights Act. *The New York Times*. Retrieved from http://www.nytimes.com/2013/06/26/us/supreme-court-ruling.html

Liptak, A. (2017, January 23). Supreme Court won't hear appeal from Texas on voter ID case. *The New York Times*. Retrieved from https://www.nytimes.com/2017/01/23/us/politics/voter-id-case-texas-supreme-court.html

Lusch, R., & Wu, C. (2012). A service science perspective on higher education: Linking service productivity theory and higher education reform. *Center for American Progress* [White Paper].

Lyotard, J.-F. (1984). *The postmodern condition: A report on knowledge*. Minneapolis, MN: University of Minnesota Press.

MacSwan, J., & Rolstad, K. (2006). How language proficiency tests mislead us about ability: Implications for English language learner placement in special education. *The Teachers College Record, 108*(11), 2304–2328.

Massey, D. (2005). *For space*. Thousand Oaks, CA: Sage.

Mehan, H. (1979). "What time is it Denise?": Asking known information questions in classroom discourse. *Theory Into Practice, 18*, 285–294.

Nespor, J. (2008). Education and place: A review essay. *Educational Theory, 58*(4), 475–489.

Ollstein, A. M. (2015, August 26). Georgia county admits to illegally disenfranchising voters. *Think Progress*. Retrieved from https://thinkprogress.org/georgia-county-admits-to-illegally-disenfranchising-voters-a51592c8b904#.b4hykf73d

Powell, A. G., Farrar, E., & Cohen, C. (1985). *The shopping mall high school: Winners and losers in the educational marketplace*. Boston, MA: Houghton Mifflin.

Rist, R. (1973). *The urban school: A factory for failure*. Cambridge, MA: Massachusetts Institute of Technology Press.

Schubert, W. H. (1986). *Curriculum: Perspective, paradigm, and possibility*. New York, NY: Macmillan.

Soja, E. (1989). *Postmodern geographies: The reassertion of space in social theory*. New York, NY: Verso.

Springer, S. (2010). Neoliberalism and geography: Expansions, variegations, formations. *Geography Compass, 4*(8), 1025–1038.

Toeplitz, S. (2011, November 10). Top 5 ugliest districts: Partisan gerrymandering 101. *Roll Call*. Retrieved from http://www.rollcall.com/features/Election-Preview_2011/election/top-5-ugliest-districts-210224-1.html

Tsing, A. L. (2005). *Friction: An ethnography of global connection*. Princeton, NJ: Princeton University Press.

Tuck, E., & McKenzie, M. (2015). *Place in research: Theory, methodology, and methods*. New York, NY: Routledge.

Tyler, R. W. (1949). *Basic principles of curriculum and instruction*. Chicago, IL: The University of Chicago Press.

Weinberg, B. H., & Utrecht, L. (2001). Problems in America's polling places: How they can be stopped. *Temple Political & Civil Rights Law Review, 11*(2), 401–499.

Wechsler, H. S. (2007). *The chosen: The hidden history of admission and exclusion at Harvard, Yale, and Princeton*. Baltimore, MD: Johns Hopkins University Press. doi:10.1353/ajh.2007.0044

Wilson, M. (2015). Note: Piercing the umbrella: The dangerous paradox of Shelby County v. Holder. *Seton Hall Legislative Journal, 39*, 188–201. Retrieved from http://scholarship.shu.edu/shlj/vol39/iss1/8

Wood, D. (2010). *Everything sings: Maps for a narrative atlas*. Los Angeles, CA: Siglio.

Woodson, C. G. (1933). *The mis-education of the Negro*. N.P.

Wormser, R. (2003). *The rise and fall of Jim Crow*. New York, NY: Macmillan.

Walter S. Gershon
Kent State University

GABRIEL HUDDLESTON

10. WELCOME TO ZOMBIE CITY

A Study of a Full Service Community School and School Choice

The center of neoliberal education reform in both a literal and figurative sense is the urban public school. As such, the surrounding communities feel the effects of such reforms. Indeed, neoliberal education reform has ties to larger efforts to re(de)form the city (Helfenbein, 2011). These education reforms are situated with(in) a larger movement that seeks to undermine public services and shift the balance of democracy firmly away from any communitarian principles onto a hyper-realized individual. This looms large in the future of urban areas. While the discussions surrounding the policy effects of such reforms are important (Apple, 2001; Ravitch, 2010; Taubman, 2009; Watkins, 2012), this chapter seeks to engage Soja's (2010) call to "rebalance the ontological triad" by discussing the spatial alongside the historical and the social in terms of knowledge production and ways of being. The battle lines between so called "education reformers" and the communities they seek to reform are not solely about public education, but about the right to shape the schools' cities themselves. As Harvey (2003) notes, "The right to the city is not merely a right of access to what already exists, but a right to change it after our heart's desire" (p. 939). Such a desire to change the city is inherently powerful, as it cannot only utterly transform those within, but has larger ramifications as well. Examples include segregation and marginalization of people of color, a further stratification of class structures, and the increased influence of corporations on how cities are built and developed (see Dyja, 2014). This chapter presents a Full Service Community School (FSCS) in a Midwest city as a contentious battlefield for this right and posits a complex picture of how the FSCS model's emphasis on community, combined with neoliberal education reform's insistence on the right to choose one's school, leads to a process of "othering" students not solely based on socio-historical considerations such as race and class, but also on spatial grounds such as where a student lives. To elucidate this point further, this chapter relies on the conceptual metaphor of the zombie. Built on Quiggan's (2010) concept of zombie economics and the most current popular culture iteration of the zombie, *The Walking Dead* graphic novel and television series (Darabont, 2010; Kirkman, Adlard, Moore, & Rathburn, 2009), the zombie offers an insightful examination of the context of the neoliberal times in which U.S. public schools now exist.

N. Ares et al. (Eds.), Deterritorializing/Reterritorializing, 151–174.

The FSCS model (Dryfoos, 2000; Dryfoos & Maguire, 2002) is based upon a communitarian ideal that emphasizes caring for the whole child in terms of her academic, health, and social needs. As such, the school is seen as a centerpiece for the entire community, housing various socio-educational services for the community's children and families. At face value, such a model seems to be at odds with neoliberal education reform. More specifically, the emphasis on the individual's right to choose based on an accountability system which relies heavily on standardized testing to deem schools and teachers failing, adequate, or exceptional in terms of providing a quality education undercut any efforts to judge schools on more communitarian ideals, such as benefits for the growth of a community, social justice, and providing services to fight poverty. While not discounting the ways in which the stated goals of both are at odds, this chapter utilizes qualitative research, focusing on teachers at Polk High, to uncover the relationship between a FSCS and neoliberal education reform. Furthermore, it considers the ways in which the spatial lines of community interact with student transiency in terms of school choice. As Buras, Randels, Salaam, and Students at the Center (2010) demonstrate, neoliberal education reform effects are not simply monolithic and absolute, but rather, morph depending on the context to which they are applied. In the case of James K. Polk Community High School, I argue that its FSCS status and the reliance upon the model's understood definition of community dictated how teachers responded to an influx of new students to the school as a result of school-choice. In turn, such a reaction speaks to larger ramifications of how neoliberal education reform is not only changing schools, but how it is changing cities as well. It is the contention here, as Helfenbein (2011) notes, that the changes brought forth by neoliberal reform efforts in both schools and cities work together in transforming the urban right before our very eyes by removing any consideration for communities within and replacing them with a worshipping of individual rights above all else.

Zombies are a useful conceptual metaphor for two reasons. First, Quiggan (2010) uses zombies to examine how neoliberal ideas persist beyond their deaths in the face of continued proof of their ineffectiveness or outright danger within economic reforms. Secondly, the popularity of *The Walking Dead* television and graphic novel series mark a moment in which zombies speak to both societal and ideological changes in the United States context. More specifically, the ways in which the graphic novel and television treat spatial concerns makes the zombie metaphor an apt lens in which to discuss how choice not only re(de)forms pedagogy and curriculum, but also the spatial relationship between schools and surrounding communities.

Ironically, neoliberal reform seeks to bestow the right to choose on students while simultaneously denying their right to shape and/or change the city in which they live. Similar to Fataar's (2013) "way of apprehending the dynamic interaction between the rapidly reconfiguring city and young people's exercise of school choice in it" (p. 11), this chapter utilizes the zombie metaphor to trouble the concept of school choice as it relates to the geographic considerations of public schools, communities, and the residents therein. In the end, this chapter is a move "towards the concrete" (Helfenbein & Huddleston, 2013) and seeks to expand the urban as a dynamic concept that moves beyond simplistic categorizations (see Buendía, 2011; Irby, 2015).

FULL SERVICE COMMUNITY SCHOOLS

A Full Service Community School (FSCS) offers a study in a specific theoretical approach towards pedagogy and curriculum combined with a material application of these theories in both the everyday goings-on and the overall organization of the school. It is certainly possible that there are additional tenets of FSCSs not mentioned within this chapter, as FSCSs are diverse not only in the applications of a FSCS framework but also in how they view the framework itself. Additionally, some FSCSs characteristics have a connection to literature that harkens back to traditional progressive ideas as they relate to public education. As such, discussions of FSCSs often include scholars not normally associated with FSCS such as John Dewey (2008, 2012; Hickman & Alexander, 1998) and Nel Noddings (1992, 2006, 2007).

The literature on FSCSs typically focuses on three theoretical pieces and the ways in which these pieces should manifest themselves in the school. To begin, FSCSs propose that the education of a student extends beyond a concern for the mind to include a mind-body connection contending that the well being of a student's health, both mentally and physically, directly relate to the ability to learn (Beuhring, Blum, & Rinehart, 2000; Blank & Berg, 2006; Epstein, 2005; Lewis & Schaps, 1995; Weiner, 1993). This is often referred to as a holistic approach to education. An outgrowth of this connection is that student achievement can be measured beyond the academic and, most often, take into account the students' lives outside of school as a means to measure the success and scope of the school's responsibilities (Harkayy & Blank, 2001). Lastly, FSCSs are the centerpieces of the communities where the typical boundaries between schools and communities (locked doors, set hours, lack of resource space for non-students, etc.) are removed to offer the school as a resource for all community members, not just students (Belenardo, 2001; Blank, Melaville, & Shah, 2003; Epstein, 1995; Hatch, 1998; Henderson & Mapp, 2002; Lareau, 1987).

In the end, FSCSs offer a model that addresses concerns as they relate to a holistic approach to education—such an approach is in service to the general wellbeing of the child inasmuch as it relates to academic achievement. Additionally, the community/school partnerships are forged so that all community and school members have an equal stake in the development and success of the students as they move through the school. Of interest in this chapter are the conceptions of a FSCS as "open" and a centerpiece of a community. The concept of an *open* school encourages community members to consider the school borderless as it relates to the surrounding neighborhoods. In other words, the school is a welcoming place full of resources not just for students, but for everyone. Paradoxically, while FSCS advocates see the school as borderless, to position the school as the centerpiece of a community means school leaders must rely on static, traditional, and oftentimes,

153

geographic boundaries. This is a crucial element of the framework. As mentioned previously, FSCS advocates stress the importance of adapting the model to address the specific needs and goals of the community. Additionally, the community services upon which the school will rely to provide support for students and community members are oftentimes close in proximity to the school itself. As will be discussed later, adhering to an *open* concept left Polk High vulnerable to new students who, through the neoliberal concept of choice, would erode the very definition of community upon which the school relied. In the minds of the participants, the FSCS model had become such a major part of the school's identity and culture, the fact that the new students lived outside of clearly defined markers of community made it easy to mark them as "other". While race, class, and gender certainly could also be a factor in this othering process, participants' foregrounded location because of Polk's status as a FSCS.

CHOICE

While the FSCS model accounts for an othering centered on where the students lived, school choice, in the context of Polk, explains their ability to freely transgress defined boundaries of community in the first place. The state in which Polk is situated can be described as one deeply committed to the neoliberal idea of school choice. Therefore, it is helpful to pull apart not only the ideology surrounding school choice, but also how such an ideology discursively works on public schools.

Whereas the locus of a FSCS is the community, school choice centers on the individual. It would be a fair assumption that "choice" in the lexicon of neoliberal reform efforts would mean a choice amongst public schools. However, to make such an assumption ignores the massive influx of private investment, either in the form of startup money for charter schools or vouchers for private and parochial schools, that results in private choices alongside the public ones. It also ignores that the majority of the money in the political debate surrounding school choice is in favor of privatizing public education and comes from a small contingent of think tanks and political organizations tied to private businesses (Chi, 2008). As Apple (2001) and Kohn (2012) point out, one of the results of neoliberal reform audit culture, where schools are only concerned with meeting the accountability standards regardless of whether it translates to quality education for their students, is that public institutions become labeled as bad, and privately funded options must be provided to give the consumer, in this case students and parents, options that are good. In the case of schools, these private options are mainly provided in the form of vouchers and charter schools with other choices in the form of online/virtual schools, home schooling, and different public school options, such as magnets (Gam & Cobb, 2008). In the cases of the first two, a dollar amount is attached to a student—in principle. It is the amount of tax dollars set aside for that student's education. When a child attends school, the school can use that money as a resource. In the case of vouchers, this money can be used to pay for private school tuition. In the case of charter schools, the money follows the student to the school, so it can use that money as a resource. In a sense, charter schools are public schools in that they receive public money; however, they are often started through private investment, which is looking to turn a profit (Buras, 2012; Ravitch, 2010). In both cases, vouchers and charters have had mixed results (Cobb, 2012; Raymond, 2009). In addition, presenting private options as inherently better obscures important differences between public, private, and charter schools, such as the fact that a higher percentage of teachers in public schools are certified and have Master's degrees than in charter schools (Cannata, 2008). Regardless, vouchers and charters are often presented as solutions to the public schools that have failed accountability standards set forth by the state.

The two major assumptions of school choice are that most people will exercise their right to choose, and if they do make a choice, it will be a well-informed one. These assumptions are built upon an audit culture meant to result in a free market where choices are clear and equal. However, this foundation is nothing but shifting sand, ignoring problems inherent within a free market system and the purpose of public institutions within a democratic society. As Apple (2001) writes:

> Public institutions are the defining features of a caring and democratic society. The market relations that are sponsored by capitalism should exist to pay for these institutions, not the other way around. It should be clear by now that a cynical conception of democracy that is "on sale" to voters and manipulated and marketed by political and economic elites does not adequately provide for goods such as general and higher education, objective information, media and new forms of communication that are universally accessible, well-maintained public libraries for all, public health, and universal health care. At best, markets provide these things in radically unequal ways, with class, gender, and especially race being extremely powerful markers of these inequalities. (pp. 103–104)

And therein lies the rub. If the U.S. school system relies on free market principles, such as competition, to "fix" education, the likely result is a reification of the gross inequalities education is supposed to help overcome. Research has not shown a clear-cut positive effect on public schools as a result of more competition (Arsen & Ni, 2008). Indeed, such a reliance on free market ideals ignores the corruptibility of the marketplace that is often seen in other sectors (Giroux, 2010). For example, there has already been evidence of general misconduct in the manipulation of test scores (Ravitch, 2010). Moreover, if parents and students do not exercise their right to "choose," what happens to the schools in which they stay? The entire choice model assumes there are better choices than the school they are currently in, to say nothing of the likelihood of them returning to the public schools they leave. Indeed, the actual percentage of parents who choose to enroll their child in another school is small (Ravitch, 2010). Additionally, the parameters of school choice are shaped by legislation and litigation, making for a volatile landscape wherein making an informed decision becomes difficult depending on the changing laws in regards to choice (Mead, 2008). In short, "choice" is a false and empty promise built on an idea that the individual must make his or her way in the world with little or no help from public resources. Such a "survival of the fittest" strategy harkens back to the legacy of eugenics and its influence on ideas of education and social mobility. By focusing on the failure of an individual to exercise his or her liberty thereby improving their situation, we, as a society, can ignore the systemic change needed to combat poverty and oppression (Winfield, 2007, 2012).

If the freedom of the individual to choose is illusory at best, choice does provide for the free flow of money, in the form of private investment, into the public sphere of education. By allowing public funding to follow students to other school options, be it vouchers or charter schools, private investment has an opportunity to make money by increasing student enrollment and lowering costs in the form of teachers' salaries. Indeed, while the number of charter schools has leveled off, the enrollment in these schools has increased (Molnar, Miron, & Urschel, 2010) and the salaries of teachers in charter schools, on average, are lower than those in public schools (Cannata, 2008). The achievement of students is not the number one concern—profitability is (Buras, 2012). All the while, this new sphere of a public/private hybrid becomes more segregated, more full of inequality than ever before, with an increased role of business in public education. Such an increase is detrimental to the overall growth of students (Molnar, Boninger, & Fogarty, 2011). Indeed, this is just the beginning. As a majority of the affected public schools are urban schools, the foray of private investment can expand into a variety of urban public areas resulting in gentrification. As Helfenbein (2011) writes, choice is part of an overall

> …rhetoric of making urban areas as attractive to the global marketplace continually echoes in media outlets and statements from the statehouse. The urban core, or ghetto as some might call it, has become attractive again, resulting in escalating property taxes and economic incentives to move the people that reside there out. (p. 322)

The larger implications here cannot be ignored as attacks on public schools in the U.S. echo other attacks on the public sector across the world (Giroux, 2010). A transformation is taking place, and as the teachers of Polk noted, it is straight out of a dystopian nightmare.

STUDY CONTEXT

James K. Polk Community High School

James K. Polk Community High School (JPCHS)[1] is a Full Service Community public high school on the near eastside of the state capitol of a Midwestern state, founded in 1927. Due to budget cuts and shrinking enrollments the school was closed in 1995. In 1998, a grassroots community movement made up of several organizations—including the alumni of the school, the local university, and various religious and social groups—came together with goals in mind to revitalize the surrounding neighborhood. Among those goals was a plan to reopen the school. In 2000, the school was reopened as a full-service middle school, and in 2001 it added a high school to become JPCHS.[2] This move to revitalize the school and community was within a context familiar to many urban school districts—a pattern of white flight to the suburbs after desegregation greatly diminished the core of the city, leaving Polk's district underfunded and ill-equipped to serve the communities of color that remained.

Teachers

Six teachers agreed to participate in this study (Mr. Blackburn, Ms. Smith, Ms. Borkowski, Mr. Perry, Mr. Jones, and Mr. Garvey). Demographic information about the participants is presented generally, rather than specific to individual teachers. This is done to protect the privacy of the individuals. The age of the participants ranged from 25 to 57; all participants self-identified as white or Caucasian. Four of the participants were male and two were female. The participants' teaching experience ranged from two years to fifteen with their years at Polk ranging from one to eleven. Participants taught in the following areas: English, Social Studies, Math, and Special Education. At the end of the 2012–2013 school year, three teachers would still be teaching at Polk in the following year, one got a job at a different school, one left to pursue an advanced degree in education (MA or Ph.D.), and one left the teaching profession completely. Interviews (1 to 2 one hour interviews with each participant and a 90 minute focus group) make up the bulk of the data collection, but these were also supplemented by observations of the teachers' classrooms.

POLK HIGH'S NEW STUDENTS

This study covered many different topics from fidelity, to the FSCS model, to discussions of neoliberal reform tenets. However, a central theme emerged in which teachers lamented recent changes to the school that coalesced around an influx of new students who lived outside of the traditionally drawn community boundaries of the existing Polk students. The discussion of new students was in stark contrast to how teachers spoke of years prior to their arrival. Teachers would speak with some sense of pride in which progress was made in terms of student achievement and in serving the mission of the school's reopening by revitalizing the surrounding neighborhood. However, participants described a school that had devolved into chaos and was struggling to deal with this new reality in the form of new students. While the causes for the chaos within the school is multidimensional and complex, this section zeroes in on the enrollment of new students at Polk as one of the major factors. Participants did not paint a perfect picture of the school's past as they fully admitted challenges and problems existed, however, they contended that the school had changed for the worse. Examples of this chaos included an increase in behavior issues (cursing out teachers and fellow students, fighting, skipping classes, rowdiness during passing periods), student motivation was markedly lower, curriculum changes were unmonitored resulting in students lacking significant prior knowledge for higher level classes, classrooms were overpopulated and the school was woefully understaffed. Participants felt the influx of new students into Polk was the main cause of the past year's instability and chaos they described.

The influx of new students resulted from the closing of four other district schools that were reopened under the control of three for-profit Educational Management Organizations (EMOs). Regardless of its status as a school choice state, the state's Department of Education held the position that students would have to remain in the takeover schools. The district challenged this position by filing a lawsuit that would allow students to exercise their right to choose by either staying in the district or enrolling in the new for-profit schools. The district won the lawsuit and a large percentage of those students chose to stay in the district, but, without the now-closed schools, it had few options as to where those students would go. To get a sense of the change in student population, Figure 1 is a map of students' homes prior to the influx of new students and after.

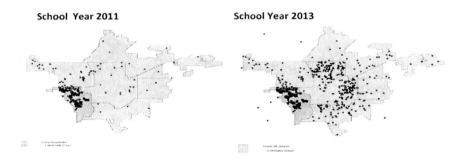

Figure 1. Polk High School student data

It is important to note that in the map on the left, the homes of students were mainly in the school's traditional boundary (represented in blue) with some students' homes in other areas of the district (represented in gray). As noted in the map on the right, in the following year, those students remained, but many more students were added whose homes were outside of the blue region. In some cases, students' homes were outside of the other drawn regions of the map altogether.

The school ill-prepared to handle the influx of new students in terms of their numbers and the teachers who participated in this study saw a multitude of problems associated with the new enrollees. These issues ranged from disciplinary (tardiness, skipping class, fights, disrespect to teachers, crude language), to lack of resources (not enough desks, textbooks, or supplies), to administrative (lack of proper Individual Education Program paperwork for new students), and curricular and pedagogical (insufficient prior knowledge or study skills, large student to teacher ratio). It should be stated that teachers did not present a utopian version of the school prior to the arrival of the new students. In other words, Polk students presented their own challenges prior to the influx of new students. Indeed, I had conducted previous research projects in the same school and witnessed many of the same problems associated with urban schools: discipline issues, academic achievement, dropouts, etc. However, the participants felt (and I would agree) that even with these problems, the school was making positive strides and the influx of new students set them back enormously. During the focus group interview, one telling excerpt encapsulated how the participants felt about the new students—tying the chaos and instability in the school specifically to them. This exchange came about when participants were asked, "How would you tell the story of this past year at Polk?"

According to the participants, the trouble began with a crucial error the year before, when the administration projected that Polk was going to lose students, not gain them. The reality was that Polk did not lose any students, but rather, gained more than they could have ever imagined and were woefully underprepared for the influx. It should be noted that while the participants saw the new students as a root cause for the chaos within the school, they still had sympathy for the students— lamenting the long bus trips they had to endure and the effect it would have on their behavior and attitudes as they entered the school—understanding what might be one of the many causes for their attitudes as they came into school every day. Much of the information discussed thus far is drawn from individual interviews, but I want to turn the attention on the focus group conducted with five of the participants. This interview was wide-ranging but an interesting conversation took place when I asked them, "How would you tell the story of the past year at Polk?" The conversation became impassioned when the participants discussed how the administration handled the difficulties the school was facing. The answers to this question set the year in stark contrast to the previous ones as Polk, almost to the point where nothing that came before really mattered. One participant started the group on a path of using dystopian descriptors by metaphorically invoking FEMA to posit the school as a disaster site. These dystopian metaphors varied, but a recurring iteration was zombies, especially as it relates to the participants' "othering" of the new students to Polk:

I:	*And it doesn't sound like there was ever a recognition of like we are in a, an official "we are in a crisis".*
Perry:	*Nobody declared it a crisis.*
Borkowski:	*No.*
I:	*Everybody knew we were in a crisis?*
Perry:	*We were waiting for FEMA and FEMA never showed up.*
I:	*Right. Everybody knew we were in a crisis, everybody there, but nobody officially or had the power to do anything about it came out and said...*

> *Borkowski:* It was almost like a minor zombie apocalypse movie. The middle
> schoolers were the zombies. Attack each other and blood going
> everywhere. Yeah. No, it was seriously like it felt that way
> sometimes. In the back of my head I would feel like you know this
> is pretty much...

This is the first mention of the new students as zombies and it is not the last. It is helpful to pause here and consider why the zombie metaphor is used. As will be discussed later the zombie metaphor is apt because the participants saw their school as being invaded from the outside and, as Figure 1 demonstrates, in terms of traditional community boundaries in relation to the school, they were. While the othering of students isn't a novel discovery, it is often, and correctly, centered on race.[3] In the example of Polk High, the spatial element of this othering is brought into focus. However, as Soja (2010) discusses, space shouldn't supersede race or any other potential elements, but rather work in conjunction to create a complex analysis. Due to the location of the students' homes, their rights as it pertained to entry to the school were immediately questioned. The focus group conversation continues, as zombies become a starting point for further dystopian language in the section below.

> *I:* So would you tell the story of a zombie movie?
> *Borkowski:* Oh, [now] we are talking. It makes more sense. You are coming
> into like this disaster movie with all these, it is sort of like Lord of
> the Flies with Mad Max.
> *Blackburn:* I can get on board with that
> *Borkowski:* With Mad Max you know two may enter one may leave. It was
> more like...
> *Perry:* Thunderdome!
> *Borkowski:* Yeah two may enter and two may leave. It was more like 42 may
> enter, 42 may leave.

The metaphors used here are telling. The dystopian vision associated with each one underscores a level of chaos, destruction, and uncertainty that had a lasting impact on the teachers as they dealt with the rash of new problems they were seeing on a daily basis. At the same time, while they were looking for help, help never came. The metaphors of disaster movies note the swiftness and extent to which the new students' presence was having on the school. This was not a slow moving problem, but rather an epidemic that never stopped long enough for those affected to come to terms with its causes, let alone its effects. Additionally, by increasing the stakes of the present crisis, the frame of the problems at Polk were centered narrowly on the arrival of these new students. In a way, the participants' focus on the current state of chaos reflect a presentist outlook and as such, the causes and solutions to the current state of problems were only considered in their immediacy to the chaos at hand. The teachers made it clear that everyone knew the school was in trouble, but few knew what to do about it:

I: *But there also seemed like there was a conspiracy element to it as well like no one is listening to me that this is happening and like people like Chicken Little like the sky is falling—*

Borkowski: *I would say more Hotel Rwanda was more of the way, as gruesome as that sounds it was, if we look at the battlefield the stuff that you know from day one. It was like ok here you go. This is a new game of Survivor Siberia. And it seriously felt like ok if any of them start getting up and doing weird stuff this is over.*

Smith: *I guess it became incredibly reactive and priorities were backwards; at least at the high school level where we didn't have the severe behavior problems.*

Perry: *Yeah, we got the back burner.*

The new students were creating a list of challenges for the school that attracted much of the administration's focus. However, participants were quick to point out that there were still other items of instability that were ignored. Smith raises a point she made in a previous interview about a specific class offered solely online, but notice how the conversation eventually makes its way back to zombies in the school:

Smith: *Yeah like, it is ok that we had major classes that feed into other classes all year on a computer.*

Perry: *I was a fly on the wall in that meeting when that was decided.*

I: *Right you were telling me about that. There were certain classes.*

Perry: *Yeah, all [that subject's classes] was online.*

Smith: *Yeah and then they started just, they finished in weeks because they were all cheating. And then taking all these classes, it was no longer we are here to learn. We are here to excel in our future classes.*

Jones: *We are here to pass.*

Perry: *We are here to Google our way through high school.*

Smith: *Yeah. And that was ok because there was so, I mean middle school needed...*

I: *There was no oversight of that?*

Perry: *Not at all*

Jones: *They weren't, the wheels were not really squeaking very loud in the beginning.*

Blackburn: *Even if they were squeaking very loud.*

Perry: *They had to be on fire (laughter).*

Perry: *And they...you did put oil on the fire.*

Borkowski: *The wheels couldn't be heard over the zombie screams*

Blackburn: *The wheel didn't squeak anymore (laughter).*

Perry: *No more squeaking.*

The problems with the online class are mentioned and specifically linked to the new students. Here, the respondents believed that all of the school administrators'

161

attention (and in the participants' minds, this was justified to a certain extent) was being directed toward the new students, so it was hard to get someone to pay attention to any problems outside of that immediate scope. If this is the case, one could see how other problems within the school would continue to mount. Indeed, the participants note that the pleas of teachers were no longer heard and they became frustrated enough not to share them. The main takeaway here is that in the mind of the participants, the most severe problems emanated from the new students' arrival to Polk. This epicenter of crisis was so disruptive that all other school issues not directly tied to dealing with the new students were given a lower priority or ignored completely. The participants believed that teachers gave up trying to have the administrators help them with these other issues and resigned themselves to living in the new normal of a zombie apocalypse. It is certainly a question as to whether these new students were the main cause of Polk's chaos, but of interest here is how the arrival of these new students resulted in the participants in this study viewing both their school and their lives within it *differently*. This viewpoint contains unique perspectives on space as it relates to the FSCS model and the new students themselves.

ZOMBIE CITY

John Quiggin (2010), in his book *Zombie Economics: How Dead Ideas Walk Among Us*, describes the ways in which ideas associated with market liberalism[4] continue beyond their lifespan. In other words, even though these ideas are proven wrong by facts and research, they continue to have a major influence in furthering the ideology of market liberalism. Quiggin uses the term *zombie* for various reasons, mainly for the quintessential characteristic of zombies—they continue on past their death. He focuses on how such ideas become zombies through a political and larger societal process in which they are championed by certain schools of economics and the political elite. This chapter has taken his conception of ideas as zombies and applied it to neoliberal education reforms. The difference is that while Quiggin focuses on how the undead are reanimated through larger discourses, this chapter focuses specifically on how zombie ideas continue on in the embodiment of teachers and students at Polk High, which, in turn, has spatial ramifications.

The use of zombies as a means to discuss neoliberal reform is not happenstance. In the focus group excerpt mentioned earlier, Ms. Borkowski made use of zombies as a metaphor to describe the circumstances of the school year as chaotic, overwhelming, and discouraging. So why was the zombie metaphor so apt to describe the year? More specifically, why did she describe the students as zombies? To begin, it would be useful to discuss specific traits of the zombie and then discuss these traits as they relate to how neoliberal ideas are both embodied and spatial.

There are many variations on the zombie theme throughout popular culture, but for the purposes of this chapter, the focus is on the most prominent, recent popular culture iteration of the zombie, *The Walking Dead* comic book (Kirkman et al., 2009) and television series (Darabont, 2010). While fascinating, the particulars of the storyline are not germane here, but how zombies are portrayed is. The first characteristic, mentioned previously, is that zombies are the undead—bodies that live beyond their mortal death in an altered state. Secondly, zombies are not benign creatures walking amongst us; they feed on living humans, attacking and eating them alive. In both the comic book and the television series, the zombie condition is the result of a disease that is spread through humans—if infected, a human will become a zombie upon his death. In the television series it is revealed that the infection, previously thought to only spread by a zombie bite, has infected the entire human race so that all the living are condemned to become zombies once they die. The virus itself reanimates the body by triggering the lower functions of the brain, only enough to move the body to its next feeding. Therefore, the monsters are inarticulate and incapable of human thought or emotion. Once a zombie, the monster is difficult to "kill." Since they are already dead, the only true way to stop a zombie is to cut its head off. This is difficult to do, as zombies are at their most dangerous when travelling in packs—the more zombies there are, the less likely one is to escape alive. Finally, becoming a zombie transforms a human from that which makes them inherently human into a monster that lives on base instincts. However, the transformation is incomplete enough that the person's body remains in human form. In other words, while a zombie is easily recognized as such, the living can still see the person it used to be. Indeed, in the television series, various characters struggle with this dissonance and cannot bring themselves to kill zombies in the hopes that their dead loved ones might return to them. Regardless of the ambivalence generated by the zombie's presence, it isn't enough to confer rights and privileges to zombies typically reserved for humans. There is no judge, jury, or group of physicians that determine the condition of zombies and whether they deserve either due process or medical treatment; the only options are either to contain or destroy them.

To be clear, zombies are mindless monsters causing destruction and chaos and the people within Polk High are human beings with agency, albeit limited due to the contrainsts of living in a society built on structures of power and control. Humans have thoughts, emotions, and feelings, whereas zombies typically do not. Zombies and, more specifically, *The Walking Dead*, are employed to discuss how ideas that make up the ideological framework of neoliberal education reform live on past their own life. Moreover, because the participants themselves used the zombie metaphor, it serves as a link back to their voices and stories.

Similar to how Taubman (2009) examines teachers' concepts of self aid in the implementation of neoliberal reform, it is the contention of this chapter that in the case of Polk High, "choice" continues on because of the powerful resonance in the lived experiences of those within the school—especially in spatial terms. Due to the FSCS framework's reliance on spatial notions of community as a foundational resource *that was bounded geographically,* Polk's identity and culture was directly tied to them. Choice easily transgressed and eroded these notions, which in turn, solidified its place as a defining characteristic of public schools. In other words, the individual transgressing community-as-space defined it as something Polk could not rely on as a means to holistically help any of its current students, let alone the new ones. If such ideas had a way of becoming ingrained into the beings of those within Polk, there is nothing special about those of us outside of the school walls that would make us immune to becoming zombies ourselves. It is reasonable to assume that the swiftness to which neoliberal education reform has attacked public education is a result of its ability to become embodied on a larger scale and change the very places we live.

So how does a zombie metaphor help us understand the ways in which neoliberal reforms become embodied by teachers and students? First, neoliberalism's ideas continue even though they are "killed" by research that shows them to be dangerous and ineffective (Quiggin, 2010). The neoliberal concept of choice continues on despite evidence of its dangerous effects, mainly due to the continuing support of major political and business leaders who espouse the merits of such reforms, enacting laws to implement them. In the case of Polk High, choice was negatively impacting the participants' practice. However, what is interesting is how these reforms come to be embodied in the teachers and students themselves through their actions and perceptions of each other. Much like how the virus of the television series infects the living and leads to an eventual transformation, neoliberal reform infects teachers and students, forcing them to transform to something other than their human nature, a neoliberal zombie as it were.

The first of these infections can be seen in the quote from Borkowski in which she describes the middle school students as zombies. How did these students become infected? As mentioned earlier, all of the participants remarked on the influx of students from outside of the Polk's community as a major factor in the chaos within the school. Furthermore, the students' status as living outside of the surrounding neighborhoods marked them as "other" from the rest of the student population as soon as they walked in the door. This "otherness," at least according to the participants in this study, seemed to eschew all the usual marks of difference—race, class, gender, and sexuality—concentrating solely on the geographical location of the students' homes. It does not discount those marks of difference could have been at play on some level; however, the willingness to admit new students as different spatially first and foremost is noteworthy as it relates to Polk's status as a FSCS. As mentioned before, the most likely explanation that geography became the dominant "other" marker was Polk's status as a Full-Service Community School. This status, before the influx of new students, made a point of emphasizing the school's various services as designed with the proximity of surrounding students' communities in mind. These new students, due to their distance from the school, represented an antithesis to the traditional Polk student. They looked like Polk students, but participants saw them as qualitatively different—as zombies.

Regardless of the specific demographic differences between new and old students, participants believed students from the surrounding communities often suffered from the chaos or joined the new students in creating it (but not originating it). The students were not "from here" and could be easily marked as not an original Polk High student. Furthering this distinction was the perception among teachers that the effectiveness of the school was directly related to the proximity of the homes of students and teachers.

However, what accounts for their presence at the school? The cause of infection here is the zombie idea of choice in public schools. As mentioned earlier, choice relies on the concept that individuals, when given the freedom to do so, will make informed decisions about where they should go to school. In the case of Polk, because the boundaries between schools in the district were porous, these new students could choose (or be moved there regardless of their choice) to attend Polk High.

In the abstract, the concept of choice is discussed in terms of the freedom it grants upon parents and students to send or attend whatever school they deem fit (Giroux, 2010; Mead, 2008). However, here we see that such choices result in the material movement of bodies from one school to another, affecting the number of students in the school, the ability of the staff to deal with that population flux, and how such movement into a community school like Polk marks these new students as different. Choice as an embodiment results in the allocation of material resources such as textbooks, desks, and classrooms. Urban schools, whose resources are already limited, must now decide how to marshal such resources effectively dependent on the movement of students due to the choices that they either make or that are made for them. In addition to all of this, not only can bodies move, but they can also move freely, increasing the mobility of what the participants viewed as an already highly transient population. Such movement easily transgressed any preconceived notions of community or neighborhood. As such, the bodies were not only differentiated for their presence and quantity, but also because of their instantaneous appearance in the school. The epidemic quality that these bodies of new students came to represent is indeed zombie-like, with the driving force of choice to spur them onward. While choice might be a zombie idea, its true effect on Polk Community High School was felt by its presence in terms of the bodies of new students, their ability to infect the rest of the inhabits of the school, but—most strikingly—their ability to appear in the school in spite of the carefully constructed boundaries of community the school had built.

Ironically, according to the participants in this study, most of the new students were not there through an active exercise in choice, but rather because the schools they attended previously were taken over by the state and assigned a corporate school agency to run the school. As a result, students chose not to attend their former school, but stay in Polk's district, leaving them with Polk as their only choice. Here, choice is active and passive. It is active in the sense that the students chose to stay in the district and therefore in a public school, but passive in that they did not choose *which* public school within the district. In other words, the government intervenes first by making movement of students easier, thus setting the stage for active choice. However, those students who do not actively choose their school can be moved from school to school within a district. Polk High was closed and the other high schools in its district were magnet schools with application processes, so it was the only place for these students to go. Their choice was made for them. Participants in this study began to see Polk as a dumping ground (see excerpt below), a place for the zombies to be quarantined. The spatial transformation was apparent in many of the participants' comments. Prior descriptions of the school depicted it as a school in the purest sense, a place of learning that was making real strides to improve the community. Descriptions of the school after the new students' arrival were post-apocalyptic and chaotic, with any semblance of a school difficult to discern:

> *Jones:*   *Well, the thing I would say is that we are a dumping ground school, we are getting kids all the time who are not connected to the school, who've been kicked out of other schools and that makes it problematic. We have serious, really serious, discipline issues here. It's gotten better, because some of the worst of the worse were removed and put on different programs; they're just no longer in school here. But I have never in my life seen the influx of dysfunctional individuals into a building like this. This is just amazing to me.*

And yet, even though these students were marked as different, they were still recognized as students. Perhaps the most effective way to deal with these students would have been to shut them out, in effect cutting off choice as the infectious driving force behind their zombie-like state to save the other inhabits inside. Obviously, structural factors in both the district and the school prevented this from happening. However, what is telling is that participants tended to put the decision to shut these students off outside of their purview—their own feelings of how to deal with these students was a mixture of sympathy and remorse. Similar to how humans view zombies in *The Walking Dead* in the context of a zombie apocalypse, participants did not blame these students for their infection, but recognized the context of public education as the major cause. The ambivalent status of the new students being both a cause of chaos, but also the victims of the new reality of public education can be seen in this passage:

> *Borkowski:*   *New population, yeah, the charter schools, the magnet school basically—to be completely rude about it—we turned into a dumping ground. I mean we have a middle school and high school here that the influx of new students has affected the middle school more than the high school. Oh, it's a huge effect, what happens when they get kicked out of charter schools? What happens when they get kicked out of the magnet? They have to find a school that isn't within their boundaries that will accept them. That's just it, charter schools, uh, private schools can decide whether or not they want to accept who they want to accept. We don't get that option; we have to say, "Okay, time to fill out the paperwork."*

Even if we know, we know that these kids are bad news. We still have to bring them in. And that's where the problem becomes, we are going to have all these specialized schools going well you have to...this schools deals with this or this school will only accept these kids. What happens to the kids that don't fit those charter schools? No, so what happens to the kids that get kicked out of charter schools when there is no more district dumping schools? What are those kids going to do then? End up locked up? And, they have got that far. That's in the next couple of years what we'll see. And that's sad because, it's not so much the kids' fault.

This brings us to the way in which the zombie metaphor helps us think about place and space as it relates to "choice." In the context of Polk High as a FSCS, one that took great pains to define what community means both in a literal and figurative sense, a battle was taking place for the right to the city (Harvey, 2003). In *The Walking Dead* series, survivors were in a constant search for safe spaces within the new zombie apocalypse landscape—places that were secure against both zombies and humans who were sometimes equally dangerous. At one seminal point in the story, the protagonists happen upon an (mostly) abandoned prison and realize the original design meant to keep inmates within is now perfect for keeping zombies out. As they do with other spaces throughout the series, the characters look to define this safe area as home, fortifying its defenses to deal with the newly infected bodies. These reinforced boundaries not only protected those inside from zombies and other dangers, but also clearly defined *anything* outside those walls as threats. In the case of Polk High, by adhering to a model that emphasized supporting surrounding communities, its very existence defined students outside of those communities as "other." As mentioned before, Figure 1 demonstrates that in some cases the distance to the school, in terms of their homes, was so striking it would be easy to note how *not of this community* a student could be. Furthermore, by continually relying on this model, the distinction was increased to the point that the new students could only be seen as threats that had somehow climbed over a carefully constructed fence specifically to endanger the safety of those inside. In the case of Polk, this wall was mainly a social construct built with words like "community," "parental involvement," and "partnerships". School choice was the ladder these new students used to scale those walls and ultimately bring them down.

Polk High was not only fighting to hold fidelity to their FSCS model in spite of the influx of new students, but also being undermined with how choice was redefining its city. By knocking down traditional community barriers that schools oftentimes mirror or support, choice made for a fluid landscape in which students could move freely intra-districtly, from school to school, as well as from public schools to charter schools to private schools. Choice became a solidified characteristic of Polk's city because of the bodies it freed to move and the boundaries it transgressed. These bodies, by moving from school to school, cut through traditional geographical markers of community, making them meaningless when Polk High, as a FSCS, was trying to make community meaningful. Similar to the ways in which Fataar (2013) posits, the movement of bodies within a city have both a material and discursive effect on how the city evolves, changes, grows, etc. These movements are simultaneously restricted by material and discursive barriers of the cities themselves and can also erode those same boundaries, resulting in new dividing lines.

CONCLUSION

It is not something inherent about the ideas within neoliberal education reform that makes them immortal zombie ideas. Perhaps it is their ability to become spatially embodied by those within public education that is the real source of their zombie power to live beyond death. Regardless of the reasons, it must be noted that something beyond the merits of their arguments extends the life of these ideas beyond mortality (Quiggin, 2010). At least in the case of this study, the zombie ideas became strengthened by the people they infect. In the case of the students, choice became solidified as a characteristic of public education not because of its effectiveness in terms of improving student learning or public education, but because students become the embodiment of choice, making spatial changes of the schools they attend, thereby solidifying itself within public education. However, it wasn't only the embodiment of choice that changed the school but also that the concept of "community" changed the moment "students of choice" trumped "students of the community." This leads to another reason why the zombie metaphor is useful, as it marks the negotiated process of distinguishing who is infected and who is not.

There is a specific passage in *The Walking Dead* comic book (Kirkman et al., 2009) in which the main character, Rick, questions which are truly the walking dead, the zombies or the living. He says (emphasis in bold is the author's);

> We *already are* savages. The second we put a bullet in the head of one of these monsters—the *moment* one of us drove a hammer into one of their faces—or cut a head off. We became what we are! And that's just it. *That's* what this comes down to. You people don't know what we are. We're *surrounded* by the *dead.* We're *among* them—and when we finally give up *we become them!* We're living on *borrowed time* here. Every minute of our life is a minute we steal from *them!* You see them out there. You *know* that when we die—we become them. You think we hide behind walls to protect us from the *walking dead!* Don't you *get it? We* are *the walking dead! We* are the walking dead.

Here we see the character of Rick encapsulating an overarching theme of the comic and, to a lesser extent, the television show. Delineating who exactly is the walking dead, zombies or humans, is difficult at best, especially when the zombie virus infects all. While the spectacle nature of the zombies' horrific state is certainly the premise of *The Walking Dead*, it is not necessarily the focus. The most compelling stories are born from the interactions of the living as they deal with the ramifications of life in a zombie apocalypse, questioning and challenging traditional definitions of what being human means. In the end, both zombie and human become floating signifiers and the differences between both become non-distinguishable (and maybe besides the point). The only differences are the material and spatial ones, and as stated earlier, even those are not enough to make a clear line.

So what does this mean for those inside of Polk High? While the use of zombies as a mode of understanding clarifies the implications of neoliberal education reforms, perhaps the best understanding can be gleaned when applying zombies in their most current pop culture iteration. More specifically, *The Walking Dead's* theme is the lack of distinction between the living and the dead. In other words, the ways in which neoliberalism infects the lives of teachers and students is ambivalent at best; even more so when deciding who is *more* infected—the teachers or the students? In the end, the concept of zombie, as presented by *The Walking Dead,* captures an ontological and spatial uncertainty not by trying to define the condition of the neoliberal body, but by focusing on the affect of such a condition. It is an uncertain state of being that ebbs and flows depending on the specifics of the relationships to other bodies (both zombie and human) and the space of the schools they inhabit. Indeed, it is the ways in which those bodies interact with each other as zombie/ human or human/zombie within specific places that makes the ability to define them as either zombie or human increasingly difficult. I would contend that attempting to define teachers and students as either zombies or humans misses the point, as it is more important to try and understand the state of flux represented in their identities as they relate to each other, to the schools in which they find themselves, and to neoliberal education reforms.

This state of flux problematizes the very basic notions of "open" and "community" in a way that makes adherence to these FSCS tenets challenging. To begin, while a FSCS might be "open" as a resource to those within a specific community it is still closed based on the parameters of the community itself. Community is defined by mainly physical limitations, thereby closing a FSCS to those outside of those definitions. When this is done, bodies within that school become inscribed with the very limitations in which the community defines themselves. This could be relied upon as a strength, reinforcing the bond between those in the school and those in the community. However, as this chapter has demonstrated, the characteristics of a given community are a small part of a greater assemblage that makes up the individual's identity. As mentioned before with neoliberal education reform, the ability of these characteristics to transmit themselves between bodies depends on the context of place and complex relationships to other bodies. In the case of Polk, when students outside of the community become enrolled in the school, these static definitions of community become even more problematic. As others (Harvey, 1989; Lefebvre, 1991; Massey, 1994; Smith, 1990; Soja, 1989, 2010) have discussed, geography is not static at all, but rather a negotiated creation of both material and discursive elements.

Polk High became a school of shifting borders determined by the "original" Polk students and the zombie students. Limited by the social and political capital to shield the school from students outside of the community, those inside relied upon subtler means to hold the line by placing the problems of the schools squarely on the shoulders of the new students themselves. The definitions of community as crystalized by Polk's classification as a FSCS served as the tools to continually distinguish the new problem students as different bodies. In the end, these new students could never be a part of Polk, as long as Polk was a community school. Additionally, by having a constant presence of students who offered a means by which to define them as belonging, students and teachers were able to deny their own infection of the neoliberal zombie virus. At the same time, no matter how much effort was made to keep the zombie students at bay, their constant presence was a haunting reminder that by "othering" them, the teachers had betrayed what it meant to be an "open" school.

Returning to a moment when the lack of social and political capital Polk's administration had in preventing students from outside of the community from coming in brings to bear the ways in which neoliberal education reforms not only shape the discourse around public education, but also around community. When students embody school choice as demonstrated by the ease with which they can move from school to school, be they public, charter, or private, the students are transgressing the physical, social, and historical boundaries of communities. With such transgression comes the degradation of those same boundaries—boundaries by which FSCS rely upon to define what it means to be a community school. If the concept of communities is changing, or even eroding, what does this mean for the FSCS model itself? Combine these border erosions with the simple notion that neoliberalism places emphasis on the individual at the expense of the community, and it becomes increasingly apparent that Polk must come to terms with what community means in a neoliberal context or join in a struggle to seek spatial justice. As Soja (2010) discusses, seeking spatial justice is to recognize the material and discursive elements of the places we live and join in the fight to utilize those elements in order to achieve social justice. To do so would radically redefine what "community" means in a FSCS such as Polk.

So, how would Polk High engage in a fight for spatial justice? To begin, perhaps a shift away from trying to shield the school from the zombies—it is a lost cause to fortify oneself from students outside of the community from attending the school. It is doubtful, given the proliferation of school choice and the eroding of community boundaries, that a school could successfully do so. Additionally, it is not conclusive that these new students are the apparent cause of problems though they were perceived to be by teachers. The fact that a school must go out of its way to categorize itself as a "Community School" shows that the traditional notion of the school as a centerpiece of a community is long gone. Instead, FSCS advocates should join the battle to define what "community" means, recognizing that they cannot simply call for a return to traditional materially static notions of community.

For starters, community can no longer be defined strictly on the proximity from which a student lives to a school. Rather, community can be defined in terms of political and social interests in which the affinity of its members are defined by the various ways in which neoliberal education reforms continue to disenfranchise and oppress them. In this scenario, new students are no longer seen as outsiders infecting a school, but as additional support in the stand against oppression. Regardless of the ways FSCS advocates for a more nuanced understanding of community upon which to base their framework, it can no longer be apolitical. FSCS advocates must claim "community" as a part of a school's identity in strict defiance of neoliberal education reforms' destruction of the communities from which their students come. To do otherwise renders the word "community" in a school's name meaningless.

NOTES

[1] Pseudonyms will be used to protect privacy of individuals in the study.
[2] The information in this paragraph was taken from the school's website, but has been left out of the reference section to maintain privacy of the participants.
[3] While not an exhaustive list, see Delpit (1995); Laura (2014); Noguera (2008); Tatum (2003) for examples.
[4] Quiggan (2010) equates market liberalism with neoliberalism, Thatcherism, Reaganism, economic rationalism, and Washington Consensus (p. 4).

REFERENCES

Apple, M. W. (2001). *Educating the "right" way: Markets, standards, god, and inequality*. New York, NY: Routledge Falmer.

Arsen, D., & Ni, Y. (2008). *The competitive effect of school choice policies on performance in traditional public schools*. Tempe, AZ & Boulder, CO: Education Policy Research Unit, Arizona State University & Education and the Public Interest Center, University of Colorado. Retrieved from http://nepc.colorado.edu/publication/the-competitive-effect-school-choice-policies-performance-traditional-public-schools

Belenardo, S. J. (2001). Practices and conditions that lead to a sense of community in middle schools. *NASSP Bulletin, 85*(627), 33–45. doi:10.1177/019263650108562704

Beuhring, T., Blum, R. W., & Rinehart, P. M. (2000). *Protecting teens: Beyond race, income and family structure*. Minneapolis, MN: Center for Adolescent Health. Retrieved from http://eric.ed.gov/?id=ED450075

Blank, M. J, & Berg, A. (2006). *All together now: Sharing responsibility for the whole child*. Alexandria, VA: Commission on the Whole Child, Association for Supervision and Curriculum Development. Retrieved from : http://www.ascd.org/ASCD/pdf/sharingresponsibility.pdf

Blank, M. J., Melaville, A., & Shah, B. P. (2003). *Making the difference: Research and practice in community schools* (ISBN-0-937846-11-2). Washington, DC: Coalition for Community Schools. Retrieved from http://www.eric.ed.gov/ERICWebPortal/detail?accno=ED499103

Buendía, E. (2011). Reconsidering the urban in urban education: Interdisciplinary conversations. *Urban Review, 43*(1), 1–21. doi:10.1007/s11256-010-0152-z

Buras, K. L. (2012). "It's all about the dollars": Charter schools, educational policy, and the racial market in New Orleans. In W. H. Watkins (Ed.), *The assault on public education: Confronting the politics of corporate school reform* (pp. 160–188). New York, NY: Teachers College Press.

Buras, K. L., Randels, J., ya Salaam, K. (Eds.). (2010). *Pedagogy, policy, and the privatized city: Stories of dispossession and defiance from New Orleans*. New York, NY: Teachers College Press.

Cannata, M. (2008). *Teacher qualifications and work environments across school types*. Boulder, CO & Tempe, AZ: Education and the Public Interest Center & Education Policy Research Unit. Retrieved from http://nepc.colorado.edu/publication/teacher-qualifications-and-work-environments-across-school-types

Chi, W. C. (2008). *The impact of advocacy funding on the school choice debate*. Boulder, CO & Tempe, AZ: Education Policy Research Unit. Retrieved from http://nepc.colorado.edu/publication/the-impact-advocacy-funding-school-choice-debate

Cobb, C. D. (2012). *Review of SCDP Milwaukee evaluation report*. Boulder, CO: National Education Policy Center. Retrieved from http://nepc.colorado.edu/thinktank/review-Milwaukee-Choice-Year-5

Darabont, F.(Writer), Dickerson, E., Nicotero, G., Ferland, G., & Gierhart, B. (Directors). (2010). The walking dead. In D. Alpert, G. A. Hurd, & R. Kirkman (Producer), *The walking dead*. Beverly Hills, CA: Anchor Bay Entertainment.

Delpit, L. D. (1995). *Other people's children: Cultural conflict in the classroom*. New York, NY: New Press, Distributed by W.W. Norton.

Dewey, J. (2008). *Experience and education* . New York, NY: Touchstone.

Dewey, J. (2012). *Democracy and education: An introduction to the philosophy of education*. New York, NY: Simon & Brown.

Dryfoos, J. G. (2000). *Evaluation of community schools: Findings to date*. Washington, DC: Coalition of Community Schools. Retrieved from http://www.communityschools.org/assets/1/AssetManager/HCS Final Report (2-6-12).pdf

Dryfoos, J. G., & Maguire, S. (2002). *Inside full-service community schools*. Thousand Oaks, CA: Corwin Press.

Dyja, T. (2014). *The third coast: When Chicago built the American dream*. New York City, NY: Penguin Books.

Epstein, J. L. (1995). School/family/community partnerships. *Phi Delta Kappan, 76*(9), 701. Retrieved from http://ezproxy.lib.indiana.edu/login?url=http://search.ebscohost.com/login.aspx?direct=true& db=tfh&AN=9505161662&site=ehost-live&scope=site

Epstein, J. L. (2005). A case study of the partnership schools comprehensive school reform (CSR) model. *The Elementary School Journal, 106*(2), 151–170. Retrieved from http://www.jstor.org/stable/10.1086/499196

Fataar, A. (2013). Students' bodily carvings in school spaces of the post-apartheid city. *Taboo, 13*(1), 11. Retrieved from http://proxyiub.uits.iu.edu/login?url=http://search.ebscohost.com/login.aspx?direct= true&db=edsggo&AN=edsgcl.358057145&site=eds-live&scope=site

Garn, G., & Cobb, C. (2008). *School choice and accountability*. Boulder, CO & Tempe, AZ: Education Policy Research Unit. Retrieved from http://nepc.colorado.edu/publication/school-choice-and-accountability

Giroux, H. A. (2010). Dumbing down teachers: Rethinking the crisis of public education and the demise of the social state. *Review of Education, Pedagogy & Cultural Studies, 32*(4–5), 339–381. Retrieved from http://ezproxy.lib.indiana.edu/login?url=http://search.ebscohost.com/login.aspx?direct=true&d b=eric&AN=EJ901129&site=eds-live&scope=site

Harkavy, I., & Blank, M. (2001). Community schools: A vision of learning that goes beyond testing. *Education Week, 21*(31), 38–52.

Harvey, D. (1989). *The urban experience*. Baltimore, MD: The Johns Hopkins University Press.

Harvey, D. (2003). The right to the city. *International Journal of Urban and Regional Research, 27*(4), 939–941.

Hatch, T. (1998). How community action contributes to achievement. *Educational Leadership, 55*(8), 15–16. Retrieved from http://www.eric.ed.gov/ERICWebPortal/detail?accno=EJ565120

Helfenbein, R. J. (2011). The urbanization of everything: Thoughts on globalization and education. In S. Tozer, B. P. Gallegos, & A. Henry (Eds.), *Handbook of research in the social foundations of education*. New York, NY: Routledge.

Helfenbein, R. J., & Huddleston, G. (2013). Youth, space, cities: Toward the concrete. *Taboo, 13*(1), 5. Retrieved from http://proxyiub.uits.iu.edu/login?url=http://search.ebscohost.com/login.aspx?direct= true&db=edsggo&AN=edsgcl.358057144&site=eds-live&scope=site

Henderson, A. T., & Mapp, K. L. (2002). *A new wave of evidence: The impact of school, family, and community connections on student achievement.* Retrieved from http://www.eric.ed.gov/ERICWebPortal/detail?accno=ED474521

Hickman, L. A., & Alexander, T. M. (Eds.). (1998). *The essential Dewey.* Bloomington, IN: Indiana University Press.

Irby, D. J. (2015). Urban is floating face down in the mainstream: Using hip-hop-based education research to resurrect "the urban" in urban education. *Urban Education, 50*(1), 7–30. doi:10.1177/0042085914563183

Kirkman, R., Adlard, C., Moore, T., & Rathburn, C. (2009). *The walking dead compendium one.* Berkeley, CA: Image Comics.

Kohn, A. (2012). Test today, privatize tomorrow: Using accountability to "reform" public schools to death. In W. H. Watkins (Ed.), *The assault on public education: Confronting the politics of corporate school reform.* New York, NY: Teachers College Press.

Lareau, A. (1987). Social class differences in family-school relationships: The importance of cultural capital. *Sociology of Education, 60*(2), 73–85. Retrieved from http://www.jstor.org/stable/2112583

Laura, C. T. (2014). *Being bad : My baby brother and the school-to-prison pipeline.* New York, NY: Teachers College Press.

Lefebvre, H. (1991). *The production of space.* Oxford: Blackwell Publishers.

Lewis, C. C., & Schaps, E. (1995). Beyond the pendulum. *Phi Delta Kappan, 76*(7), 547. Retrieved from http://ezproxy.lib.indiana.edu/login?url=http://search.ebscohost.com/login.aspx?direct=true&db=tfh&AN=9503202271&site=ehost-live&scope=site

Massey, D. (1994). *Space, place, and gender.* Minneapolis, MN: University of Minnesota Press.

Mead, J. (2008). *How legislation and litigation shape school choice.* Boulder, CO & Tempe, AZ: Education and the Public Interest Center and Education Policy Research Unit. Retrieved from http://nepc.colorado.edu/publication/how-legislation-and-litigation-shape-school-choice

Molnar, A., Miron, G., & Urschel, J. L. (2010). *Profiles of for-profit education management organizations: Twelfth annual report, 2009–2010.* Boulder, CO. National Education Policy Center. Retrieved from http://ezproxy.lib.indiana.edu/login?url=http://search.ebscohost.com/login.aspx?direct=true&db=eric&AN=ED513917&site=eds-live&scope=site

Molnar, A., Boninger, F., & Fogarty, J. (2011). *The educational cost of schoolhouse commericialism: The fourteenth annual report on schoolhouse commercializing trends: 2010–2011.* Boulder, CO: National Education Ploicy Center. Retrieved from http://nepc.colorado.edu/publication/schoolhouse-commercialism-2011

Noddings, N. (1992). *The challenge to care in schools: An alternative approach to education.* New York, NY: Teachers College Press.

Noddings, N. (2006). *Critical lessons: What our schools should teach.* Cambridge, NY: Cambridge University Press.

Noddings, N. (2007). *When school reform goes wrong.* New York, NY & London: Teachers College Press.

Noguera, P. A. (2008). *The trouble with Black boys: And other reflections on race, equity, and the future of public education.* San Francisco, CA: Jossey-Bass.

Quiggin, J. (2010). *Zombie economics: How dead ideas still walk among us.* Princeton, NJ: Princeton University Press.

Ravitch, D. (2010). *The death and life of the great American school system: How testing and choice are undermining education.* New York, NY: Basic Books.

Raymond, M. (2009). *Multiple choice: Charter school performance in 16 states.* Stanford, CA: Center for Research on Education Outcomes. Retrieved from https://credo.stanford.edu/reports/MULTIPLE_CHOICE_CREDO.pdf

Smith, N. (1990). *Uneven development: Nature, capital, and the production of space.* Athens, GA: The University of Georgia Press.

Soja, E. W. (1989). *Postmodern geographies: The reassertion of space in critical social theory.* London, UK: Verso.

Soja, E. W. (2010). *Seeking spatial justice* (Vol. 16). Minneapolis, MN: University of Minnesota Press.

Tatum, B. D. (2003). *Why are all the Black kids sitting together in the cafeteria: And other conversations about race.* New York, NY: Basic Books.

173

Taubman, P. M. (2009). *Teaching by numbers: Deconstructing the discourse of standards and accountability in education*. New York, NY: Routledge.

Watkins, W. H. (2012). The new social order: An educator looks at economics, politics, and race. In W. H. Watkins (Ed.), *The assault on public education: Confronting the politics of corporate school reform* (pp. 7–32). New York, NY: Teachers College Press.

Weiner, L. (1993). *Preparing teachers for urban schools: Lessons from thirty years of school reform*. New York, NY: Teachers College Press.

Winfield, A. G. (2007). *Eugenics and education in America: Institutionalized racism and the implications of history, ideology, and memory*. New York, NY: Peter Lang.

Winfield, A. G. (2012). Resuscitating bad science: Eugenics past and present. In W. H. Watkins (Ed.), *The assault on public education: Confronting the politics of corporate school reform*. New York, NY: Teachers College Press.

Gabriel Huddleston
Texas Christian University

EDWARD BUENDÍA AND PAUL FISK

11. THE SCALES OF POWER IN SCHOOL DISTRICT SECESSION

Research focused on the processes and effects of educational segregation has consistently centered school district and municipal boundaries as conceptual units that are critical to understanding the dividing mechanisms of different racial and economic groups across U.S. schools. The two prongs constituting this line of inquiry—demographic and policy focused research—have emphasized the effects of these political units, particularly in how they sort different racial groups and structure access to high status educational programs. This focus has been useful in helping researchers and policy makers understand and appraise the state of isolation of racially and ethnically distinct populations, as well as mark the effects of desegregation reforms. As all frameworks do, however, it has placed particular dimensions of these processes in the background. This line of inquiry has diminished the interaction of the multiplicity of social relations and processes at work to create social sorting mechanisms, or what might be seen as the alignment of spatial and political relations that cohere through activity. Put differently, the field has concentrated on the end-effects of these mechanisms while sidelining the complexity of how local actors, policies, and the appendages of glocal capital—constituting nested contexts—destruct, reconstruct, and re-institutionalize spatial relationships in creating the mechanisms of contemporary educational segregation. The significance of bringing these productive processes to the foreground lies in expanding the potential for groups and/or individuals to intervene in the machination underlying the creation of these borders and boundaries as well as to amplify the field's tool kit towards spatial relationships.

This chapter's goal is to expand the conceptual tools employed in these conversations by advancing a framework of scalar production. In its simplest form, scale is the bracketing of spatial relationships to define a level of resolution (Marston, 2000). Scalar production is a unit employed in human and physical geography scholarship and its adoption in educational research has the potential to allow researchers to attend to and represent the complexity of socio-spatial creation in forming educational segregation processes. The concept can attune researchers to the processes of interplay and realignment of local and national spatial relations of power. These processes shift the political and educational landscape towards the reproduction of separate educational spaces. Most importantly, this concept can move us towards identifying the dynamics at work prior to their coherence as durable structures.

N. Ares et al. (Eds.), Deterritorializing/Reterritorializing, 175–189.

To advance this framework, we analyzed a suburban school district secession movement in a medium size metropolitan region in the western U.S. The focus of this study was on mayoral political processes of reconstructing the field of political-educational relations to create a new school district. The case helps to show how the creation of segregated school places necessitated an analysis of scale making processes of spatial production, one in which actors re-aligned and created material and discursive relations to enact divisions in educational spaces.

This chapter begins with a discussion of the relationship between scale and space as key educational and political units in studying segregation. We then use these constructs to discuss the political and educational relationships that were in place prior to the secession. This discussion is followed by a mapping of the political processes and players that restructured pre-secession relationships in order to alter the scales of power and ultimately, practice. Finally, the chapter turns to the institutionalization of the new relationships that politicians, policy makers, and parents structured.

SPACE, SCALE, AND EDUCATIONAL RELATIONSHIPS OF POWER

If there were ever an area ripe for talking about spatial production and spatial relationships, educational segregation research would be a primary candidate. In a field clustered into demographic and policy inquiry, the analytical unit of space and its production is muted in these conversations. On the demographic side of segregation research, the relationship between population distribution and political boundaries—principally mobilized through census tract analysis—has been the central focus (Reardon & O'Sullivan, 2004). The field created and employed, beginning in the late 1950's, indices that measured population evenness, exposure, clustering, and concentration (York et al., 2011; Massey & Denton, 1993). Demographers and sociologists foregrounded these units as a way of assessing racial distribution in relation to national level structural (e.g., housing, education) relationships (Reardon, Yun, & Eitle, 2000).

Equally, policy researchers defined a robust branch of policy analyses that sought to identify how federal and state law bolstered educational isolation and undermined the Brown mandate (Orfield & Lee, 2005). The objective was, and continues currently be, to propel the federal and state level governance structures to advance Post-Brown Civil Rights integration initiatives by appraising and dismantling educational segregation between different racial and ethnic populations at a national scale.

The focal points and methodologies continue to be honed and expanded within educational sociology. Over the last fifteen years, the field has seen an expansion in the scope of research, ranging from the proliferation of municipalities and their effect on the sorting processes shaping educational segregation (Bischoff, 2008; Richards & Stroub, 2014), to the expansion of segregation into suburbs (Frankenberg & Orfield, 2012; Gumus-Dawes, Orfield, & Luce, 2013), to the ideologies driving self-sorting (Holme, 2002; Rhodes & DeLuca, 2014). With a few exceptions (Reardon & O'Sullivan, 2004), the focus of this line of research has maintained its sights on the artifacts of spatial creation. The populational and policy emphasis of our frameworks have provided us with either federal level school district desegregation policies or boundary line adjustments to act as the principal intervening points in processes of reproduction of educational inequality. Considering the intransigence of segregation, new tools that amplify the spheres of action and allow the public to intervene and disrupt these patterns are needed to accompany macro-oriented methodologies.

Other fields such as human and cultural geography have offered constructs that make available the production dimensions that create segregated spaces and places. Vigorous discussions of spatial and scalar production have been underway that point to networks of interconnected actors and processes that constitute and construct space (Jessop, 2006; Marston, 2000). The diversity of relations and processes that this research has linked has included state and federal governance entities, individual actors, collectives such as trade unions, and different forms of capital. The latter has been a prominent unit in these discussions, with much of the theorizing grounded within Marxian and neo-Marxian theoretical traditions (Marston, 2000).

Educational segregation researchers have been slow adopters of these socio-spatial tools, for the most. This may be due, in part, to the limits of these frameworks in facilitating large, macro-scale national analyses that restrict the definition of clear policy mandates that propel federal-level mechanisms. Equally, the Marxian roots of these frameworks may also be a detractor. The manner in which Marxism de-centers the state and its incremental policy-driven approach to social change and places, instead, the diverse forms of capitalism as a central focal point of inversion may constrain the focus on policy.

Yet, the turn towards spatial analysis has been underway in educational research that is not squarely situated in educational segregation streams of inquiry. Key pieces in the field of urban school district reform have amplified the conceptual frameworks typically found in educational segregation, nudging the field towards examining the creation dimensions of segregation. For example, Tate (2012) and his co-authors have asserted conversations of complex and integrated ecologies, highlighting how complex processes "are situated in place, in neighborhoods and communities" (p. 1). Lipman (2011) and Buras (2011) have amplified the field of spatial networks and have centered the creation of "glocalized" economic mechanisms by highlighting relationships between neighborhood and educational segregation that are linked to global economic relationships, expanding the discussion beyond political boundaries. This activation of intersecting relationships—global and local—has primed the field for a spatial turn by marrying these conversations.

Scale & Spatial Power

As discussed in the introduction of this volume, scale broadly refers to the level of representation (Marston, 2000), or the bracketing of relationships. Geographers have brought a high degree of nuance to the concept by introducing the concepts of geographic scale, cartographic scale, and operational scale (Marston, 2000). While the first two are important in physical geography, human geography has offered operational scale, which is the unit mobilized in this case. Many human geographers define it as the principal plane in which different social entities intermingle, or "the level at which relevant processes operate" to create a social activity or event (Marston, 2000, 220).[1] Operational scale centers the socio-spatial relations and processes that actors and knowledge frameworks link and create, attending to production and their end effects. Alongside this, we link the concept of political scale (McCann, 2003), which identifies the strategic choices and alignments that propel the relations constituting operational scale. Political scale is focused on actor-driven processes and discursive frames, or the actions and frameworks that persuade others, conjoin to find commonality, and shape alignments, or politics. Taken together, they put into motion actors and their processes, as well as the interests and motivations propelling linkages.

Relations defined here can be operationalized broadly as individuals, institutions, social structures, or texts. Various theorists have rejected static, or ontologically given, qualities to explain scale and have emphasized the relational facets of scale construction (see Howitt, 1998; Marston, 2000). Consequently, the focus on the relational prompts researchers to identify how different social-spatial relations intermingle, de- and re-construct, exercise and embody power, contradict and/or conjoin, and transform action and context. Some have represented the interface of these dimensions as a spatial fix (Harvey, 1981a; Jessop, 2006), a concept that explains the processes of (dis)connection of relations within and constituted through space, time, and practice.

The intent of examining operational and political scale is to explain the complexity and contingency of interaction that is inherent in the production of space-time. This theme of the indeterminacy of interaction can be found in various social-spatial concepts such as the discussions of networks (Castells, 1996), rhizomes (Deleuze & Guattari, 1987; Jessop, Brenner, & Jones, 2008) and processes of deterritorialization/reterritorializatrion (Appadurai, 1996). Spaces and places are secreted and embodied, to paraphrase Henri Lefebvre, through these relations.

While the analytical unit of power is embedded within operational scale, it warrants a bit of clarification considering its prominent place and role across different theories of spatial production. Many theorists have offered competing spatial theories of power (for different position see Foucault, 1980; Harvey, 1996b; Soja, 1998) in analyzing processes of spatial construction. The thrust of theorizing power in social activity is seeking to explain the nature of force in interaction, particularly in terms of levels and states of human agency and consciousness. A dividing line in this debate is the weight given to the material or the cultural realms, even though the line has softened as theorists assert frameworks of new materialism (see Cheah, 2015). Those foregrounding materialist groundings of power tend to privilege a humanist concept of sovereign power, a concept in which power can be held and wielded (see Harvey, 1996b). Power is framed as a tool wielded consciously, privileging humanist concepts of agency.

The emphasis is on the force that individuals and groups exert through economic and structural power. A key unit of analysis is on determining how these mechanisms dictate who is empowered or disempowered. In spatial analyses, the general goal has been to understand how space has been constituted by elites in order to harness it for economic production as well as consolidate and isolate groups by race and social class to create a pool of surplus labor (see Davis, 1990; Harvey, 1996b; Lipman, 2011).

In contrast, culturalists conceive of power as a spatial complex of processes and relations, which can be rendered as both power and its effects. A key premise that theorists advancing this position emphasize is the idea that there is a force of knowledge and bodily practices that are both constituting and constituted by spatial relations. Rather than envisioning power as isolated in the hands of a few, discursive power is theorized as distributed throughout as ensembles of cultural meanings, knowledge, bodies, and socio-material relations (Foucault, 1972). These propel the material as well as the bodily as part of, and effects of, space. Theorists have advanced a dispersed, horizontal network of spatial relations as the model, rather than a vertical arrangement of relations (see Buendía & Ares, 2006; Foucault, 1972). Power is conceptualized as both an act and affect in which individuals are involved through bodily, material and discursive complexes.

THE SHIFTING OF OPERATIONAL SCALE IN A SCHOOL DISTRICT SECESSION MOVEMENT

School district secession movements are a mode of "gloves off", or confrontational and contentious, educational reform that involve the political fragmentation, or "the proliferation of autonomous political jurisdictions" (Bischoff, 2008, p. 182), of an existing service unit. Members of a city or community seek to politically sever a relationship by redrawing district boundary lines as well as redistributing material resources of an established, and typically large, school district in order to create a new school district. While redefining school district boundary lines and autonomous governance structures are the objective of these initiatives, individual and group actors participate in processes of redefining operational scale that involve the destruction and reconstruction of spatial relationships that expand beyond merely boundaries. We explore the case of the Jordan School District (Utah, USA) secession to explore the methodologies of scalar production. The following questions drove the study: What socio-political elements drove the fragmentation of a large, multi-citied, suburban school district? In light of contemporary mayoral take-over movements in central cities, what overlaps and departures marked suburban mayors' roles in this case? Lastly, what implications do these initiatives have for continuing or rupturing patterns of segregation considering the demographic shifts taking place in these suburban areas? To grasp how processes of operational scale were destroyed and recreated we focused on the activities of mayors and spatial relationships with which they disconnected and connected in order to create a new order of operational scale that facilitated the creation of a new school district.

Rescaling Alliances

Mapping the shifts, or creation, in socio-spatial relations needed to create a new school district is an entry point to identifying the production of operational scale. Specifically, researchers might seek to identify and represent the breakages in alignments and the creation of new spatial fixes that constitute successive arrangements of operational scale. Contemporary methodologies such as actor network theory offer a complimentary version to mapping the rescaling of such relationships (Latour, 2005). While individuals and groups have been the principal focus in many of these frameworks, researchers need to amplify these frameworks and maintain a sense of openness to the manner in which cultural facets such as discourse, not just material and individual entities, enter into these relationships.

Secession movements involve individuals and groups located within and engaged in reconstructing space and place. This is done actively in order to realign the field of social relationships that exist at one particular moment to a different configuration that reflects as well as furthers their interests. Four mayors of a multi-municipality school district engaged in such an activity. The school district was composed of nine municipalities prior to the secession (Map 1). It was one of five school districts in the region. Spatially, it spanned from one side of the foothills to the opposing mountainside on the other end of the valley. The district was divided geographically by a river and an interstate freeway that split the district east and west.

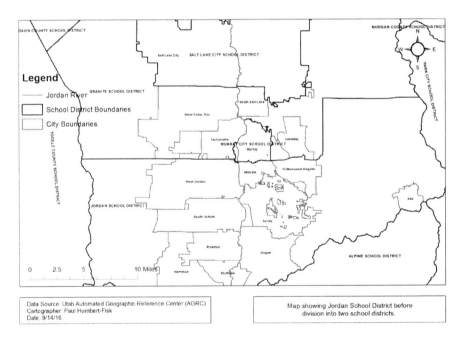

Map 1. Pre-secession boundaries of JSD

Taken together, the municipalities composed both a spatial and institutional relationship whose activities and alignment partly constituted a unified district. A diagram of the network of pre-secession relations identifies some of the connections constituting the district's political and operational scale as well as the activities and practices that linked the parties together (see Diagram 1). Some of these were put into place as recent initiatives that complimented and expanded long established historical relationships. Notable relationships to the pre- and post-secession included an elected school board that networked these independent entities together to constitute the governance structure for the school district. Representatives hailed from precincts that cut across the different municipal units. Underlying this was the Utah state government apparatus and policy code that facilitated, at the turn of the century, an intergovernmental cooperation mechanism allowing the union of entities legitimacy as well as permitting it to levy itself and distribute resources across municipal lines. A county level board mechanism termed the County Commission, which weighed-in on tax adjustments, residential and school growth plans, and modifications to municipal and school boundary lines was equally linked into the ensemble by Founders.

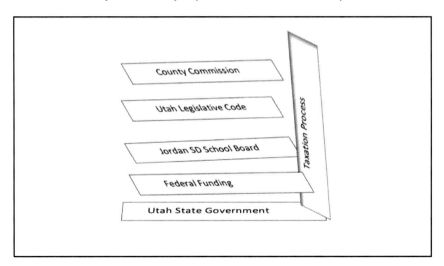

Diagram 1. Pre-secession structural relationships

The pre-secession politics of scale foregrounded a discursive framing of a unified, multi-city school district whose cities co-existed to share resources. The superintendent of the pre-secession district described the prevailing framework undergirding district politics as "one district" (Interview, Superintendent), signifying a set of municipal, fiscal, and educational relationships constituting a space of interdependence. The framework advanced an image of an institutional unit functioning from a coherent and uncontested mission, specifically working to serve all the cities' children within its borders. This framing set the competing municipal interests and political boundaries that constituted it in the background. This politics of scale of an enmeshed network of relationships tempered city mayors' proclivities towards a city-centered, or insular, framing when addressing educational issues.

An operational scale within these networked relations was constructed through the one district discourse. Property taxation, for the purposes of funding schools, as well as the ensuing distribution of collected resources was one of these key activities. It directly activated multiple governance levels, specifically the school board, the County Commission, and the municipal-level administrative structure. Each body was a formal approving and oversight body of changes to the tax structure. The linkage of these units lied embedded in the fabric of daily life, surfacing in the construction, maintenance, and operation of schools, or was made apparent on bi-yearly property tax statements.

The political work that the one district discourse accomplished was also significant in forging political relations to maintain and expand the district's operational scale. The district's administration mobilized it to create a coalition of mayors and parent groups to support a $20-million-dollar school bond measure. The documents making the case for the bond foregrounded the Jordan School District infrastructure and its student body as the subjects and recipients, never a specific city. Yet, its ability to convince stakeholders showed fissures as the superintendent sought to build political partners across the various city mayors. The mayors of the four eastern region cities, which ultimately left the school district, interjected arguments and forged agreements that shifted the terms towards a city centered discourse, asserting a scale giving primacy to municipal and regional interests. An example of this was evident in one mayor's description of the arrangement that was put into place between mayors constituting cities on the eastern side of the district. Note in this quote how spatial signifiers such as 'east side' and 'north eastern' partitioned the district into different regions that impose a tension in the sense of a unified institution.

> With the high growth in the west side, the pressure was mounting to move resources over there at the expense of east side schools. We, mayors, extracted promises from the school district at the time of agreeing to the bond. One was that savings generated from the closing of schools would be re-deployed in schools in the same north eastern sector, so that it wasn't money being saved and being sent to open a new west side school. Secondly, they promised that there wouldn't be any more conversations about school closures. (Mayor, Interview).

Mayors made apparent the cleavages in the "one district" framing through the partitioning put into place by spatial distinctions such as the "east side" and "west side". The assurances that the administration put into place to distribute resources to all regions of the school district were enough to build the backing needing to pass the bond, however.

While the bond initiative represented an instance of affirming the link across municipalities, it also demonstrated the network of relations needing to be engaged in order to sustain this scale, which had to be repeatedly reproduced and asserted to sustain vibrancy in the district's political relations. District administrators not only engaged mayors but also had to sell the proposal to school board members that represented different regions of the district as well as the County Commission and State Office of Education. These practices sought to be re-connective and scale affirming processes that bolstered the assemblage of actors and governmental bodies.

Fracture of the Existing Spatial Order

We've highlighted, in my explanation of the theoretical elements, the processes of fracturing of existing ensembles of relations as key to moments of the production of new orders of scale. The operational scale of JSD political relationships was shaken and ultimately fractured in 2009 as four cities from the network broke away and created a coalition that sought to secede from the school district. Three mayors led the coalition (Cottonwood Heights, Draper, Sandy) whose city boundary lines were contiguous and spatially consolidated along one side of the school district. Midway through the process, they included a fourth city, Midvale, to the coalition. Midvale's borders also buttressed two of the municipalities involved which accounted for all of the political units that constituted a spatial cluster wedged between the mountain and a freeway that partitioned the district east to west (see Map 2). The three mayors proposed the creation of a new school district that was smaller in size than the fifty thousand student, eight city shared district that they had belonged to since they were established.

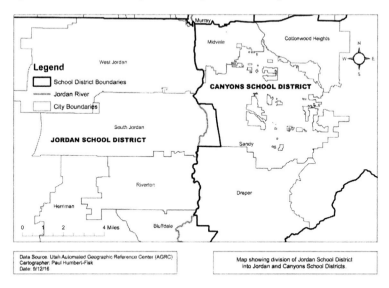

Map 2. Post-secession boundaries

The act of seceding and creating a new school district involved creating a different scale than what was in place when these municipalities were aligned as part of the union composing the school district. The pre-existing scale of the Jordan School district did not serve the municipalities in the reform/creation process, principally because the procedural-legal mechanisms either opposed the secession or did not permit cities of their size to create new social entities such as school districts, or to enter into unions to share services, or inter-local agreements.

The genesis of this secession is marked by the cleavages in the one district framework. The fracture in the union became more pronounced after the school district closed one elementary school in Cottonwood Heights and fell short of distributing the bond monies promised to schools located on the eastern side of the district. These measures, in addition to the prospect of the school board enacting other closures in the same region, proved to be the tipping point that set the secession from exploratory to fully in-motion (Toomer-Cook & Swinyard, 2005).

The act of these cities seceding and creating a new school district involved creating a different scale than what was in place when these municipalities were aligned as part of the unified district. The configuration of discursive and social relations of the Jordan School district did not serve the municipalities seeking to split-off. First, the discursive framing of "one district" did not serve the coalition of mayors that needed to convince constituents to dissolve the existing district relationship. Mayors needed to assert to constituents that their city's schools were not treated equally on the financial or curricular front. Second, many of the legal-procedural mechanisms constituting the operational scale presented legal hurdles or outright opposed the secession. The principal legal obstacle presented itself in the form of the state policy or code, which did not permit cities of their size to create new service units such as school districts or to enter into shared resource agreements, or what is termed inter-local agreements. Third, the political opposition manifested from regional jurisdictional entities such as the County Commission and the full district referendum process, which would have been voted down the secession due to its impact on local property taxes. The coalition of mayors worked with key state level political representatives to dismantle the existing network and affix a new scale of political and operational relations.

The coalition enacted a discursive shift in the politics of scale that negated the one district framing and asserted, instead, one of "local control." It appeared in statements as either a "local control" or a "my city" framing. The discourse foregrounded municipality centered decision-making of educational issues as well as fiscal containment within city borders. As an example:

> We wanted to not have to face the potential of closing schools. People don't want their school closed, and by having local control and taking it amongst a smaller school district, their chance of not having their neighborhood school closed diminishes, regardless of whether it means increasing taxes or not for them. (Mayor, Interview)

The discourse activated the units of neighborhood, small service units and decision-making processes that did not have competing interests to weigh. This is a historical

184

discourse that suburban cities have employed to legitimize a broad spectrum of actions, ranging from tax base isolation to racial exclusion (Frug, 1999). The appearance of this construct within the secession context not only indexed historical national-level meanings but also had a dialogic link to the local city incorporation movement that one of the pro-secession cities enacted in order to become a city.

The politics of competing framings was not lost on the district's superintendent. He continuously found himself in conflict with the new politics of scale that the coalition drove. He identified a change in the value system, or ethic, of how mayors framed the dynamics of shared public institutions. The superintendent reflected upon the focus on municipality and mayoral control contributing to the deterioration in the relationship between mayors, district administration and school board members:

> And you could no longer convince mayors that decisions based on what's best for the common good was worth anything. It became all about my city, my city. (Interview)

The "common good" referred to in this excerpt pointed to a scale and framework that foregrounded collectivity and shared interest that moved beyond municipal politics. The framework was the proverbial glue that kept the large district intact over the last century by keeping municipal self-interest in check. The deterioration reflected a change in the value system of viewing the school district and its corresponding constituents.

While the mayors were effective in offering a different vision of educational accountability, the material-legal dimensions required to structure a consonant operational scale remained tethered to an order that did not permit the coalition to secede and create a new district. Utah's legal-policy domain defined the parameters of who could and could not create a school district, specifically it stated that this realm belonged to citizen groups not municipal governments. Equally, state policy dictated a process that included approvals by each city's respective city council, a county commission, and a district-wide vote on the referendum by residents affected by the secession. These legal relationships had remained dormant yet ever-present in the architecture until the four cities sought to create their own district.

Upon engaging the legal relationships, the mayors realized the scope of prohibitions that state level policies placed upon them as well as the opposition to the split—particularly with majority approval needed from the County Commission as well as the majority of voters constituting the district. The leadership decided that rather than work within the same operational scale structuring the parameters they would reconstruct it, circumventing particular governing bodies and adding others in their place. Working with state level legislative partners, they eliminated approval bodies that provided regional checks-and-balances. The new operational scale removed the County Commission, the Utah State Board of Education, and restricted eligible voters to only those cities seeking to secede. They added policy provisions that placed cities, where mayors functioned as proxies, as initiating agents and that centrally located the state legislature as a pivotal approving body, which was inclined to small government (see Diagram 2).

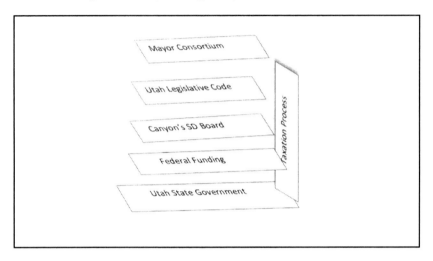

Diagram 2. Post-secession structural relationships

The details of how operational scale was mapped through policy can be seen in the verbiage of the approved 2007 Utah state code. The absences and presences of key relationships are significant in defining operational scale. Track how municipalities and the legislative body are given prominence in the network. It stated:

> After conducting a feasibility study, a city of the first or second class as defined under Section 10-2-301, may by majority vote of the legislative body, submit for approval a measure to create a new school district....

> By majority vote of the legislative body, a city of any class, a town, or a county, may, together with one or more other cities, towns, or the county enter into an interlocal agreement, in accordance with Title 11, Chapter 13, Interlocal Cooperation Act, for the purpose of submitting for voter approval a measure to create a new school district. (https://le.utah.gov/xcode/Title53A/Chapter2, p. 1)

The city unit was provided legal entitlements that were not possible prior to this bill. First, cities were granted the authority to "create" a school district. The appropriation of existing buildings and capital from existing school districts was subsumed under the process of creation. Second, the policy reframed mayors as well as city councils as active agents with rights in the process of secession, a role held for parents and voters. Third, the legislature became the only sanctioning body, outside of those seeking to split. Last, the policy permitted cities and towns of any size to create legal unions, or inter-local collaborations, which created opportunities for other secession attempts in the future to be pursued to create smaller school districts.

The elimination of the various approving bodies produced a scale that limited dissension and, importantly, homogenized the population of decision makers. Within the JSD secession movement, this sorting translated into muting from the deliberations and decisions populations whose economic and family size attributes did not generally correspond to those within the four pro-secession cities. Residential choices at the level of housing and cities pre-sorted the population with the new organizational scale following to institutionalize the distribution of educational dollars. The long-term implications of these changes were a demographic and policy context that were prone to foster racial segregation. The demographic trend in the region suggests that low to moderate income ethnically and racially diverse populations are migrating and settling into the cities and neighborhoods that already have experienced contested institutional contexts. Very little is left to stand in the way of cities and their residents in creating additional boundaries.

CONCLUSION

This chapter has argued that research focused on educational segregation should amplify its tools to study not solely the sorting effects of political boundaries, but also to investigate the processes that create these mechanisms. A focus on the production of scale provides the field with a generative option that facilitates documenting the confluence and intermingling of different social actors, institutions, and forces that construct socio-educational divisions. This spatial turn initiates its work from the premise that the creation of segregated spaces is brought about by a multitude of relationships that function in concert as well as, at times, in a contradictory fashion. It acknowledges that educational processes, in some degree, are rhizomatic and dynamic in nature, involving the entanglement of a multitude of social relations that can shift in how they produce social phenomenon. Put differently, this chapter has sought to show and argue that entities that appear disconnected can be significant in operational processes.

Our argument for asserting a spatial turn into conversations of educational segregation research as well as other lines of educational inquiry is not to push a fashion trend of space and spatial thinking into educational research or debilitate the objectives of social justice oriented inquiry currently undergirding macro-demographic and policy approaches. The politics of advancing social justice and access issues, which are the aims of educational segregation inquiry, remain intact within a scalar conceptual framing. As the analysis of this case study has sought to demonstrate, the openings for increased civic engagement and social justice oriented activity can be expanded through these lenses. Opportunities for intervention can be made available that provide actors possibilities to democratize educational reform. This stands in contrast to projects rendering educational reform as structural relationships that appear out of the hands of regular individuals and organizations other than the policy elite.

Finally, educational researchers' employment of spatial tools can provide us with the conceptual scaffolding to bridge local and global processes. While the case study examined here demonstrated how school district, municipal, regional, and state-level institutions and actors were linked, others have demonstrated persuasively how global capital finds its way into these processes (see Buras, 2011; Lipman, 2011). The prominence of the themes of globalization, neoliberalism, and the ecologies of supporting children's well-being in educational research necessitates a spatial oriented took kit that can map broadly yet retain a focus on actors and processes.

NOTE

[1] Different concepts of scale are employed in the field of Geography. Cartographic scale and geographic scale also are employed in sub-fields (see Marston, 2000).

REFERENCES

Appadurai, A. (1996). *Modernity at large: Cultural dimensions of globalization.* New York, NY: University of Minnesota Press.

Bischoff, K. (2008). School district fragmentation and racial residential: How do boundaries matter. *Urban Affairs Review, 44*(1), 182–217. doi:10.1177/1078087408320651

Buendía, E., & Ares, N. (2006). *Geographies of difference: The social production of the east side, west side and central city school.* New York, NY: Peter Lang.

Buras, K. (2011). Race, charter schools, and conscious capitalism: On the spatial politics of whines as property (and the unconscionable assault on black New Orleans). *Harvard Educational Review, 81*(2), 296–331.

Castells, M. (1996). *The rise of the network society: The information age: Economy, society and culture, volume I.* Malden, MA: Blackwell.

Cheah, P. (2010). Non-dialectical materialism. In D. Coole & S. Frost (Eds.), *New materialisms: Ontology, agency, and politics* (pp. 70–91). London: Duke University Press.

Davis, M. (1990). *City of quartz: Excavating the future of Los Angeles.* New York, NY: Verso.

Deleuze, G., & Guattari, F. (1987). *A thousand plateaus: Capitalism and schizophrenia.* New York, NY: University of Minnesotta Press.

Foucault, M. (1972). *Archeology of knowledge and the discourse on language.* New York, NY: Pantheon.

Foucault, M. (1980). *Power/Knowledge: Selected interviews and other writings, 1972–1977.* New York, NY: Pantheon.

Frankenberg, E., & Orfield, G. (2012). *The resegregation of suburban schools: A hidden crisis in American education.* Cambridge, MA: Harvard Educational Press.

Frug, G. (1999). *City making: Building communities without building walls.* Princeton, NJ: Princeton University Press.

Gumas-Dawes, B., Orfield, M., & Luce, T. F. (2013). The state of public schools in post-Katrina New Orleans: The challenge of creating equal opportunity. In E. Frankenberg & G. Orfield and associates (Eds.), *Educational delusions?: Why choice can deepen inequality and how to make schools fair* (pp. 159–186). Berkeley, CA: University of California Press.

Harvey, D. (1981). Hegel, Von Thunen and Marx. *Antipode, 13*(3), 1–12.

Harvey, D. (1996). *Justice, nature and the geography of difference.* Boston, MA: Basil Blackwell.

Holme, J. J. (2002). Buying homes, buying schools: School choice and the social construction of school quality. *Harvard Educational Review, 72*(2), 177–205.

Howitt, R. (1998). Scale as relation: Musical metaphors of geographical scale. *Area, 30*(1), 49–58.

Jessop, B. (2006). Spatial fixes, temporal fixes, and spatio-temporal fixes. In N. Castree & D. Gregory (Eds.), *David Harvey: A critical reader* (pp. 142–166). Oxford: Blackwell.

Jessop, B., Brenner, N., & Jones, M. (2008). Theorizing sociospatial relations. *Environment and Planning D: Society and Space, 26*, 389–401. doi:10.1068/d9107

Latour, B. (2005). *Reassembling the social: An introduction to actor-network-theory.* Oxford: Oxford University Press.

Lipman, P. (2011, January 10). The case for board control of public schools. *Chicago Tribune.* Retrieved from http://articles.chicagotribune.com/2011-01-10/news/chi-110110lipman_briefs_1_low-performing-schools-school-closings-school-boards

Marston, S. A. (2000). The social construction of scale. *Progress in Human Geography, 24*(2), 219–242. doi:10.1191/030913200674086272

Massey, D., & Denton, N. S. (1993). *American apartheid: Segregation and the making of the underclass.* Cambridge, MA: Harvard University Press.

McCann, E. J. (2003). Framing space and time in the city: Urban policy and the politics of spatial and temporal scale. *Journal of Urban Affairs, 25*(2), 159–178.

Orfield, G., & Lee, C. (2005). Why segregation matters: Poverty and educational inequality. *The Civil Rights Project.* Retrieved from http://escholarship.org/uc/item/4xr8z4wb

Reardon, S. F., & O'Sullivan, D. (2004). Measures of spatial segregation. *Sociological Methodology, 34*(1), 121–162. doi:10.1111/j.0081-1750.2004.00150.x

Reardon, S. F., & Yun, J. T., & Eitle, T. M. (2000). The changing structure of school segregation: Measurement and evidence of multiracial metropolitan-area school segregation, 1989–1995. *Demography, 37*(3), 351–364. doi:10.2307/2648047

Richards, M. P., & Stroub, K. J. (2014). The fragmentation of metropolitan public school districts and the segregation of American schools: A longitudinal analysis. *Teachers College Record, 116*(12), 1–30.

Rhodes, A., & DeLuca, S. (2014). Residential mobility and school choice among poor families. In A. Lareau & K. Goyette (Eds.), *Choosing homes, choosing schools* (pp. 137–166). New York, NY: Russell Sage Foundation.

Soja, E. (1998). *Thirdspace: Journeys to Los Angeles and other real-and-imagined places.* Cambridge, MA: Blackwell.

Tate, W. F. (2011). Introduction. In W. F. Tate IV (Ed.), *Research on schools, neighborhoods and communities* (pp. 1–11). Lanham, MD: AERA.

Toomer-Cook, J., & Swinyard, K. (2005, March 9). Jordan school district to close two schools. *Desert News.*

York, A. M., Smith, M. E., Stanley B. W., Stark, B. L., Novic, J., Harlan, S. L., Cowgill, G. L., & Boone, C. G. (2011). Ethnic and class clustering through the ages: A transdisciplinary approach to neighbourhood social patterns. *Urban Studies, 48*(11), 2399–2415. doi:10.1177/0042098010384517

Edward Buendía
University of Washington – Bothell

Paul Fisk
University of Utah

ADAI A. TEFERA, CECILIA RIOS AGUILAR, ALFREDO J. ARTILES,
CATHERINE KRAMARCZUK VOULGARIDES AND
VERONICA VÉLEZ

12. DEVELOPING A CRITICAL SPACE PERSPECTIVE IN THE EXAMINATION OF THE RACIALIZATION OF DISABILITIES

Researchers have long argued that the spatial dimensions of our lives, in addition to the social and historical, have important practical and policy significance (Lefebvre, 1991; Soja, 1989, 2010). Although theorizing space has increased in recent years in a number of disciplines, including sociology, anthropology, postcolonial studies, and economics, to name a few (Peake & Schein, 2000), it has been relatively under-theorized in education (Tate, 2008). Yet, "we are, and always have been, intrinsically spatial beings, active participants in the social construction of our embracing spatialities" (Soja, 1996, p. 1). A critical examination of space provides important opportunities for new insights and understandings to emerge, particularly in addressing racial inequities in education. Indeed, deep educational inequities continue to be documented in urban locales where poverty and racial segregation have been present across generations. More recently, evidence points to growing educational inequalities in suburban spaces (Orfield & Frankenberg, 2014; Tefera, Frankenberg, & Siegel-Hawley, 2011) with alarming trends of racial disproportionality in special education[1] in suburban locales (Kramarczuk, Voulgarides, Aylward, & Noguera, 2014). Although research on racial disproportionality has documented a number of explanations that include biased assessments and referral practices, lack of quality instruction, and the impact of poverty on students' academic achievement, narrow methodological and theoretical approaches have contributed to limited critical understandings of educational inequities, particularly related to disproportionality (Waitoller, Artiles, & Cheney, 2010). More recently, however, a growing number of scholars are considering the role of space in racial disproportionality (Annamma, Morrison, & Jackson, 2014; Artiles, 2011; 2003). In light of this, in this chapter we situate racial disproportionality in special education within a critical spatial perspective by demonstrating how the consequences of changing patterns of residential segregation, particularly in suburban communities, are marked by differentiations along axes of race and disability, thus increasingly influencing the racialization of disabilities. Specifically, we demonstrate how teachers and leaders contributed to material and discursive landscapes of exclusion (Trudeau &

N. Ares et al. (Eds.), Deterritorializing/Reterritorializing, 191–207.

McMorran, 2011) for students at the intersection of racial and ability differences that were heavily shaped by the shifting demographics of suburban space.

We posit that analyses of educational equity and disproportionality must be enriched with critical examinations of space that include social and cultural dimensions, while simultaneously focusing on race, disability, and other markers of so called difference. This affords important possibilities to identify both enabling and disabling geographies of opportunity (Tate, 2008) in discourses related to racial disproportionality in special education. In this chapter, we therefore examine the questions: How can a critical spatial perspective advance the study of disproportionality in demographically changing school spaces? How can geographical mapping tools be used to supplement a critical spatial perspective to assist educational researchers and policymakers in understanding and addressing racial disproportionality in special education?

In order to examine these questions it is important to first take note that the U.S. today is more ethnically, racially, and linguistically diverse than any other time in its history. In fact, during the next 40 years it is expected that as the White population steadily declines, the Latina/o and Asian populations will gradually rise, with Black, American Indian, and American Pacific Islander populations remaining comparatively constant (U.S. Census, 2015). These changes in racial demographics are shifting historically White spaces—particularly suburban communities—and bringing new questions related to educational inequality to the fore. In *Seeking Spatial Justice* (2010), Soja makes the case that the geographies we live in "are not just dead background or a neutral physical stage for the human drama but are filled with material and imagined forces that affect events and experiences, forces that can hurt us or help us" (p. 19). Similarly, Tate (2008) argues that we need to consider the role of space and uneven geographies of opportunity in the U.S., where both cities and suburbs are simultaneously examined. Uneven geographies include disparate spaces that afford or limit key resources and thus opportunities such as adequate schooling and health facilities, fair and affordable housing, transportation, green space, and the like. Essentially, if we are serious about addressing the inequities facing our students, we must consider the spatial, as well as cultural, social, and historical factors.

Critical considerations of geography or space can be applied to understand these educational inequities. While FirstSpace includes what is visible and physical, and SecondSpace includes an ideational or imagined space, the concept of "ThirdSpace" (Soja, 1996) provides an exploratory, multidisciplinary, and flexible framework to examine the dynamism embedded in our spatial imaginations. Depending on events, meanings and circumstances constantly shift. Therefore, "ThirdSpace is a space where issues of race, class, gender, disability, and other intersections can be addressed simultaneously without privileging one over the other; where one can be Marxist and post-Marxist, materialist and idealist, structuralist and humanist, disciplined and transdisciplinary at the same time" (Soja, 1996, p. 5). This perspective has enabled a greater understanding of the role of space in the production of educational inequities and the racialization of disabilities in particular (Artiles, 2011; 2003).

This is important given that recent research points to a series of racialized consequences influenced by spatial and social relations, some of which include the persistence of racially segregated communities and schools (Orfield & Frankenberg, 2014; Richards, 2014), particularly in suburban spaces (Diem, Cleary, Ali, & Frankenberg, 2014), the relegation of English Learners to separate classrooms due to English-only laws (Gándara & Aldana, 2014; Gándara & Hopkins, 2010), enduring challenges related to the disproportionate placement of students of color in special education classrooms (Artiles, 2011; Harry & Klingner, 2014; Losen & Orfield, 2002), and the disproportionate suspensions and expulsions of primarily young Black men and boys labeled with disabilities (Losen, Ee, Hodson, & Martinez, 2015). These challenges speak to just a few of the critical ways in which the future of educational equity in the U.S. intimately ties to historical, racial, and spatial dimensions with significant material consequences.

With this in mind, we intentionally bring structures of privilege to the spatial surface (Soja, 2010) as they relate to race, disability, and disproportionality in special education in demographically changing suburban communities. Indeed, it was just over one decade ago that Artiles (2003) posed a series of enduring questions that foreshadowed some of today's most pressing challenges related to the racialization of disabilities (Artiles, 2011). Poignantly, he asked, "how will special education's identity change as this system serves more racially and linguistically diverse students with disabilities in general education contexts?" And, "as understandings of inclusion shift from a focus on spatial location (the general education classroom) to the alignment of educational philosophies with visions of organizational arrangements, how will this new identity account for racial differences, culture, and space?" (2003, p. 165). In this chapter, we heed the importance of these questions given these epochal racial, ethnic, and linguistic demographic shifts.

To do this, we begin the chapter by setting up the policy context and illuminating the paradoxes in special education policy and the law as they pertain to racial disproportionality in special education. First, we detail how policies often reify inequities given the lack of consideration for the relationship between educational inequities and space. Next, we discuss emerging research that demonstrates the relationship between recent racial demographic shifts in suburban spaces and the consequences of racialized or racially segregated communities on racial disproportionality in special education. We do this by exploring the significance between shifting racial demographics, racial disproportionality, and space. Specifically, we focus in on one case study conducted in the town of Middleton (a pseudonym), a suburban community in a northeastern region of the U.S., and demonstrate how teachers and leaders contributed to material and discursive landscapes of exclusion (Trudeau & McMorran, 2011) shaped by a residentially segregated community. We then provide an outline of the possibilities and promises of infusing a critical spatial perspective with mapping as a potential tool for researchers and policymakers to critically assess and address larger spatial and structural factors that influence educational inequities. In particular, we focus on spatial dynamics of disability identification for students of color and their families, namely the concepts of enabling and disabling geographies in the context of quickly changing demographic suburban communities.

FOREGROUNDING SPACE: PARADOXES & INEQUALITIES IN SPECIAL EDUCATION POLICY & LAW

A significant portion of disproportionality research has focused on what Soja (1996) calls the FirstSpace, or what is visible and physical. As a result, research has tended to emphasize placement patterns in special education focusing on the relationships among indicators such as race, poverty, achievement, and location (Artiles, 2003). Significantly, this prior research has rarely considered the social, discursive and structural dynamics that affect practice as well as students' experiences. On the other hand, considerations for SecondSpace, an ideational, conceptual, or imagined space is focused on what is possible (Lefebvre, 1991; Soja, 1996). Artiles (2003) argues that disproportionality research should focus in this nexus between the First and SecondSpace in order to develop new visions of spaces for students in more equitable classrooms and schools. While this ThirdSpace is often one of contestation, struggle, and messiness, particularly when it comes to issues of educational equity, it can also be one of shared understanding, meaning, and possibility for historically marginalized students. This lens therefore provides important possibilities in understanding the sociological, political, and cultural contexts that contribute to disproportionality (Artiles, 2011). Essentially, a ThirdSpace perspective in the examination of disproportionality provides a strategic opportunity to bridge the gap between the goals of educational equity, particularly for students of color with disabilities, and its actual enactment.

It is important to note, however, that the historic intent of special education policy, most notably the Individuals with Disabilities Education Act (IDEA, 1975), which expanded the educational opportunities for and civil rights of students with disabilities, has not always lived up to its promise. Persistent trends in racial disproportionality in special education have limited educational opportunities for many students of color. For example, Black students are between 24% and 26% more likely to be identified for special education than White students (D'Agord, Munk, & O'Hara, 2012). It has also been well documented that Black students with disabilities do not receive high-quality special education services compared to White students with disabilities (Harry & Klingner, 2014; Losen & Orfield, 2002). Furthermore, although Black and American Indian students have been most affected by disproportionality, Latinas/os and Dual Language Learners (DLLs) are overrepresented in some disability categories, particularly in specific regions of the U.S. (Artiles, Rueda, & Salazar, 2005). There is also evidence that disproportionality patterns vary by disability category, race, school location, and socioeconomic level. For example, Oswald, Coutinho, Best, and Singh (1999) reported that Black students' overrepresentation in intellectual disabilities *declined* as community poverty levels *increased*. Interestingly, Latina/o and Black students' overrepresentation in learning disabled (LD) and emotional behavioral disorders (EBD) *increased* as community poverty level *increased*. "American Indian students tend to be overrepresented, particularly in EBD, if they live in predominantly non-White communities" (Artiles et al., 2005, p. 723). In other words, these alarming correlations between the high placement of students of color—or racial disproportionality in disability categories—defy the all too common logic that poverty is the primary rationale for disproportionality and highlight the need to use of innovative educational research practices and tools to reveal spatial along with sociocultural and contextual factors that together help explain the persistence of these equity challenges.

Despite these trends in educational inequities, discussions of a "post-racial" society abound (Bobo, 2011; powell, 2012) and are evidenced in the growing number of educational laws and policies that espouse so called "colorblind" ideals (Bonilla-Silva, 2006). For example, the Supreme Court ruling, *Parents Involved in Community Schools v. Seattle School District No. 1* (2007), limited the use of race—effectively seeking to be "colorblind"—in school boundary decision-making despite a plethora of evidence of the negative consequences of racially segregated schools (Orfield & Frankenberg, 2014; Tefera, Frankenberg, & Siegel-Hawley, 2011). The notion of colorblindness has been critiqued by a number of scholars (Bonilla-Silva, 2016; Bobo, 2011) who have described the concept as a sort of "new racism" whereby race is erased and presumed to no longer matter, but remains equally detrimental to the opportunities available to historically marginalized groups as overt acts of racism. Similarly, the current reauthorization of the Elementary and Secondary Education Act (1965) reaffirms neoliberal ideologies that continue to evaluate equity through national standards, school choice, and mandates for equal outcomes among all so called "subgroups" (i.e., racial/ethnic, linguistic, socioeconomic, and ability groups) on standardized tests, an insidious pattern that reifies colorblind ideologies and avoids systemic and institutional analysis (Apple, 2006; Au, 2013; Lipman, 2004; Picower & Mayorga, 2015). Essentially, educational policies that promise inclusion and equity with such narrowly conceived policy prescriptions are commonplace in the rhetoric and implementation of educational policies today (Gonzalez, Tefera, & Artiles, 2015).

Furthermore, national educational policy seldom considers the ways that complex local spaces and structures influence the implementation of educational policies on schools (Ball, Maguire, & Braun, 2012; Tefera & Kramarczuk Voulgarides, in press). In the case of racial disproportionality in special education, problematic federal policies have myopically focused on technical considerations (Cavendish, Artiles, & Harry, 2015) and adhered to overly simplistic explanations of poverty and psychological frameworks, rather than pursue an understanding of the dysfunction of local socio-institutional relationships and spatial dimensions that contribute to racial disproportionality. For example, in taking a closer look at how states comply with federal policy efforts to track disproportionality, Cavendish et al. (2015) provide evidence of varying policy requirements across the country. The authors explain how federal policy dictates that each state currently defines disproportionality with various numerical calculations to establish the relative risk of different racial groups being disproportionally placed in special education. After analyzing states' reporting data, the authors found a number of differences in threshold designations by region. From 2006 to 2009, while the average relative risk ratio[2] for states across the country was 2.8, Southern states featured a slightly higher average of 3.1.[3] Since states set their risk ratios higher to avoid being federally cited, they mask potential regional inequities and underscore the relevance of a critical space analysis.

Based on these emerging trends in disproportionality research, we contend that more attention must be given to the enabling and equally important disabling geographies of opportunity (Annamma, Morrison, & Jackson, 2014; Artiles, 2011; Pacheco & Vélez, 2009; Tate, 2008) that shape racial inequities in education, particularly in spaces that are demographically shifting with significant consequences for students of color in suburban spaces. Next, we summarize research that suggests racial disproportionality in special education may be taking a new "spatial turn" in U.S. suburbs. By zooming in on one study conducted in a racially and economically diverse suburb, we outline the prevailing sentiments of "colorblind" or "color evasive" racism (Annamma et al., 2014) and the consequences of racialized communities on racial disproportionality in special education.

LANDSCAPES OF EXCLUSION IN THE NEW U.S. SUBURB: CONSEQUENCES FOR DISPROPORTIONALITY IN SPECIAL EDUCATION

The idea that space matters to how people live their lives and that it affects their relationships is not new. One particular dimension of space that has been studied in detail among educators is that of residential segregation because of the impact it has on significant social and spatial aspects (Soja, 2010) that shape schooling inequities (Frankenberg & Orfield, 2012). In the context of racial disproportionality in special education, growing demographic changes in racially segregated spaces are creating new forms of exclusion whereby students of color, particularly those with disabilities, experience marginalization and exclusion "through multiple nodes of difference that compound and complicate marginality" (Trudeau & McMorran, 2010, p. 446). We detail this dynamic in this section by discussing the relationship between segregation and disproportionality in suburban districts. We demonstrate how competing narratives contributed to material and discursive landscapes of exclusion (Trudeau & McMorran, 2011) within the context of a segregated suburban district.

It is important to remember that residential racial segregation is complex and should be considered "contextually as arising from underlying spatial structures and structural advantage and disadvantage" (Soja, 2010, p. 55). In addition to the rapidly changing racial, ethnic, and economic landscape of the U.S, suburban spaces are experiencing unprecedented demographic shifts. In fact, a significant number

(> 50%) of students of color and of low-income students attend suburban schools (Orfield & Frankenberg, 2008). These suburban spaces are increasingly becoming more Latina/o (Frey, 2011) and less white (Frankenberg & Orfield, 2012). Amidst these demographic trends throughout suburbs, corresponding results include important shifts in the students that educational leaders and practitioners are used to serving. In other words, increased cultural diversity can contribute to cultural dissonance and misunderstandings about students' abilities (Frankenberg & Orfield, 2012). Frankenberg and Orfield (2012) point out that few policies exist to support suburban educators contending with these rapid demographic shifts. Further, few policies address the ways in which these changes contribute to residential segregation in areas with little civil rights coordination within various locales.

Racial disproportionality in special education increasingly relates to shifting suburban demographics and segregated school districts. For example, Kramarczuk Voulgarides et al. (2014) correlated the size of a school district, its geographic space or *locale* (rural, suburban, urban),[4] and the timeframe within which a school district was removed from a citation[5] for racial disproportionality in special education. Kramarczuk Voulgarides et al. (2014) analyzed school district-level data from 2005 to 2011 to identify the sociodemographic variables that contributed to the likelihood of entering and exiting a citation for disproportionality. They found that while larger and urban school districts took the longest time to exit a citation, smaller and rural school districts took the least amount of time.

In addition, the authors found numerous districts had entered, exited, and re-entered a citation in urban and suburban defined spaces, with approximately 40%—the vast majority in suburban districts—following this citation pattern. The researchers found that suburban districts appeared to have complex and contrasting social forces that shaped movement in and out of a citation for disproportionality, more so than urban and rural spaces in the study. It is important to understand how these social forces within the new suburban landscape shape disproportionality. Micro-relational focused qualitative research on the subject has identified some of these forces associated with the persistence of racialized outcomes in special education in suburban school districts. For example, Kramarczuk Voulgarides (2015) conducted a comparative ethnography on disproportionality and found that segregation *within* suburban spaces greatly affected practitioners' perceptions of racial minority students, how educational services were delivered, and the ways in which practitioners understood racialized inequities. Three specific themes in practitioners' responses emerged: (a) one group of district leaders and teachers and staff were aware of segregation within the district, often adhering to colorblind sentiments; (b) another group of practitioners discussed segregation and expressed outrage at the racialized outcomes of students with disabilities; and (c) the third and most prevailing group normalized disproportionality and believed its occurrence to be expected. In other words, these perceptions contributed to material and discursive landscapes of exclusion (Trudeau & McMorran, 2011) for students at the intersection of racial and ability differences that were heavily shaped by the shifting demographic of suburban space. Concomitantly, these findings suggest the need to "spatially examine how structural and institutional factors divide, constrict, and construct space to impact the educational experiences and opportunities available to students based on race" (Pacheco & Vélez, 2009, p. 293) and other markers of so-called difference. This includes important school factors that influence racial disproportionality, such as deficit thinking, school practices and leadership, and acknowledging and addressing school bias (Skiba, Chung, Trachok, Baker, Sheya, & Hughes, 2015).

To highlight the landscapes of exclusion within Middleton, we provide findings from Kramarczuk Voulgarides et al.'s (2014) study by focusing in on one suburban school district. Within Middletown, the district operated under the Princeton Plan desegregation strategy that organized student attendance according to grade level rather than where students resided. Two of the district's four school buildings cited for disproportionality in special education were located within the most segregated areas, where primarily families of color resided; the other two bordered the white community. To the point of increasing levels of segregation, Soja (2010) discusses the formation of unjust suburban geographies and institutionalized racial segregation, identifying a "sophisticated strategy specifically designed to produce beneficial geographies for the hegemonic few while creating spatial structures of disadvantage for the rest" (p. 40). Similarly, Voulgarides et al. (2015) found that Middletown's racial segregation contributed to educators' lack of understanding of diverse bodies, namely Black bodies with disabilities, and as a result the district received a citation for disproportionally disciplining Black students with disabilities. The district's sophisticated strategy of segregation not only separated the community racially but also led to the segregation of students within the school through disciplinary practices that forced students out of the school.

Indeed, the community of Middleton was fiercely divided. Its business center looked like a typical small-town main street, characterized by elements of visual cohesion. Storefronts blended together and several signs hung on the streets boasting Middletown's pride. However, the idyllic façade of the business core was fleeting, depending upon which way you travelled. A five-minute drive in either direction presented two very different communities. Traveling east, the storefronts became less uniform while the road widened and became busier with speeding traffic, car shops, temporary housing structures, discount retailers, and fewer manicured lawns. This community was made up predominately of families of color. Traveling west, in a predominately White community, however, the lawns maintained a distinct uniformity. Stores boasted products such as organic produce and teeth-whitening services, and roads meandered in various directions leading to cul-de-sacs that each nestled a semicircle of large houses. These singular racial and cultural enclaves impacted the ways that teachers considered racial and ability differences in the classroom within a shifting suburban demographic landscape.

District staff were also highly aware of these divisions in the community. Yet it was rare for district employees to address the effects of residential segregation on practice and effectively meet the needs students of color with disabilities. The fieldwork yielded three prevailing sentiments about the influence of racial and economic segregation on district practices that influenced disproportionality. The first group glossed over issues of race or residential segregation, deeming them inconsequential and adhering to so called "color-blind" or color evasive sentiments. For example, one White high school staff member described the "real mix" of races and socioeconomic groups in Middletown. At the same time, she referred to the West Side as a "million dollar neighborhood," "beautiful," "very affluent," and "mostly White." Very few White students enrolled in the public school system. Another interviewee, a White woman, said she purposefully did not "see race" and instead just saw "a kid in need." In fact, she discussed her frustration when people would tell her race mattered in the district, and she could not understand why race was even brought up as an issue. These types of responses were commonplace. One interviewee even went so far as to say disproportionality was "an idea concocted by the state to get teachers in trouble." This group of professionals often tried to confide that they saw no issues with how students of color with disabilities were treated, disciplined, or educated in Middletown; rather, the issues were solely the students' problems.

The second group involved several staff members who were outraged by the racial inequities in the district. Some were very straightforward about their anger. One employee proclaimed that, "Middletown is a racist place" and lamented that students of color and low-income students were treated as if "they were nothing." Others acknowledged feeling connected to the community but were saddened by how the district operated. One staff member was very clear about her frustration with the district: "It is an act of God that we [Middletown] have not been in the newspapers more. The way kids are treated here, it is like 'I'm done with you.' I'm surprised nothing worse has happened (in reference to the district's citation for disproportionality)."

The third prevailing response on the effect of racial and economic segregation on practice came from the largest group of district staff members encountered in the field. This group seemed to accept the citation for disproportionality as a simple fact. In Middleton, school officials readily admitted that the district had racial and economic divisions and expressed little to no surprise about the citation. One grade school employee noted issues in Middletown surrounding "things like race and disproportionality," have "been going on for decades." She added, "it is a divided community" and "there has always been a big difference between East Middletown and West Middletown." Another interviewee thought Middletown was "very stable" with "legacies of families." When probed on what he meant by "legacy," he elaborated, "it is a very segregated community with the Whites in the west and Blacks in the east," implicating the lack of integration in the community. He promptly added explicit analysis of racism:

There is racism here in this community. It's not overt but it is there. No one really talks about how segregated it is, but I mean the district lives like we are separate but equal, just as long as equal means you don't join us! I think the community chooses to live like it is the 1950s because it is easier and making changes costs money.

His comments illustrate how this group of employees paradoxically recognized racial divisions in the community but failed to connect how these divisions influenced district practices, particularly those related to the district's citation for the disproportionate suspension of Black students with disabilities.

The disparate understandings of the community context in Middletown greatly affected practice and contributed to a systemic lack of coordination between buildings, staff members, school district polices, and leadership to address disproportionality. Essentially, the deep-rooted effects of residential segregation on practice coupled with staff and leadership that was dissociated from student outcomes stifled a significant systematic response to address the issue. Each individual in the district was left to his/her own devices to act as he/she pleased and needed. Furthermore, parents had little influence or say over the schooling practices within Middleton.

Collectively, the series of interview data from district employees, coupled with evidence from field notes and historical records on residential patterns, showed Middletown had a complicated social context characterized by racial and economic demarcations of difference. Differences between the White and racially diverse populations in the community were perceived by most as relatively normal; disproportionality was therefore perceived as a logical outcome given the social context of the district.

Perceptions of teachers and leaders were heavily shaped by the spatial segregation of the community, demonstrating how social forces within the town of Middleton constructed space and impacted the educational experiences and opportunities available to the students based on race and disability. Though these discursive landscapes of exclusion were significant in shaping understandings of disproportionality within the segregated suburban context, Soja (2010) reminds us that not all forms of residential segregation have to be unjust. That is, "residential segregation can be voluntary and beneficial, with people of similar background choosing to live together for many different purposes" (Soja, 2010, p. 55). Though beyond the purposes of this chapter, building on and understanding the cultural assets that exist within these segregated spaces may hold significant opportunities to understand how to better serve students of color with disabilities in ways that have as of yet been relatively underexplored.

In the next section we argue that infusing a *critical* space perspective can aid in the analyses and understanding of how complex forces shape dis/abling geographies and inequities in education. We outline specific steps scholars can take to examine these geographies of enabling and dis/abling geographies, particularly in increasingly diverse communities. We argue that understanding these spaces provide the possibility for a ThirdSpace perspective in addressing the racialization of disabilities.

HOW CAN A CRITICAL SPACE PERSPECTIVE BE USED TO EXAMINE (DIS)ABLING GEOGRAPHIES?

A focus on the spatial distribution of opportunities enables us to study how educational equity is constituted by opportunities and constraints outside, as well as inside, the educational system. Geographies of opportunity (Tate, 2008) can serve as a powerful set of conceptual and methodological approaches to contextualize inequities in education. More concretely, we assert that such a tactic could help educators examine the disability identification practices of educators and administrators, particularly of culturally and linguistically diverse students in various spatial contexts, including suburban communities. This is a significant area that deserves to be studied more carefully and rigorously from a critical spatial perspective. Increasingly in suburban locales, we know that students of color are disproportionately identified with disabilities. The research to date has relied primarily on psychological concepts that focus on child factors, rather than on critical spatial analyses that document the interplay of psychological forces with geographic, sociological, political, and cultural contexts and processes that contribute to disproportionality and the roles played by the various stakeholders (Artiles, 2003). Research has also underexplored how families—culturally and linguistically diverse families in particular—engage with the special education system, and the degree of agency these families have in seeking or resisting a disability identification for their child.

Given this context, how do we engage in research focused on understanding enabling and disabling geographies using a critical space perspective? We offer the following concrete steps scholars must consider when examining the spatial dynamics of disability identification in increasingly diverse locales:

1. Use various data (i.e., U.S. Census, ECLS, NELS, OCR, etc.) to examine the ways in which neighborhood and school structures affect the educational opportunities of students with disabilities. A critical spatial analysis could benefit from multiple databases to create variables that truly capture the dynamics of the educational processes and contexts experienced by under-represented students.
2. Critically examine identification practices and processes in schools by looking at school datasets and by interviewing school stakeholders, including district and school administrators and teachers. Doing this allows key stakeholders to regularly reflect on how their practices affect outcomes related to equity, including racial disproportionality.
3. Employ qualitative data to contextualize inequities and as visual representations on maps. These data include interviews with families and students to understand how they (a) make sense of a disability diagnosis, (b) interact with the special education system, and (c) utilize resources (in their schools and neighborhoods/

communities) to navigate the system. Such qualitative data could be coded as categorical variables by geographic unit on a map or hyperlinked through interactive technologies. While digital mapping has traditionally been a quantitative science, new technological advances allow users to embed and layer qualitative data in creative ways (see https://storymaps.arcgis.com/en/).

4. Map the interplay of *enabling* and *disabling* geographies by focusing on the spatial distribution of resources and opportunities in the neighborhoods or communities in which families live and its relationship with schools and other resources. This step often combines traditional census data with qualitative data from interviews to create maps that capture the geographies of opportunity in which students and families live. The contrast of traditional neighborhood boundaries with families' subjective neighborhood borders will enable scholars to identify resources and constraints that are not visible given the limitations of existing research. By connecting rich contextual measures to quantitative and qualitative individual-level student and school data, scholars will be able to provide a nuanced portrait of students' school, family, and neighborhood environments.

5. Tell the stories of families with children with disabilities and their students navigating (dis)abling geographies. Use qualitative data and GIS maps to provide a non-deficit approach to identification practices and its consequences for students labeled with disabilities.

By identifying the intersections among individual, family, community, and school strengths and constraints, scholars and practitioners can pinpoint factors and processes to frame community and school partnerships on behalf of students of color with disabilities. Moreover, such a spatial perspective of (dis)abling geographies will contribute to a strengths-based, culturally responsive perspective in the design and reform of educational programs that enhance learning opportunities, prevent school failure and dropout, and strengthen preparation for social participation and citizenship. Such an approach provides opportunities for a critical ThirdSpace perspective.

In the next section, we posit that the development of a critical spatial perspective can be facilitated with mapping tools such as geographic information systems (GIS), which provides an important tool to account for racially and economically shifting suburban spaces like Middleton, and then examine the consequences for students of color with disabilities.

POSSIBILITIES OF A CRITICAL SPACE PERSPECTIVE WITH THE USE OF MAPPING TOOLS

Suburban communities like Middleton will continue to grow around the country with significant racialized consequences for the increasing number of demographically diverse students entering the school system. A critical space perspective reveals persistent racialized outcomes for students with disabilities in these changing spaces and closely examines how power and domination are entrenched in the creation of geographic boundaries (Soja, 1989). As researchers who strive to understand "geographies of opportunity" (Tate, 2008) for under-represented students, families, and communities, we believe that a critical spatial perspective and mapping tools can help to broaden our range of conceptual frameworks and methodologies to study the relationship between space and equity in much-needed educational research and policy.

One example of a spatial mapping tool is the Geographic Information System (GIS). GIS simplifies the use of multiple types of data across a variety of locales, revealing socio-spatial relationships visually. Due to its broad appeal, increased accessibility, and ability to display complex data with ease, GIS is being employed more and more by "nontraditional" users, such as grassroots and community groups (Elwood, 2002; Ghose, 2001; Kellogg, 1999), as well as policymakers and researchers. With these new alliances, GIS can address the complexities of disproportionality and, ideally, facilitate examination of disproportionality to affect practitioners in schools and learners with disabilities.

As previously mentioned, educational researchers have not fully utilized the conceptualization of space and mapping tools to the same degree as other disciplines. When maps are used, moreover, there is an overwhelming enthusiasm to engage in the practice of mapping just for the sake of mapping (Rios-Aguilar, 2013) without carefully considering its intent or paying sufficient attention to the consequences of producing such maps (Crampton & Krygier, 2006; Knigge & Cope, 2006; Kwan, 2002a). We believe it is urgent to use map-making beyond visual representations of quantitative data because maps reveal deeply rooted educational inequities (Pacheco & Vélez, 2009; Vélez & Solórzano, in press).

More specifically, we believe a critical space perspective and the use of mapping offers educational researchers a range of exciting possibilities to answer critical questions that explore the spatial dynamics and complexities of the relationship between schools and neighborhoods, particularly in underserved communities. Mapping tools such as GIS can help us conceive new avenues for examining the important social, cultural, political, and historic role of space as it relates to schools, student experience, and academic outcomes (Pacheco & Vélez, 2009; Vélez & Solórzano, 2015). Yet, to do so requires some "re-imagining." As Vélez and Solórzano (in press) argue, we must treat the technique of map-making as both an *epistemological* and *methodological* approach in educational research that is situated within a broader spatial consciousness.

In suburban Middleton, applying a critical spatial perspective in the study of racial disproportionality highlights varied spatial contexts in which students, teachers, leaders, families and communities occupy and engage with—and against—structural forces that shape how opportunity is distributed across homes, schools, classrooms, and communities. It also provides a way to represent diverse perspectives of the world and encourages researchers to assess how people contest space differently (Knigge & Cope, 2006; Kwan, 2002b; Vélez & Solórzano, in press). Through the emerging field known as Critical GIS, Vélez and Solórzano (in press) note the importance of renegotiating critical perspectives on space and mapmaking as a discursive tactic that employs both quantitative and qualitative data to create "counter-maps" that challenge dominant representations of the world. Recently within the field of education, critical race scholars (Pacheco & Vélez, 2009; Solórzano & Vélez, 2007; Vélez & Solórzano, in press) introduced critical race spatial analysis (CRSA), which draws from critical race theory and re-imagines GIS to examine how structural and institutional factors impact the educational experiences and opportunities available to students based on race and other markers of difference, including disability. These examples suggest that a critical race perspective in the study of space—precisely using tools such as GIS—should aim to challenge the power-laden aspects that are part and parcel of students' varied ways of life.

CONCLUSION

In this chapter we outline the benefits of infusing a critical space perspective in research to address the persistence of racial disproportionality in special education in order to uncover and map the racialized consequences of (dis)abling geographies of opportunity. This, we contend, will provide new insights for researchers and policy makers to attend to the important and, as of yet, poorly understood roles of space, structures, and everyday educational practices. Middleton's example sheds light on possible answers to the questions posed just over a decade ago by Artiles (2003), which asked how special education will change amidst rapid growth among culturally and linguistically diverse students in changing spatial landscapes. As suburbs like Middleton expand across the U.S., students will likely be caught between competing and converging cultural, political, and economic forces, leading to serious consequences for historically marginalized students, particularly students of color with disabilities. Therefore, considering how students, families, educational practitioners, and communities respond to, occupy, and engage in varied spatial contexts within larger contextual forces becomes increasingly important. We believe that doing this will invite opportunities for new insights in research and more adequate policy responses to the racialization of disability and the advancement of educational equity and opportunity.

NOTES

[1]   Racial disproportionality in special education is the over- or under-representation of a racial/ethnic group in special education programs relative to the presence of this group in the overall student population.

[2]   The relative risk ratio (RRR) is a comparison of the risks of a racial/ethnic population being placed in special education to the relative risk of a comparison population. Typically, the comparison population is white. For example, a RRR of 2.0 means that a racial/ethnic group is twice as likely to be placed in special education compared to their white peers.

[3]   Southern states include Alabama, Arkansas, Georgia, Mississippi, North Carolina, South Carolina, Tennessee, and West Virginia. Because Texas and Virginia do not use the Relative Risk Ratio, they were excluded.

[4] District size refers to how many students are in a school district and locale is defined as the proximity an address or school district has to a densely populated urban center.

[5] Disproportionality is currently monitored through legal mechanisms found in the Individuals with Disabilities Education Act (IDEA). The 1997 and 2004 reauthorizations of IDEA have included three disproportionality indicators that monitor discipline, classification, and placement patterns of students with disabilities by race. When a local education agency is found to have disproportionality, a "citation" is issued. When given a citation, a district is required by federal and state law to monitor its compliance with IDEA procedural protections.

REFERENCES

Annamma, S., Morrison, D., & Jackson, D. (2014). Disproportionality fills in the gaps: Connections between achievement, discipline, and special education in the school-to-prison pipeline. *Berkeley Review of Education, 5*(1), 53–87.

Apple, M. W. (2006). *Educating the "right" way: Markets, standards, God, and inequality* (2nd ed.). New York, NY: RoutledgeFalmar.

Artiles, A. J. (2003). Special education's changing identity: Paradoxes and dilemmas in views of culture and space. *Harvard Educational Review, 73*(2), 164–202. doi:10.17763/haer.73.2.j78t573x377j7106

Artiles, A. J. (2011). Toward an interdisciplinary understanding of educational equity and difference: The case of the racialization of ability. *Educational Researcher, 40*(9), 431–445. doi:10.3102/0013189X11429391

Artiles, A. J., Rueda, R., & Salazar, J. J. (2005). Within-group diversity in minority disproportionate representation: English language learners in urban school districts. *Exceptional Children, 71*(3), 283–300. doi:10.1177/001440290507100305

Au, W. (2013). Coring social studies within corporate education reform: The Common Core state standards, social justice, and the politics of knowledge in U.S. schools. *Critical Education, 4*(5), 1–15.

Ball, S. J., Maguire, M., & Braun, A. (2012). *How schools do policy: Policy enactments in secondary schools.* New York, NY: Routledge.

Bobo, L. D. (2011). Somewhere between Jim Crow & post-racialism: Reflections on the racial divide in America today. *Daedalus, 140*(2), 11–36. doi:10.1162/DAED_a_00091

Bonilla-Silva, E. (2015). The structure of racism in color-blind, "post-racial" America. *American Behavioral Scientist, 59*(11), 1358–1376.

Bonilla-Silva, E. (2006). *Racism without racists: Color-blind racism and the persistence of racial inequality* (2nd ed.). Lanham, MD: Rowman & Littlefield.

Cavendish, W., Artiles, A. J., & Harry, B. (2014). Tracking inequality 60 years after *Brown:* Does policy legitimize the racialization of disability? *Multiple Voices for Ethnically Diverse Exceptional Learners, 14*(2), 30–40.

Crampton, J. W., & Krygier, J. (2005). An introduction to critical cartography. *ACME: An International E-Journal for Critical Geographies, 4*(1), 11–33.

D'Agord, C., Munk, T., & O'Hara, N. (2012). *Looking at race/ethnicity disproportionality in special education from the student outcomes side of the educational system: Why analyzing disproportionality matters for results improvement planning.* Paper presented at the meeting of the IDEA Leadership Conference, Washington, DC.

Diem, S., Cleary, C., Ali, N., & Frankenberg, E. (2014). The politics of maintaining diversity policies in demographically changing urban-suburban school districts. *American Journal of Education, 120*(3), 351–389. doi:10.1086/675532

Elwood, S. A. (2002). GIS use in community planning: A multidimensional analysis of empowerment. *Environment and Planning, 34*(5), 905–922.

Frankenberg, E., & Orfield, G. (2012). *The resegregation of suburban schools: A hidden crisis in American education.* Cambridge, MA: Harvard Education Press.

Frey, W. H. (2011). *Melting pot cities and suburbs: Racial and ethnic change in metro America in the 2000s.* Washington, DC: Brookings Institution Report. Retrieved from http://www.brookings.edu/research/papers/2011/04/06-census-diversity-frey

Gándara, P. C., & Aldana, U. S. (2014). Who's segregated now? Latinos, language, and the future of integrated schools. *Educational Administration Quarterly, 50*(5), 735–748. doi:10.1177/0013161X14549957

Gándara, P. C., & Hopkins, M. (Eds.). (2010). *Forbidden languages: English learners and restrictive language policies.* New York, NY: Teachers College Press.

Ghose, R. (2001). Use of information technology for community empowerment: Transforming geographic information systems into community information systems. *Transactions in GIS, 5*(2), 141–163.

Gonzalez, T., Tefera, A., & Artiles, A. J. (2015). The intersections of language differences and learning disabilities: Narratives in action. In M. Bigelow & J. Ennser-Kananen (Eds.), *Handbook of educational linguistics* (pp. 145–157). New York, NY: Routledge.

Harry, B., & Klingner, J. (2014). *Why are so many minority students in special education? Understanding race and disability in schools* (2nd ed.). New York, NY: Teachers College Press.

Kellogg, W. A. (1999). From the field: Observations on using GIS to develop a neighborhood environmental information system for community-based organizations. *Urisa Journal, 11*(1), 15–32.

Knigge, D., & Cope, M. (2006). Grounded visualization: Integrating the analysis of qualitative and quantitative data through grounded theory and visualization. *Environment and Planning, 38*(11), 2021–2037.

Kramarczuk Voulgarides, C. (2015). *Special education law and disproportionality: Does compliance matter?* (Unpublished doctoral dissertation). New York University, New York, NY.

Kramarczuk Voulgarides, C., Aylward, A., & Noguera, P. A. (2014). The elusive quest for equity: An analysis of how contextual factors contribute to the likelihood of school districts being legally cited for racial disproportionality in special education. *The Journal of Law in Society, 15*(2), 241–274.

Kwan, M. (2002a). Feminist visualization: Re-envisioning GIS as a method in feminist geographic research. *Annals of the Association of American Geographers, 92*(4), 645–661. doi:10.1111/1467-8306.00309

Kwan, M. (2002b). Is GIS for women? Reflection on the critical discourse in the 1990s. *Gender, Place & Culture: A Journal of Feminist Geography, 9*(3), 271–279. doi:10.1080/0966369022000003888

Lefebvre, H. (1991). *The production of space* (D. Nicholson-Smith, Trans.). Malden, MA: Blackwell. (Original work published 1991)

Lipman, P. (2004). *High-stakes testing: Inequality, globalization, and urban school reform.* New York, NY: RoutledgeFalmer.

Losen, D. J., Ee, J., Hodson, C., & Martinez, T. E. (2015). Disturbing inequities: Exploring the relationship between racial disparities in special education identification and discipline. In D. J. Losen (Ed.), *Closing the school discipline gap: Equitable remedies for excessive exclusion* (pp. 89–106). New York, NY: Teachers College Press.

Losen, D. J., & Orfield, G. (2002). *Racial inequity in special education.* Cambridge, MA: Harvard Education Press.

Orfield G., & Frankenberg, E. (2008). *The last have become first: Rural and small town America lead way the way on desegregation.* Los Angeles, CA: Civil Rights Project/Proyecto Derechos Civiles.

Orfield, G., & Frankenberg, E. (2014). Increasingly segregated and unequal schools as courts reverse policy. *Educational Administration Quarterly, 50*(5), 718–734. doi:10.1177/0013161X14548942

Oswald, D. P., Coutinho, M. J., Best, A. M., & Singh, N. N. (1999). Ethnic representation in special education: The influence of school-related economic and demographic variables. *The Journal of Special Education, 32*, 194–206.

Pacheco, D., & Vélez, V. N. (2009). Maps, mapmaking, and critical pedagogy: Exploring GIS and maps as a teaching tool for social change. *Seattle Journal for Social Justice, 8*(1), 273–302.

Peake, L., & Schein, R. H. (2000). Racing geography into the new millennium: Studies of "race" and North American geographies. *Social & Cultural Geography, 1*(2), 133–142. doi:10.1080/14649360020010158

Picower, B., & Mayorga, E. (Eds.). (2015). *What's race got to do with it? How current school reform policy maintains racial and economic inequality.* New York, NY: Peter Lang.

Powell, J. (2012). *Racing to justice: Transforming our conceptions of self and other to build an inclusive society.* Bloomington, IN: Indiana University Press.

Richards, M. P. (2014). The gerrymandering of school attendance zones and the segregation of public schools: A geospatial analysis. *American Educational Research Journal, 51*(6), 1119–1157. doi:10.3102/0002831214553652

Rios-Aguilar, C. (2013). Mapping (in)opportunity in educational research [Web log post]. Retrieved from http://www.niusileadscape.org/bl/page/4/

Skiba, R. J., Chung, C. G., Trachok, M., Baker, T., Sheya, A., & Hughes, R. (2015). Where should we intervene? Contributions of behavior, student, and school characteristics to out-of-school suspension. In D. J. Losen (Ed.), *Closing the school discipline gap: Equitable remedies for excessive exclusion* (pp. 132–146). New York, NY: Teachers College Press.

Soja. E. W. (1989). *Postmodern geographies: The reassertion of space in critical social theory.* Brooklyn, NY: Verso.

Soja, E. W. (1996). *Thirdspace: Journeys to Los Angeles and other real-and-imagined places.* Malden, MA: Blackwell.

Soja, E. W. (2010). *Seeking spatial justice.* Minneapolis, MN: University of Minneapolis Press.

Solórzano, D., & Vélez, V. N. (2007). *Critical race spatial analysis along the Alameda Corridor in Los Angeles.* Paper presented at the meeting of the American Education Research Association Conference, Chicago, IL.

Tate, W. F. IV. (2008). "Geography of opportunity": Poverty, place, and educational outcomes. *Educational Researcher, 37*(7), 397–411. doi:10.3102/0013189X08326409

Tefera, A. A., & Kramarczuk Voulgarides, C. (in press). Is educational policy alleviating or perpetuating the racialization of disabilities? An examination of "big-p" and "little-p" policies. *NSSE Yearbook, Teachers College Record, 118*(14).

Tefera, A. A., Frankenberg, E., & Siegel-Hawley, G. (2010). *Integrating suburban schools: How to benefit from growing diversity and avoid segregation.* Los Angeles, CA: The Civil Rights Project/ Proyecto Derechos Civiles.

Trudeau, D., & McMorran, C. (2011). The geographies of marginalization. In V. J. Del Casino, M. E. Thomas, P. Cloke, & R. Panelli (Eds.), *A companion to social geography* (pp. 437–457). Oxford: Wiley Blackwell.

U.S. Census. (2015). *Projections of the size and composition of the U.S. population: 2014 to 2060.* Retrieved from https://www.census.gov/content/dam/Census/library/publications/2015/demo/p25-1143.pdf

Vélez, V., & Solórzano, D. G. (in press). Critical race spatial analysis: Conceptualizing GIS as a tool for critical race research in education. In A. Morrison & D. Jackson (Eds.), *The spatial search to understand and address educational inequity to inform praxis.* Sterling, VA: Stylus.

Waitoller, F. R., Artiles, A. J., & Cheney, D. A. (2010). The miner's canary: A review of overrepresentation research and explanations. *The Journal of Special Education, 44*(1), 29–49.

Adai A. Tefera
Virginia Commonwealth University

Cecilia Rios Aguilar
University of California, Los Angeles

Alfredo J. Artiles
Arizona State University

Catherine Kramarczuk Voulgarides
New York University

Veronica Vélez
Western Washington University

SANDRA SCHMIDT

13. GENDERPLAY AND QUEER MAPPING

Heterotopia as Sites of Possible Gender Reform
as Spatial Reconstruction

Many will likely look back at June 2015 as a pivotal month for queer and trans activists. In June, Caitlyn Jenner debuted on the cover of *Vanity Fair*. This media-supported public coming out transition of the Olympic athlete and reality television star brought widespread attention to transgender issues, politics, and identities. Just weeks later, the Supreme Court overturned the Defense of Marriage Act (DOMA). Writing for the majority, Justice Kennedy opined,

> No union is more profound than marriage, for it embodies the highest ideals of love, fidelity, devotion, sacrifice, and family. In forming a marital union, two people become something greater than once they were. As some of the petitioners in these cases demonstrate, marriage embodies a love that may endure even past death. It would misunderstand these men and women to say they disrespect the idea of marriage. Their plea is that they do respect it, respect it so deeply that they seek to find its fulfillment for themselves. Their hope is not to be condemned to live in loneliness, excluded from one of civilization's oldest institutions. They ask for equal dignity in the eyes of the law. The Constitution grants them that right. (*Obergfell v. Hodges,* 2015, p. 28)

We can jointly read the events as queer penetrations into mainstream culture. As such, they disturb familiar paradigms of marriage and woman. Normal is expanded/ questioned/repositioned. Jenner is a visible referent of the entanglement of sex, gender, and sexuality. The rejection of DOMA strengthens the hetero- and homo-normative definitions of marriage, but expands who can access such unions.

If June was coded as a moment of progress, then fall 2015 was a time to put deviance back in its place. Backlash reflected the refusal of spaces to be redefined based on the events of June. Queer critiques have long been concerned about same-sex marriage and its homonormative misrecognition of queer that does not fit the paradigm (Conrad, 2011; Warner, 2000). Although same-sex marriage was legal, some county clerks refused to issue marriage licenses. Following a well-publicized case in Kentucky, the newly-elected governor noted that his priority in January was to amend marriage certificates such that clerks whose religious beliefs do not support same-sex marriage will not be forced to sign them (Brydum, 2015). Election day also saw the city of Houston overturn an ordinance protecting spatial access and

N. Ares et al. (Eds.), Deterritorializing/Reterritorializing, 209–232.

other equity measures for transgendered persons (Fernandez & Smith, 2015). This comes amidst the struggles of schools across the US to wrestle with whether to allow trans youth access to locker rooms aligned with their sex identity (Reuters, 2015). Perhaps the best reading of these months, consistent with those that preceded and will follow, is the failure of utopian discourse. "Equity" is always contested, moving, and not quite reachable.

As society addresses a changing imagination related to gender and sexuality, we must turn to schools as social institutions. Schools are spaces wherein social constructions, lived experiences, and identities come together to build physical and abstract environments that invite participation based on accordance with rules of the space. Literature proposes their spatiality is regulated by a male-female binary and heteronormativity. The result is that redresses to gender-based inequality focuses on improved LGBT recognition – the identification of guardians, curriculum, dance policies, etc. – and bullying. More recently (social) media has been abuzz and embroiled with news/stories of parents allowing children to live the gender they identify, decisions by single-sex colleges to allow or not allow transmen and transwomen to apply/attend, decisions by schools about how to determine access to sex-specific bathrooms and locker rooms, and other challenges to gender norms in social policies. These changes are necessary but rarely sufficient. Schools are filled with gendered performances and embodiments that are beyond the realm of school (and social) policy. These performances disrupt the categories and even the categorization of gender and sexuality embedded in school regulations and curricula. This chapter looks beyond dominant narratives of the space of school, using heterotopia to examine performances and arrangements that transgress. I hope to give importance to spatial analysis and explore the limitations of reform (in all its forms) to account for the queer practices and performances that create instability. The chapter begins with a theoretical overview of gender as a spatial experience. It then considers two examples from research that examine how young people use schools as spaces of gender play. It concludes with a discussion of the possibilities for heterotopia as sites for recreating the imagination of gender in school policy.

DYSTOPIC EXPERIENCE? GENDER, SEXUALITY AND SPACE

Gender and sexuality are complex social constructions. In the effort to redress inequity through policy, the dominant constructions tend to emphasize marginality. The most common portrayal of LGBT youth in schools reinforces a "martyr-target-victim" narrative (Ingrey, 2013; Rofes, 2004). The narrative offers three possible subject positions for LGBT youth – the target of bullying, the victim who has been bullied, and the martyr who is sacrificed to oppressive conditions. GLSEN[1] regularly conducts national surveys that offer data to support these conclusions (Kosciw, Greytak, Palmer, & Boesen, 2014). These subject positions, the harassment that create them, and the alienation that results make LGBT youth at-risk for suicide. As suicides by targeted youth became frequent in the early 2010s, interventions took multiple forms. For example, gay columnist Dan Savage and his husband launched the *It Gets Better* (IGB) project (Savage & Miller, 2012). The thousands of videos uploaded to the website by celebrities and ordinary citizens sought to reassure young people that the experiences in school and in their small-minded hometowns were merely part of a trajectory that concludes with surrounding oneself with accepting friends in college and beyond and relocating to open-minded urban areas.

The "martyr-target-victim" narrative is corroborated by curricular absence. Much attention has been given to the omission of gay issues, people, events, and identity as themes and descriptors of what is studied in literature, history, and art (Schmidt, 2010; Thornton, 2003). This may arise in the failure to identify an author as gay or the decision not to include gay rights activism in a unit on 1960s social movements. Further curricular research examines the use of male and female binaries to produce a specific way of understanding gender and sexuality (Sumara & Davis, 1999). The result is a curriculum that normalizes gender-sex categories and heterosexuality.

LGBTQ scholars, educators, and activists offer various solutions that redress the experiences of LGBTQ youth and the narrow representation of their experiences. Much of the literature and resources for teachers and policymakers frames the issues from the perspective of LGBT studies (Sears & Letts, 1997; Unks, 1995). The LGBT studies approach recovers the queer (read marginalized and thus victimized) subject and moves him and her to a valued curricular and social position. Clearly, elements of this are needed. Caitlyn Jenner's public coming out, hate crime laws, and the circulation of IGB videos produce a discourse about equity. In so doing, queer lives and experiences are made visible and injustice and bullying are made problematic. The inclusive approach has its limitations; it does not contemplate the intersection of sexuality and gender nor allow us to conceive of the queer person as an agentive subject. A critical engagement with IGB, for example, challenges the trajectory of progress and inclusiveness. The prospect of the change of subject positions as one moves from school to society, from young person to adult presumes that schools have a different socio-spatial content that the world in which they exist, a presumption worth questioning.

Feminist and queer geographers speak directly to the socio-spatial critique of IGB and in so doing, challenge the landscape dominated by LBTQ studies. Queer geography, like its broader theoretical lens queer theory, attends to queer subjectivity (Bell & Valentine, 1995; Browne, Lim, & Brown, 2007; Doan, 2007; Hubbard, 2002). The queer subject is a body that refuses or transgresses categorization. Butler (1990) importantly theorized gender as performativity. The queer subject is the girl who kisses her girlfriend at the school dance that sold tickets to heterosexual couples, the lesbian youth who is not victim, the male body in a skirt and high heels, the gay boy who performs a queer reading of *My Antonia* in English class. These performances, rather than reifying gender categories, trouble, disrupt, and resist.

Queer geographers distinguish themselves by considering how these performances result from, respond to, and construct gendered senses of place and place-based senses of self.

The meanings attached to and rules that regulate space may be produced in their original form through a particular conception of gender and/or sexuality, but such intentions are complicated by and complicate everyday gender and sexuality performances (Binnie, 1995; Brown, Browne, & Lim, 2007; Knopp, 2007). Many producers of space have thoroughly embedded their gender and sexual ideologies in the landscapes they build, understandings that are often hetero/homonormative and rely on the binary distinction of male and female. The distinctions (and resultant heights of tables and/or location of restrooms) between public and private space, the arrangements of shopping spaces and their contingent locations all arise from distinctions between female and male roles in society. The physical possibilities and expectations reproduce male and female constructions (Butler, 1990). Social negotiations entrench these constructions. Systems of surveillance, refusal of entry based on clothing or sex, and the geography of fear force those entering to take up the "right" gender and sex cues when/if they decide to enter. When women are denied entry to a nightclub for wearing "male" attire or men acquiesce to laughter shopping alone in a baby store, they reaffirm a gendered sense of the space and a sense of their genders. Surveillance monitors heteronormativity and homonormativity. Schroeder (2012) examines how adult negotiation of LGBT friendly spaces erases both queer and youth. Uni-directional flow of the meaning of space overlooks how people perceive and manipulate space for their uses. But many places are unable to control so strictly. The penetrations and resistances of space are critical to the assertion and development of gender and sexual identities of individual and spaces (Knopp, 2007). Women claiming the right to wear trousers on the floor of the Senate disrupted the apparatus of gender hierarchy in Congress. The gay couple kissing in the heterosexual bar is a penetration that creates a necessary stir (and perhaps stimulation) as they make visible the various ways love and sex unite people. The collective decision to build businesses that cater to gay men produced queer spaces such as Miami Beach, BoysTown (Chicago), and the West Village (New York). These counterperformances affirm positions beyond the center and change the sexual and gender identity inherent in/of space. This is the conception of gender, sexuality, and space that is central to rethinking the possibility that the space of school and the identities therein might not fit narrowly into the victim-martyr-target paradigm and heteronormativity through which school spaces are most often conceived.

Queer geography reveals the interdependency of sex, gender, and sexuality. They examine female or gay bodies and where these bodies cannot roam and more importantly, why (Doan, 2007; Valentine, 1989). What is it about how space is navigated and experienced that keeps people out, both in doing the policing of bodies and encouraging people to police themselves into the margins? The intersection of gender and sexuality begins to arise in this. The reason women's bodies take up certain locations is often because of their sexualized nature. The sexualized nature of women's bodies produce risky conditions for men – consider dress code policies that regulate women because men cannot control their desires – or risky conditions for women – the dark shadows of the street produce areas where women are more likely to be assaulted. These warnings rely on a (hetero)sexual expression of the female body and male response. Part of the manner in which we are able to "know" woman is through sexual response to male. This leads Monique Wittig (1980) to conclude that lesbians are not men; their identity does not evolve out of the gaze of the male eye, nor in response to the potential and possibility of heterosexual reproduction. Thus, while we may speak of queer sexualities and gender non-conforming persons, gender and sexuality are deeply intertwined. The performance of one's gender is often related to a performance of sexuality (this may include an asexual performance) (Butler, 1990). Thus, while gender and sexuality may be named as separate identities, they are rightfully taken together in this paper because efforts to regulate gender and sexuality in schools are mutually impactful and consequential.

HETEROTOPIC SPACES FOR GENDER AND SEXUALITY

If the world were simple, we would reform schools into gender-fluid and queer utopias. We would have school policies and cultures that evolve with ways of understanding and performing gender and sexuality. We could reduce the reliance on binaries and categories to make sense of experience and organize young people in schools. But the world is not simple and utopias are not attainable; by definition they exist just beyond what is imaginable. As utopic realizations generate new utopic ideals, queer gender and sexuality contribute performative disruptions at the moment we seem to grasp their meaning (Johnson, 2009). The same can be said of dystopias, the non-idyllic state. Although presumed to exist beyond reality, some queer and gender non-conforming students experience school as dystopia. While there are some tragic aspects of schooling, trying to confine school and experiences of school into such categories misses the instability of these spaces and the ongoing and ever-changing relationships young people have therein. To theorize this further, I turn to Michael Foucault's (1986) heterotopias as a means of synthesizing and making visible queer experiences of school.

The heterotopia is a place with multiple layers wherein the intended physical design is complicated by perceptions and lived engagement with the space (Foucault, 1986).

> What we doubtlessly encounter here is the true essence of the heterotopias. They query all other spaces, namely in two different ways: either [...] by creating an illusion which exposes the entire remaining reality as an illusion or, to the contrary, by creating another real space, in a real way, which is also perfect, meticulous and disorderly arranged like ours, badly ordered and tangled [...].

For Foucault, heterotopias are the "real" spaces, if such a thing exists. He is rethinking how we understand spaces of being as complicated. He designates specific types of heterotopias which share some general characteristics. Heterotopias of crisis are spaces wherein people and behavior that are coming into being are allowed to occur out of sight and judgment of others. Heterotopias of deviation are places (prisons, mental hospitals) wherein behaviors and people not deemed acceptable can be contained. Heterotopias of ritual are open and yet not easily penetrable; people must demonstrate their ability to participate in the ritual to gain access. These heterotopias share characteristics. First, heterotopias are contextually specific. They serve a specific function in society, particularly in relation to other spaces (Bailey & Shabazz, 2014). Second, they play with rules that simultaneously open and close the space (Kannen, 2014). The opening of the space leads to play and possibility in the reconstruction of illusion (Johnson, 2009). Finally, they bring together place-based experiences and identities that are seemingly incompatible.

I contend that schools share many of the general attributes Foucault describes. Schools serve a particular function in school. They are physically designed to organize students to be obedient. Young people enter the doors of school and are expected to learn to behave in ways that normalize citizenship, gender, sexuality, and the neoliberal worker. The environment is physically built and administratively ruled and surveilled to enforce this. Symbolically, schools are portrayed as sites of learning. The learning is largely housed within a formal curriculum and classrooms but the learning orientation enforces explicit spatial encounters that shape with rules and norms. Similar to spaces of deviation, entry to the school is limited. The brief, heavy-handed analysis of the function and location of schools as spaces positions schools as heterotopic spaces where young people, ill-prepared to be fully functioning members of society can do their time until they are prepared as citizens. We must not lose the final aspect of the heterotopia because it is at the essence of synthesizing the gendered environment of schools. Heterotopias and schools bring together the real and perceived, the intended and the lived, the abstract and the concrete. If the physical institution of learning is the real, the intended, and the concrete, then the lives of the young people who move around/in/within the classroom walls and symbols of learning use their perceptions, multiplicity of identities and experiences, to rethink, reimagine and build layers in the space. Consider the language we associate with young people – students. Young people are students when they are in school, at least in the eyes of adults. As they cross the threshold of the school, a new identity is assumed. As with all identities, we must call into question what it means and how it is taken up and complicated in the interaction with space.

"GENDER TROUBLE" IN SCHOOL

In between the utopic hopes and dystopic experiences rests a lot of gender trouble in school. The play on Butler's (1990) title is apt for this section in that it examines how young people's performances play with the space of gender and the gender space of/ in schools. Much literature that troubles gender (in schools) attempts to (re)present the experiences of gender non-conforming and/or queer youth. I propose that gender trouble in school rests in heterotopic possibilities, in the manners that youth navigate the complex layers and contradictions of gender. This section takes up schools as gendered spaces, co-constructed by the performances of youth. It shares experiences from two studies in which young people organize and engage with space and spatial categories/expectations within and against dominant discourses of gender and sexuality. Butler (1990) is useful in reminding us to examine spatial navigations as performances that are deployed to reify and counter norms and dualisms.

Embedding Sexuality in the Physical Landscape

Physical landscapes are designed such that people use and move through them intentionally. Critical geographers encourage us to examine how people speak back to and/or engage with such intentions. Schools are spaces, comprised of spaces. If they are intentionally planned, how is it that young people (the non-planners) experience and shape these spaces? To explore this, I engage with research in which young people mapped their schools.

The study discussed here involved 225 high school participants in two Southeastern (Savanna and Woodlawn) high schools. The purpose was to explore how students made spatial sense of their school. Participants were asked to complete a survey about school-based experiences and engagements, draw a map detailing their school, and indicate favorite, student friendly, and non-student friendly spaces on their maps. A subset of students[2] participated in focal interviews to explain the decisions underlying their mapping and to narrate experiences within spaces. Following the mapping, a common thread in the discussions and resulting analysis was the function and negotiation of "student-friendly spaces". Young people explained how social landscapes were embedded in the physical arrangement of these spaces. I was forbidden from asking direct questions about sexuality, but the participants evoked the concept "weirdo" and displayed discomfort when struggled to identify their LGBTQ peers, thereby bringing sexuality into the research space. This section explores "student-friendly" spaces in their oppressive and heterotopic forms in order to consider what is queer in school.

Reproducing reality. The details on maps, commentary added to maps and interviews produced strong visualization on bodies in common areas, the most prevalent "student-friendly spaces" – the commons, cafeterias, and student parking lots. These physical spaces were architecturally designed to house many bodies. Adult conceptualizations were augmented by the specified positions young bodies took in these spaces. The comparatively high student to adult ratios in these areas distinguished them from many spaces in school, spaces wherein adults had authority over organization and rules. The landscape participants described contained clear centers, margins, and distinctions between groups, socio-spatial manipulations that attempted to erase outliers from visibility. In the cafeteria, some youth sat along the walls while others took the central tables. In common areas, norms set and regulated by the students' social caste system determined access to space according to desirability. In this hierarchy, the less visible upstairs "commons" was left for groups that were unable to claim space downstairs. The parking lot also had an arrangement that cohered groups and distanced them from others. What was striking in these allocations was how otherness was written into space. The others literally sat in the margins/edges of common areas, parked the greatest distance from school, and were forced out of eyesight in the upstairs. These outliers were displaced from the center, but their existence was necessary for establishing the central position as desirable.

In combing through the interviews, multiple groups were made visible – 'jocks', 'rednecks', 'black jocks', 'freshman', 'whites', 'emos'. Of interest because of their consistent and severe marginalization were the 'weirdos' – 'it's like lesbians and gays and Emos and Goth and like homos and like just like stuff you don't…' (Woodlawn, Interview #5, Grade Level). Savanna had its 'weirdo's' too, an unnamable group that caused hushed whispers and nods of concurrence when young people described social hierarchy. When named, these students were generally called 'artistic types'. The groups that fell into the category of 'weirdo' were socially produced through the school environment regardless of their self-identification. Participants were asked to discuss this social hierarchy by describing its spatial organization.

This interview segment highlighted how social divisions were built into the landscape.

Female 1:   The atrium is divided.
Female 2:   We got a certain group of people that stand by the window, the same certain group of people.
Female 4:   Redneck.
Female 2:   I'm talking about Emos. They all sit by the window. By the guidance room door is where all the rednecks sit. Then back here, I would say is the soccer players and baseball players.
Female 4:   Yeah, that's where we all stand, like right once you walk in the door, we all stand right there.
Female 2:   There's like a group in the middle is the freshmen, like all the freshmen just sit and chill together. Back here by this window, like girls or whatever, just random girls just chill right there.
Female 4:   It's really divided up.
Female 1:   But they go to this, but see, what's so weird is you go to the same place every single day, no one like mixes up where they're going. Once you're in the atrium, I would never go stand out by the window next to the bus parking lot. I'm always going to stay right there. (Woodlawn, Interview #5, Grade Level)

In this discussion, the girls were able to articulate a clear arrangement of bodies. Their use of group names, for example, the initial choice of "certain group" rather than "emos" was read as part of the othering process. The arrangements themselves reflected social patterns and relationships that were part of school and society. The desirability of certain areas appeared as they located themselves close to the door. The ending of this clip was striking – that the student suddenly realizes the permanency of spatial arrangements. This may have been a moment of clarity for the speaker, but further interviews revealed a tendency to correct spatial transgressions.

Researcher: Say someone came over to where you sit that isn't typically there, how would your group respond to that person? Or say you went to lunch and another group was sitting where you normally sit, what would you do?

Male 1: It'd be awkward but we'd find another place to sit.

Male 3: This year, we had this girl just come and sit with us out of nowhere. We just sat there. We was whispering to each other, who is that? We were confused.

Male 2: I sit by myself so sometimes I sit with other groups and see how they react to me. People talk about you when you are there by yourself. Or they just say, "Leave". (Woodlawn, Interview #9, grade level African American boys)

The discussion indicated that the observed landscape was not accidental. It is actively, not passively maintained. Transgressions were not quiet; their visibility ensured the maintenance of the desired landscape, as evidenced in the confusion or "leave" described above when young people broke the patterns. They influenced not only the transgressor but served as deterrents to future transgressions. There were administrators present and watching, but they chose not to intervene in social practices. Their silence made them complicit in these spatial productions.

The spatial practices that dominated common areas tended toward both the obvious and the horrible, practices not distinct from social experiences beyond school. Among those reading this with disgust that adults allowed some youth to eat lunch next to the trashcans might be readers who experienced something similar in school or who wrestle with the visible practice of inequity. Those reading this as obvious may have accepted that kids will be kids or that school hierarchies are the reality of school. This section argued that an unjust (perhaps dystopic) set of spatial practices were built and maintained. This dominant reading/rendering of student-friendly spaces was produced by the youth who sat in the center tables and as reified by people who expect such hierarchy. Such acceptance is why we need a heterotopic encounter with school.

Heterotopia and new illusions. Heterotopic analysis is not focused on the concrete space, but lived experience with/in space. In looking past the center-margin binary, heterotopias depict contested space, contradictory perceptions, and penetrations of deviance into normed space. The young people designated as weirdos served a deviant position in school and society. Bailey and Shabazz (2014) note, "The spaces to whom those deemed 'deviant' are assigned, are created in order to manage these people in accordance with the norms of society" (p. 317). But, what happens therein? Heterotopias suggest that spaces are open to (re)interpretation and play, the possibility that from the closed position of deviant, new possibilities emerge

(Kannen, 2014). This subsection examines uses of space that disrupt the normalizing paradigm of school and gender in school.

The initial rendering of the maps as the reproduction of a particular reality did not indicate agency in the space or the people who claimed those marginal spaces. In the unidirectional flow of discursive power, the analysis of student maps and interviews as reifying margin-center binary produced "weird" as marginal akin to the victim narrative (Rofes, 2004). It read the margins as passive and undesirable; students would not willingly occupy such spaces. Perceiving of the margins in this manner simultaneously assigned positive attributes to the center. This reading is insufficient; queering or reading against the norms produced a different interpretation of spatial experience.

Youth challenged the crisis language assigned to queers in school. Rather than presuming the passivity of the margins, queer analysis of the data explores these voices, even if they represent a minority voice. The maps and interviews simultaneously suggest that the people who sit on the perimeters are agents of their own socio-spatial practices (hooks, 2000). Figure 1 depicts Savanna, the school wherein some young people sat on the perimeters. The student who drew the map noted that there are too few tables and long lines, situations that made this not student-friendly. He also starred his space in the cafeteria, designating this as a favorite place. Favorite seems inconsistent with crisis and undesirability. Interviews with other youth indicated why these were favorite places. Youth who sat here did not state that they sat "near the trashcans", a derogatory characterization used by those who sat in the center. They said the "sit near the stage", a familiar area for some of them. The voices from the margins construct these as spaces of opportunity not marginalization. The perimeter was unconfined by tables, allowing free movement, play and dramatics. People sat below eye level and avoided reprimands from adults and could gaze out and voice disdain for the strange happenings in the center. Occupying the upstairs area of the commons was similarly desirable for some. The upstairs allowed young people to lie down or sit and read, to play guitars and games, and to move freely. Such activities were not possible in the crowded areas downstairs, nor were they allowable activities or uses of space under the gaze of adults who hovered downstairs. The young people herein were permitted to deviate from behaving – standing orderly and talking – as adults expected and the space assumed of them. These youth were generally able to repurpose spaces in school. The band room was a cafeteria for some, the library a rowdy game space, the classroom a theater, and the journalism room for social convening. The initial interpretation indicated that student-friendly spaces in school were commonly understand and organized to reflect and maintain unequal social patterns. In examining the spaces claimed by the weirdos, there were agentive spatial practices that disrupted the meaning attached to space, deviated from intended purpose and refused the attributes or passivity and victim associated with weirdo.

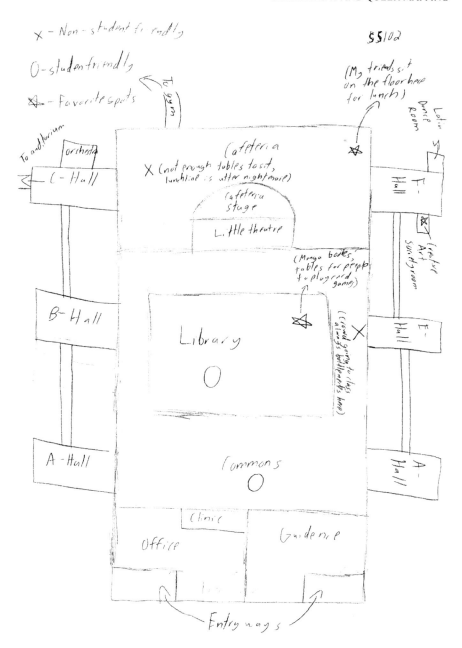

Figure 1. Savanna high cafeteria relations

Deviance did not only manifest in areas physically carved out in the margins. Another heterotopic indication was when youth holding a variety of marginal identities penetrated the dominant meaning of spaces across their schools. The movement of students from the perimeter of the cafeteria into classrooms for lunch disrupted the symbolic binary of center and margins. On one hand, their self-exile was a problematic means of erasure. Their movement away from the lunchrooms or into the invisible upper commons prevented them from being used by the center to bolster their status. The binary was broken. As these young people moved into other areas of the school, they penetrated the assigned uses of those spaces, as noted above. These visible deviant presences in school spaces occurred in many ways. Consider the young person who sleeps through class as a penetration into the concept of a classroom; her visible presence undermines the intentions a teacher has for that space. Her deviance requires the teacher to set aside teaching for reprimand. Consider the disruption of gendered space and distinction as trans youth challenge bathroom policies. In the study, a Gay Straight Alliance (GSA) member discussed the placement of GSA flyers. She placed them in close proximity to flyers for the Fellowship of Christian Athletes. This was the organization that had advocated against the GSA so the proximity of posters was a reminder of the presence of GLBTQ students. Such reminders are small, but they change the make-up of space.

This section has largely focused on the failure of the margins to marginalize. There is another significant manner in which the mappings speak to the heterotopic potential of school. A more general reading of how all participants depicted "school" shows how schools exist in multiple socio-spatial purposes. Schools, in broad terms, remove young people from public spaces when adults do not have the time to regulate them and to school them into the roles they will take as adults. While learning is central, architects and administrators recognize that schools house a variety of activities. Thus, we find academic, social, athletic, and administrative spaces in schools. What was striking across the maps was the common erasure of learning spaces and the elevation of the social areas – the commons and cafeteria. I attend to this discussion not merely to suggest that young people do not experience school as it was intended but that the uptake of schools by young people bring together simultaneous and contrasted identifications with space.

On the maps, students' de-emphasized the academic aspect of school. As modeled in Figure 2, the areas that held classrooms were left undefined, without detail, and unnamed. This map also portrays academic areas as comparatively small, a common trend. Commons and lockers rooms were often bigger than the entire academic wing of the school. Figure 3 also from Woodlawn only contains common areas. The cafeteria and library are drawn in detail. The maps from Savanna consistently drew the center of the school with commons, offices, theater, cafeteria, and library, and left the classrooms to disappear with the edge of the page. They emphasized the areas they entered by choice. Their emphasis also utilized the production of boundaries on the page. Participants drew solid lines on their maps (see Figure 4) to mark off common areas, lines that did not depict actual walls. Like the imagined boundaries on maps in their classrooms, these lines divide things by bounding things in and out. In these cases, participants most often bounded significant spaces – the area in the hallway where they eat or sit or the common areas or a division within the library or theater. Sometimes it was not the classroom of a favorite teacher that was rewarded with boundaries in an otherwise open space. The spatial claims and reconfigurations made by young people change the rules for how spaces are regulated and function within the school. I have written elsewhere that when left to young people to inscribe the rules of space, a set of uncivil practices and ideologies emerge (Schmidt, 2013). Foucault reminds us that heterotopias are situated within a broader purpose. Schools are created as sites for teaching and learning. Their heterotopic deployment suggests a necessary attention to the manners in which young people teach and learn from one another as they elevate common areas and unmonitored exchanges as the significant spaces in school.

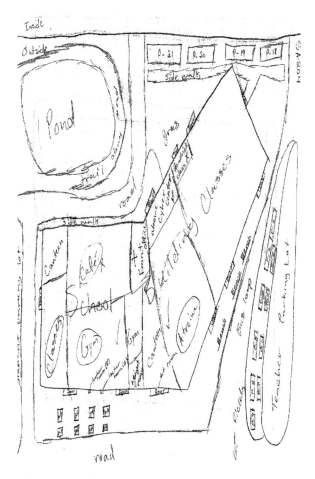

Figure 2. Woodlawn high undefined and disproportionate spaces

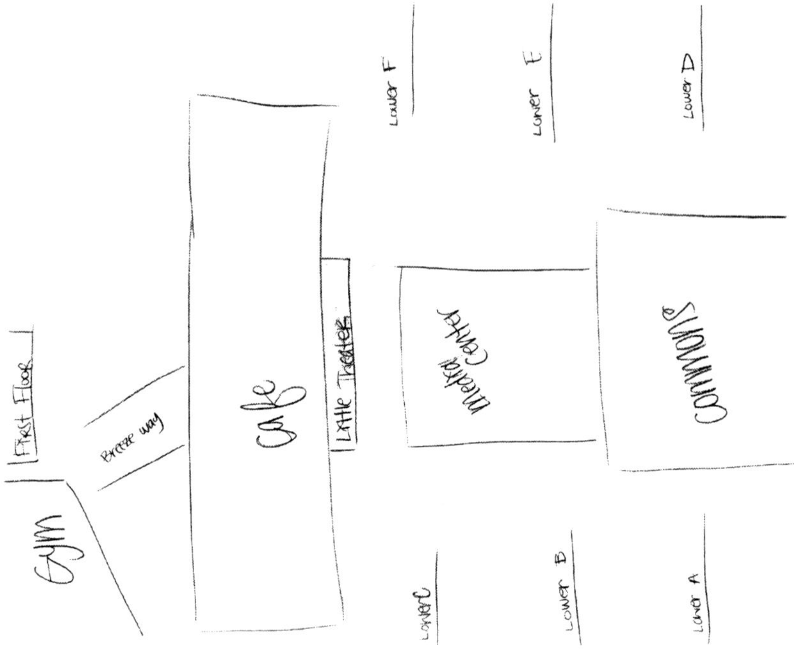

Figure 4. Savanna high bounded common areas

Figure 3. Woodlawn high depicting common areas

Summary. These depictions of the social production of school spaces explore how school as heterotopia challenges the expected relationships and uses of the physicality of the space. The physical landscape is built by architects and the rules that supposedly dictate space are produced by administrators but the actual use embodiment of that physical space and interpretation/manipulation of those rules is multiply layered by students' needs and interactions. They are influenced by intended use, by observation of what can be claimed, by penetrations of deviant identities, by experiences with other spaces and experiences they attempt to reproduce in the school. When read as heterotopia, this is not merely about the different perceptions groups have of a space. It has to do with the expectations from different players in the space that they control the illusion of reality. In constructing the center and margins and the adults and young people in the above sections, we see different intersections of space and identity. The dominant attributes fail to define the range of experiences. Such awareness is especially important as schools contemplate equity for queer youth in schools. The challenge for those contemplating regulations, particularly those that legislate identity and access is this instability and ongoing formation of the identities and rules that socially regulate school experiences.

Sex, Gender, and Complicating a Sense of Place

The previous section examined the contestations of spatial meaning. This example explores how youth people negotiate their gendered identities within a seemingly rigid sense of place. I spent a year conducting ethnography research in 7th grade single-sex classrooms[3] in a South Carolina middle school, a state that at that time contained one-third of the country's single-sex schools/classrooms. The premise behind the state policy and the school's program arose from the writings of Leonard Sax (2005). Sax presumes the existence of two sexes, assigns people based on genitalia and concludes that boys and girls have different brains and hormonal make-ups from conception that program them to learn and experience the world different rather than through social construction. He concludes that teachers should use different teaching strategies in boy and girl classrooms. The state policy allowed students to opt into these classes based upon the sex listed in their school records. At first glance, these classrooms and the policies that support them were as problematic as any school policy/space that separated students by sex. My research findings did not draw such straightforward conclusions. First, teachers were not able to create the "boy" or "girl" environment they were told they should/could create. These inabilities stemmed from learners whose needs, dispositions, and interests were more diverse than Sax claimed. The students pushed at and, sometimes, directly resisted the narrow/universal gender paradigm from which teachers drew. Second, the young people in these classes, once removed from a school space that demanded gender precision, used the space to "play" – destabilize and question – with gender. I propose that such play is made possible because of the instability created by the presumption the sex can be known and divided. In order to synthesize a short description from a years' worth of ethnographic data,

I have selected three exemplar moments from the research. I begin by sharing the three moments and then put them into conversation afterwards to discuss how the youth challenged gender boundaries and what enabled the play.

Moment 1: Be yourself

Christie: Cause whenever it's a class of girls you can be yourself. But when there's guys in the class you try to be someone else because that's just how girls are. Being in single gender, I can be myself. If I'm with a guy, I have to act different.

Carly: Jenna is way crazy and she's all out there and doesn't really care about what someone thinks about what she just said...we'll be sitting in the back of the class like talking Chinese or something. We'll be going crazy. But if a guy was in the class, they'd think that was weird and you wouldn't do that. (Honors girls)

Moment 2: Family trees

[A teacher suggested I ask students about the family trees she had seen them drawing. These are my notes following this conversation with students.] Students in three of the classes created a family tree, denoting relationships between members of the class. The family tree for the honors girls evolved out of the one the honors boys made for themselves. The family tree drawn by honors boys is made only of the boys. Boys are married to other boys in the class and some boy couples have children. Similarly, the honors girls were married to one another and also had children. In the family tree, the married boys represent close friendships, friends who are good to one another. They mimic married couples in the closeness of their friendship, the time they spend together, and the way in which they trust one another. In this manner, they are drawing characteristics of the married world they see at home and using the nonsexual parts to describe their relationships with other members of the class. Just as children in the home commonly hold an inferior position and need the support of their parents, the children in the families are the followers in the classroom hierarchy. Students who are not members of the core social clique in the classes are not on the tree at all. The parents are the group of 8 students who think of themselves as the leaders and the children are the peers who aspire to be part of the core but are, by their distinction as children, on the periphery.

Moment 3: Gender non-conforming leader

This section depicts notes and an interview moment about an African American boy, Terrell, from the grade-level boys' class. He stood out as the best-performing student and one others presumed to be gay.

Researcher notes: Terrell is a quiet outsider who craves individual success with little care for the social culture of the boys around him. He does not participate in the "games" boys' designed and play when teachers are teaching. These games connect them socially but disengage them from classroom lessons. He sits in the grass by me when teachers take boys outside to play, a reward for good group behavior. At lunch, he sneaks away from his class table and sits with a group of girls in a mixed-sex class.

Interview:

Researcher: Talk to me about....if you had to say that inside this class there was a leader of the boys. Is there any kind of leader for the boys in this class?

DeAndre: Terrell

Researcher: What?

DeAndre: Terrell

Researcher: He's a leader? What does he do to be the leader?

DeAndre: He don't talk. He don't play like some of us do. He gets his work done. He's on the honor roll.

Researcher notes following informal discussion: The boys talked about Terrell. They shared that they believe he is gay. They asked Terrell's cousin why Terrell always pretends to like girls. They laughed, acknowledging that Terrell does not like or relate to girls in the manner they do. They told the cousin they didn't care or mean disrespect. They wanted him to come out and be happy with himself.

"Single-sex" outside the binary. Single-sex classrooms are strangely complicated entities. They are created by a belief by some that gender and sex are knowable and thus stable. This beginning point has led some to criticize single-sex programs for forcing a particular sexed and thus gendered identity upon participants (Jackson, 2010). As I examine the attachments students inside had to the program and what it afforded them socially, I notice the failures of these beliefs. A strength of the program is that although it mandates a division based on bodies and sex, the social experiences operate are not confined by the heteronormative gender ideas that organize relationships and interactions in heterogeneous classrooms. The sexed-based criticisms of single-sex programs tend to overlook how strongly gender functions in schools (Eliot, 2009). Girls are constantly reminded to be girls and boys to be boys through gender-referent classroom practices and procedures. Consider reactions to bullying that "victimize"/neuter the gender non-conforming girl or boy, ultimately reinforcing the hegemonic male. The school rule must rescue the boy who cannot do it for himself (Heffernan, 2010; Payne, 2010) reminding others what happens when you are outside the norm.

The contrasting element in the single-sex classroom was that the space did not immediately contain the male and female bodies needed to utilize the binary. It rarely made sense to compare or align students with those who were not in the room. It was teachers who used language that regulated heteronormative gender practices. The moments I highlighted above – the moments of play in the sex heterotopia – were the students at play within and against the space created by teachers. Many students were relieved being removed from a heterogeneous space wherein they felt obligated to play the expected girl/boy position. Christie, Carla, and Jenna specifically tackled this issue, one that regularly appeared in dialogue with students when they discussed the "distraction" of a heterogeneous sex classroom. School was generally a space of sexual tension. Thus, young people, heterosexual and queer-identified, feel the social pressure of social-sexual performance all day. In this study, it arose when students described distractions or appropriate dress in heterogeneous spaces. The single-sex students were relieved of these pressures.

These moments also reflect that the space of single-sex contained space to play with gender norms and constructions. The family trees were one such example. The trees and relationships therein used particular gender relationships but reassigned their relationship with sex. The wives were still male, the husbands female, and uncles female. The trees did not attempt to accommodate gender non-conforming students but rather allowed the typical borders around gender and ties to be reconfigured. This was largely made possible because of the single-sex space. Because there were no girls to be wives, the boys had to consider the possibility that boys could enact such a role. It forced them to contemplate what operated in husband-wife relations that did not involve sex differences. The play may not have produced hierarchical results that we like (it may promote hierarchical thinking toward future relationships and between boys at play in their classroom), but it did allow for questioning, disruption, contemplation, and fluidity of gender-aligned categories.

The position taken up so far, the one that suggests the removal of certain gendered elements, specifically those related to sexual performance, neglect to account for the gay or lesbian student. The social sexual pressures may not be removed for these students. None of the students in this study openly identified as gay, lesbian, bisexual, queer or even questioning. Terrell was perceived by his peers and his teachers to be gay but never discussed this with me. He intimated that he was close to a girl in the group he moved to during lunch. One can presume, but not account from the data how the gendered space differed for queer youth. Sexuality and gender are often intertwined with particular gender constructions arising in relation to sexual identity. Thus, some of the scripts that surrounded Terrell are worth considering. No matter his sexuality, he did not perform the gender script assigned based upon his race and sex. He rebuked sports, quite openly. One of the rewards for the boys' classes was time outside at the end of class to play football or some other sport. While his peers took to the field, Terrell played idly with the grass. But he was not merely the displaced academic student mimicking the honors boys. He received good grades but was not competitive nor bookish nor submissive in his respect of teachers. I suspect that in a different environment, the boys who looked up to him would have picked on him and used him as the negative example to reinforce the masculine classroom culture.

Heterotopias remind us that there are penetrations. The removal of the binary that I present here as stable is not. There are clear penetrations. In the end, the space that is created is contested and in ongoing formation. Although policy presumes it was held stable, there was a clear wrestling over who, how and what determined the meaning of a girls or a boys classroom.

Heterotopia and gendered space.   Spaces have gendered connotations and as such regulate who enters and how the space is used. The most obvious are certainly bathrooms and locker rooms with labels and sometimes surveillance. Other spaces acquire such meanings when the characteristics of the space align with normed gender constructions. Meandering through schools and classrooms, we can see many examples, examples which vary across the school. In the school in this study, some teachers have colorful beanbag chairs in one corner and remnant car seats in another as reading spaces, spaces which made assumptions about the users. Colorful materials in the math class to lure girls into the classroom. Such examples were heightened in the two classrooms of two teachers who only taught boys or girls. These are intentionally created spaces imbued with and reinforcing a particular and binary relationship between gender and sex. Many of the students described above do not fit within these paradigms. They spoke back to the space, less so in the reconstruction of the physical, but in the social dynamics and relationships therein. This is the heterotopia.

HETEROTOPIAS IN CONVERSATION WITH GENDER AND SEXUALITY

In theorizing heterotopia while examining modernist institutions, Foucault considers how these institutions and the people assigned to/defined in and out of them function differently from one another in revealing something about "real" society. In examining the possibilities of gender and sexuality within heterotopic schools spaces, I consider how crisis, deviance, and ritual collapse onto/into one another.

Foucault recognizes that heterotopias are places that juxtapose several spaces in their abstract as well as concrete embodiment. School serves varying societal purposes, purposes that may not operate in accord. Most people would contend something about the preparation for economic, social, and political behavior upon reaching adulthood. This thinking is problematic in that it pretends that schools are not real spaces within the adult world. Schools do not set aside deviant subjects until age 18. Young people participate in the "real" world not merely in justifying the adult world but as actors alongside adults Designations of adulthood and the formal rights associated with it are claimed at 18 (or maybe high school graduation), but the experiences with equity, inclusion, exclusion, and spatial movement are experienced with age as only one factor. Rereading schools as heterotopia allows us to acknowledge that they exist at the confluence of social realities.

A social reality linked to the political, social, and economic intentions is the formation of gender and sexual identities. We are taught how to properly perform gender roles. Society remains divided according to a male-female hierarchy and the deployment of "queer" often shames performances of sexuality rather than welcomes their plurality. We are contesting what social and economic access queer genders and queer sexualities can have while people taking up these positions are imaging new performances (Johnson, 2009). Even as Caitlyn Jenner takes her place on reality TV and same-sex marriage is enforced, people struggle daily to access space and actualize rights that accompany trans and LGB recognition. Schools deliberate whether trans students should be allowed to enter locker rooms, whether a lesbian can be homecoming queen, whether same-sex couples can attend prom, whether a trans student is known by birth name or taken name, what dresscode a gender non-conforming student must abide by, and how to think about bullying, sexual harassment, and dresscode violations in ways that do shame the gender and sexual identities of those implicated. As young people penetrate dominant ideologies through these actions, schools label them as in crisis or feel compelled to respond the crisis resulting from their actions. The discussion of my research through heterotopia supposes that rather than fear these crises we welcome them as where new possibilities about school rules and organization seem likely to emerge.

For those in support of a radical rethinking of gender and sexuality in schools, the examples presented here, enabled through rather than closed by heterotopia, produce new illusions about gender in schools. A single-sex program that is problematic in its divisions but fluid in its construction increases the imagination of how we respond to gender performances. We are challenged to consider our sense of girl and boy and reexamine these attributes and how they are used to regulate in and out of the single-sex classroom. The ascribed categories of queer, weirdo, male, and female have embraced and questioned their deviant and crisis attributes. To be queer is not to sit in the margins, to be labelled a weirdo is not to be a victim, to be a boy does not require hegemonic posturing, and to be female is not defined through sexuality with men. Thinking in spatial terms makes visible these gendered intrusions as public performances. Even moments that are individual are performed publicly in space, impacting how the action acquires spatial meaning and uttering a transgression that must be dealt with. Through the year in the single-sex program, the regular transgressions by the young people around the gendered assumptions of their teachers forced a response by teachers. Teachers changed curriculum, teaching practices, and classroom arrangements to adapt to the refusal of girl and boy positions. Teachers found themselves "failing" because their students did not fit within the paradigm offered by Sax. Instead, the performances of students required teachers to stop seeing practices as "girl" and "boy". They were similarly forced to rethink their approach to the social environment. The emergent crises were not the moments I depicted but the struggles of teachers to adapt to the fluid gender of young people. In the high school mapping, we saw spatial claims reconfigure the spatial meaning of school and uses of school space. Students who sat in the shadows thoughtfully disrupted their identification as victim. Even as their position may uphold social hierarchy, they produce new relationships between space and identity.

Possibility exists alongside exclusions. Remember, the heterotopia allows a multiplicity of spatial practices and understandings to co-exist. Within the discourse of gender and sexuality in school, Foucault's crisis heterotopia, heterotopia of deviation and heterotopia of ritual can also be noted amongst the spatial practices of young people and adults. The crisis heterotopia places certain practices out of sight while heterotopias of deviation house people who exist beyond/outside "normal". Heterotopias of ritual are where individuals take up inclusive space and regulate entrance. In some manners, these three distinctive practices can each help us understand the unjust spatial practices and reactions to them. The promises above can be reread through these troubled heterotopias. This tension is quite visible in both examples. The "center" in the mapped schools seeks to place the development of deviant identities in school spaces that are invisible or out of sight. And in reclaiming the upper commons and the theaters, the margins allow invisibility. The reconstruction of space simultaneously forces marginalized students to take up new practices to be admitted into these new spaces. Teachers use sex to include/exclude entrance into the single-sex classroom. Youth in the program requested that their peers reject such simplistic renderings of the practices in their classroom. Social cohesion in the program was marked by the willingness to resist and play with the very assumptions about gender that brought them together. Although there moments when the experiences in the heterotopias depicted directly disrupted the presumed realty of school, these were merely moments. A remaining struggle is how to allow new illusions to be visible outside the heterotopia.

IMPLICATIONS FOR REFORMS: WHAT SHOULD GENDER AND SEXUALITY POLICIES CONSIDER?

In contemplating gender and sexuality reforms in schools, the heterotopia provides a useful tool for measuring such reforms. The spatial language reminds of the possible and impossible, the unreachable stretch toward utopia. If reforms help us envision something utopic in nature, the rejection of the moments that tend toward dystopia, we are in a troubling stance if we believe that reforms are endpoints and get us toward our "goal". Such thinking refuses dynamic nature of school spaces and the identities of the people therein and outside. The current discussion of needed gender reforms in schools could not have been imagined a few decades ago and the discussions we are having today will someday be seen as irrelevant and overly simplistic. The heterotopia embraces elements of the utopia and dystopia as it offers a mirror into the immediate institutions and produces a critical eye against/within these extremes. Reflecting toward the discussion of schools as embodying many of Foucault's heterotopias, these simultaneous means of assessing the space in school are not equally desirable as functioning spaces in society. As we contemplate the context of school within the formation of gender and sexual identities, crisis heterotopia and heterotopias of deviation seem the ones to build school reform around; to make these less visible while encouraging the space to play and to bring multiple spaces and identities into co-existence.

Consider typical examples – bathrooms and locker rooms (Ingrey, 2013). Thinking about gender justice in the physical space requires breaking the two-gender, two-sex formation that is so intrinsic to how we have learned to order, perform, and relate in society. We can simply change the physical environment in the moment by creating male, female, and gender neutral bathrooms. Perhaps, even more just would be to merely rebuild all bathrooms as gender neutral. To do so, unless of single stalls, would likely produce an outcry about the possibility for harassment. We already have sense of boys, male and sexuality alongside protecting the female purity that make this impossible that arises. Thus, the physical change struggles in implementation because of the gender dynamic we cannot escape.

Queer theory and theorizing contributes to the heterotopic paradigm. Queer as a theoretical lens is used as variation around the theme of norm. Queer can be to disrupt, to make something weird as opposed to normal, to deconstruct norms, to produce discomfort (Britzman & Gilbert, 2004). Reforms need disruption. If reforms meander toward utopia, then the queer insertion is the evaluation of what arises from the reform. Queering reform and policy has allowed us to see how reform produce new, limiting norms. For example, queer theorists conceptualize homonormativity to characterize same-sex marriage as "just like" heterosexual marriages. Warner (2000) proposes that the "trouble with normal" is that it produces new binaries, new distinction, new tensions between centers and margins. While some gay and lesbian couples celebrate the right to marry, others queers scream silently from the periphery seeking recognition of full citizenship without marrying. With each step toward utopia, we need to return attention the heterotopia and the norms they make visible. Ultimately, we must make queer each time the space around us becomes too utopic. We need to ask what is being erased, moved to the upper commons and notice the claims to space that are present but ignored. This critically reflective process is the important interplay of utopia and heterotopia in education reform.

NOTES

[1] GLSEN stands of Gay, Lesbian, & Straight Education Network.

[2] I move between student and young people/youth in this chapter. Student reflects the research design wherein youth or young people reflect that participants never used "student" is describing themselves during the study. (see Schmidt, 2015).

[3] The study involved all four single-sex classes/groupings in that grade – grade level girls, grade level boys, honors girls, and honors boys. The students travelled to their core classes together and sat together at lunch. I spent one day each week with a different "class" and travelled with them through their entire day.

REFERENCES

Bailey, M. M., & Shabazz, R. (2014). Gender and sexuality geographies of blackness: Anti-Black heterotopias. *Gender, Place, and Culture, 21*(3), 316–321.

Bell, D., & Valentine, G. (Eds.). (1995). *Mapping desire: Geographies of sexualities.* London: Routledge.

Binnie, J. (1995). Trading places: Consumption, sexuality and the production of queer space. In D. Bell & G. Valentine (Eds.), *Mapping desire: Geographies of sexualities* (pp. 182–199). London: Routledge.

Britzman, D. P., & Gilbert, J. (2004). What will have been said about gayness in teacher education? *Teaching Education, 15*(1), 81–96.

Brown, G., Browne, K., & Lim, J. (2007). Introduction, or why have a book on geographies of sexuality. In K. Browne, J. Lim, & G. Brown (Eds.), *Geographies of sexualities: Theory, practices and politics* (pp. 1–18). Burlington, VT: Ashgate.

Browne, K., Lim, J., & Brown, G. (Eds.). (2007). *Geographies of sexualities: Theory, practices and politics.* Burlington, VT: Ashgate.

Brydum, S. (2015, November 9). Kentucky's new gov. will amend marriage licenses to suit Kim Davis. *The Advocate.* Retrieved from http://www.advocate.com/marriage-equality/2015/11/09/kentuckys-new-gov-will-amend-marriage-licenses-suit-kim-davis

Butler, J. (1990). *Gender trouble.* New York, NY: Routledge.

Conrad, R. (2011). *Against equality: Queer critiques of gay marriage.* New York, NY: Against Equality Press.

de Certeau, M. (1984). *The practice of everyday life.* Berkeley, CA: University of California Press.

Doan, P. L. (2007). Queers in the American city: Transgendered perceptions of urban space. *Gender, Place, and Culture, 14*(1), 57–74.

Eliot, L. (2009). *Pink brain, Blue brain.* Boston, MA: Houghton Mifflin Company.

Fernandez, M., & Smith, M. (2015, November 3). Houston voters reject broad anti-discrimination ordinance. *New York Times.* Retrieved from http://www.nytimes.com/2015/11/04/us/houston-voters-repeal-anti-bias-measure.html?_r=0

Foucault, M. (1986). Of other spaces. *Diacritics, 16*(1), 22–27.

Heffernan, J. I. (2010). The sound of silence: Educators managing and reproducing heteronormativity in middle schools (Unpublished doctoral dissertation). University of Oregon, Eugene, OR.

hooks, b. (2000). *Feminist theory: From margin to center.* Cambridge, MA: South End Press.

Hubbard, P. (2002). Sexing the self: Geographies of engagement and encounter. *Social and Cultural Geography, 3*(4), 365–381. doi:10.1080/1464936021000032478

Ingrey, J. (2013). Shadows and light: Pursuing gender justice through students' photovoice projects of the washroom space. *Journal of Curriculum Theorizing, 29*(2), 174–190.

Jackson, J. (2010) 'Dangerous presumptions': How single-sex schooling reifies false notions of sex, gender, and sexuality. *Gender & Education, 22*(2), 227–238.

Jones, A. (2009). Queer heterotopias: Homonormativity and the future of queerness. *InterAlia: A Journal of Queer Studies, 4*, 1–20.

Kannen, V. (2014). These are not 'regular places': Womens and gender studies classrooms as heterotopias. *Gender, Place, and Culture, 21*(1), 52–67.

Knopp, L. (2007). From lesbian and gay to queer geographies: Pasts, prospects and possibilities. In K. Browne, J. Lim, & G. Brown (Eds.), *Geographies of sexualities: Theory, practices and politics* (pp. 21–28). Burlington, VT: Ashgate.

Kosciw, J. G., Greytak, E. A., Palmer, N. A., & Boesen, M. J. (2014). *The 2013 National School Climate Survey: The experiences of lesbian, gay, bisexual and transgender youth in our nation's schools.* New York, NY: GLSEN.

Lefebvre, H. (1991). *The production of space.* Oxford: Blackwell.

Obergfell v. Hodges, 576 U.S. (2015).

Payne, E. (2010). Sluts: Heteronormative policing in the stories of lesbian youth. *Educational Studies, 46*(3), 317–336.

Reuters. (2015, November 3). Feds order high school to let transgender students use girls' locker room. *Huffington Post.* Retrieved from http://www.huffingtonpost.com/entry/transgender-high-school-locker-room_56387949e4b00a4d2e0bb825

Rofes, E. (2004) Martyr-target-victim: Interrogating narratives of persecution and suffering among queer youth. In M. L. Rasmussen, E. Rofes, & S. Talburt (Eds.), *Youth and sexualities: Pleasure, subversion, and insubordination in and out of schools* (pp. 41–62). New York, NY: Palgrave MacMillan.

Savage, D., & Miller, T. (Eds.). (2012). *It gets better: Coming out, overcoming bullying, and creating a life worth living.* New York, NY: Plume.

Sax, L. (2005). *Why gender matters: What parents and teachers need to know about the emerging science of sex differences.* New York, NY: Broadway Books.

Schmidt, S. J. (2010). Queering social studies: A query of the space for sexual orientation and identity in the social studies. *Theory and Research in Social Education, 38*(3), 314–335.

Schmidt, S. J. (2013). Claiming our turf: Students' civic negotiation of the public space of school. *Theory and Research in Social Education, 41*(4), 535–551.

Schmidt, S. J. (2015). The queer arrangement of school: A spatial study of inequity. *Journal of Curriculum Studies, 47*(2), 253–273.

Schroeder, C. G. (2012). Making space for queer youth: Adolescent and adult interactions in Toledo, Ohio. *Gender, Place, and Culture, 19*(5), 635–651.

Sears, J., & Letts, W. J. (1997). *Overcoming heterosexism and homophobia: Strategies that work.* New York, NY: Columbia University Press.

Sumara, D., & Davis, B. (1999). Interrupting heteronormativity: Toward a queer curriculum theory. *Curriculum Inquiry, 29*(2), 191–208.

Thornton, S. J. (2003). Silence on gays and lesbians in social studies curriculum. *Social Education, 67*(4), 226–230.

Toomey, R. B., McGuire, J. K., & Russell, S. T. (2012). Heteronormativity, school climates and perceived safety for gender nonconforming peers. *Journal of Adolescence, 35*, 187–196.

Unks, G. (Ed.). (1995). *The gay teen: Educational Practice and theory for lesbian, gay, and Bisexual adolescents.* New York, NY: Routledge.

Valentine, G. (1989). The geography of women's fear. *AREA, 21*(4), 385–390.

Warner, M. (2000). *The trouble with normal: Sex, politics, and the ethics of queer life.* Cambridge, MA: Harvard University Press.

Wittig, M. (1980). The straight mind. *Feminist Issues, 1*(1), 103–111.

Sandra Schmidt
Columbia University

232

EDWARD BUENDÍA, ANALIZ RUIZ,
ANDREA GARAVITO MARTINEZ,
ELIOT SYKES AND PAUL FISK

14. LATINO NEIGHBORHOOD CHOICE

Suburban Relocation

INTRODUCTION

The de- and re-territoralization couplet of the global-informational economy has brought with it economic and demographic changes across many metropolitan regions in the U.S. that have altered the contexts of educational reform. The dispersion of immigrant families across metropolitan regional areas has become a pervasive trend as global economies have amplified the employment opportunities beyond central cities (Castles & Miller, 2003; Singer, 2008; Wells et al., 2014). First generation families, particularly Latinos, are bypassing U.S. central cities and settling into suburban areas (Tienda & Fuentes, 2014). This shift is complicating patterns of urbanism, urban education, and big city school reforms as "urban" organizational patterns and issues approach a regional scale (Buendía & Fisk, 2015; Katz et al., 2010; Singer, 2008). Even though this demographic shift has been in motion for over a decade and a half, the field knows very little about the selection processes that Latino immigrant families employ to choose suburban neighborhoods. While researchers have explored the neighborhood selection processes of lower socio-economic African-Americans (Rhodes & DeLuca, 2014), the field should be cautious in generalizing these patterns to other ethnic and racial groups.

Some of the key questions that researchers and policy makers have not explored are:

- What does the selection making process look like for Latino immigrant families?
- What prior information do families have about neighborhoods when selecting suburban neighborhoods, as well as what are their sources of information, if any?
- Equally, and central to the interests of educational researchers, to what degree do neighborhood services, such as schools and school districts, factor into neighborhood or city choice for families?
- Finally, at what junction and under what social and family circumstances does school quality and reputation become significant for Latino families, if not an initial selection factor?

N. Ares et al. (Eds.), Deterritorializing/Reterritorializing, 233–250.

The significance of these questions matters greatly as patterns of suburban dispersion affect how educational program and curricular placement is envisioned as well as how patterns of segregation and group isolation take shape across metropolitan school districts.

We focused on these questions and examined the neighborhood selection processes of ten Latino families who settled into a suburban city in the Salt Lake metropolitan region. A burgeoning literature has explored parent residential choice and the relationship of these decisions to perceptions of school reputation and the expansion of segregation (Rhodes & DeLuca, 2014; Holme, 2002; Lareau, 2014). The interplay of these dynamics is particularly important as neighborhood schools find themselves in the crosshairs of school quality conversations; federal policy requires school districts to publish annual yearly progress reports across community media. Building and expanding upon this work, this chapter argues that school and school district reputation is not a factor in selecting a neighborhood in initial relocation for Latino suburban transplants. The process of neighborhood choice is facilitated and pre-determined by trust networks constituted of family members and friends whose geographical location in suburban cities defined the neighborhood and, ultimately, removed the school selection process from consideration. Lastly, we also posit that school attributes do eventually become a factor in Latino families' neighborhood selection processes, typically within a two-year window of resettlement for our sample. We show how parents' priority of seeking to maintain stability and continuity for their children within a particular school, not necessarily school reputation, was a key factor in selecting a home for purchase or for rental.

The chapter begins with an overview of the key literatures situating the demographic changes taking place in suburbs, focusing on the settlement of diverse ethnic groups in suburbs, followed by the neighborhood choice literature. The chapter then describes the findings. Finally we discuss how these patterns involve educational processes across space and time.

SITUATING LITERATURES

A robust body of literature has documented the demographic changes taking hold in suburban regions of large metropolitan areas (Berube et al., 2010; Katz et al., 2010). While American suburbs have long been diverse places (Kruse & Segrue, 2006), the number of ethnic groups moving to suburban regions of metropolitan areas has been steadily on the rise since the 1980's (Li, 2012; Tienda & Fuentes, 2014). Recent analyses of the 2000 and 2010 census report that ethnic and immigrant groups represent the largest segment of growth in U.S. suburban cities (Berube et al., 2010; Fry, 2009). Immigrants, as an aggregate, comprised 30% of the national suburban general population (Suro, Wilson, & Singer, 2011). When national suburban data is further dissected along racial and ethnic lines, Latinas/-os constituted 20% of the suburban population distribution, African-Americans 15%, and Asians 5% (Fry, 2009). While many of the typical gateway cities (e.g., Los Angeles, Miami,

New York) retained their share of transplants, a pattern of national dispersion is evident as southern suburbs such as Nashville (Tennessee) and Atlanta (Georgia), as well as southwestern metropolitan regions around Las Vegas, experienced the largest and fastest demographic changes in the suburbs (Fry, 2009). Many families moving to these areas represented interstate relocation as opposed to international migration (Tienda & Fuentes, 2014). The demographic, economic, and aesthetic character of some of these cities and regions has undergone such a dramatic transition that some have termed these regions "ethnoburbs" (Li, 2009).

This shift in population has not translated into integrated communities, however. Demographers and sociologists have concluded that suburban settlement patterns have adhered to durable historical patterns of racially and economically segregated spaces (Suro, Wilson, & Singer, 2011; Reardon & Bischoff, 2011). While the field has distanced itself from spatial assimilation frameworks that interpret ethnic groups' suburban relocation as an assimilative sign-post, theories of place segregation, which foreground the effects of structural processes of sorting and division, have driven current research.

Working from this latter framework, a strand of inquiry focused specifically on an individual's neighborhood selection processes has provided researchers with a fine-grained view of the intersection of social networks, ideologies of race, and the relationship between neighborhood selection and schools. This body argues, and shows, that neighborhood schools matter greatly in the processes of neighborhood selection if a family's economic status affords them the privilege to contemplate this domain. Foregrounding the entanglement of structural and interpersonal domains, Holme (2002) documented how white, affluent families selected neighborhoods by drawing upon social networks to gauge neighborhood quality, foregoing first-hand experiences (i.e., visits, tours) with the neighborhood school. Even though the study is a little over a decade old, the work importantly linked micro-processes to structural formation in showing how peer networks weighed heavily in providing white, affluent families information about school quality, translating into neighborhood selection. Holme argued that ideologies of race prevailed in the selection process.

Subsequent work has sought to understand these processes for those from the lower to middle socio-economic ranks (Rhodes & DeLuca, 2014; Weininger & Lareau, 2014) and is focused principally on the experiences of African-Americans. The research has found that schools rarely factor in the process of neighborhood selection (Rhodes & DeLuca, 2014; Weininger & Lareau, 2014). This body has studied impoverished African-Americans and found that peer networks weighed heavily in selecting neighborhoods. The particulars of the neighborhood, much less its schools, were vague in these decisions and conversations (Weinginger & Lareau, 2014). While insightful in its contribution, this body of research has maintained a black-white binary that needs to be expanded to understand the broad range of ethnic group and classed experiences. Yet, it is clear that the place of social networks in selecting neighborhoods must be an element that is examined.

METHODOLOGY

The conceptual framework that guided this work theorized residential choice as an effect of a context composed of narrowing structural and social networks. Residential choice is theorized as an economic decision that is situated within nested structural and familial dimensions that interact with each other. Race and class are entwined in structuring the residential, economic and educational domains. Equally, informational networks, or individuals interlinked as hubs, provide information and advice, and also serve as points that facilitate and constrain what data is brought to decisions.

The framework of constrained choice mobilized here stands in contrast to rational choice models typically heralded in residential choice debates. Holton (1992) takes up the rational choice school of economic theory to argue that this branch of economics has decontextualized market choices. He notes, it has "neglected the way in which the economy has been *embedded* in wider social relations wherever reciprocity, redistribution, and the household have been dominant. Instead, economists have focused on the market which is the sole type of economy sharply *differentiated* from the remainder of society" (p. 17). Various theorists and empiricists from different disciplines (Harvey, 1996; Polanyi, 1957) make arguments that are consonant with the emphasis that Holton posits. They, too, have negated the premise that economic functions can be separated, or differentiated, from other societal realms. They have asserted the entwinement of complex socio-historical structures, leading them to proffer choice frameworks that are amplified and constrained by a broad range of structural and cultural relationships.

The concept of constrained choice aligns well with place segregation frameworks. The latter eschews 19th and 20th century Romanticist views of economic autonomy and, instead, foregrounds the socio-historical structural dimensions of race, residential markets, economic processes, and social class to theorize and study the spatial organization and reproduction of people and resources.

An addition that we make to the socio-historical is amending to it the social-interpersonal dimensions of networks. The empirical literature has emphasized the manner in which trust networks function as gateways to expanding social capital. These relational facets of interpersonal networks are equally situated within and constitute structural realms. Consequently, we conceptualize choice as located in the interplay of these components.

Methods

This study employed qualitative research methods as well as GIS mapping to study the relationships of Latino immigrant families' residential choice and settlement. The participants for the study were chosen through a purposive sampling process (Robson, 2011). The ten families were selected because they satisfied two requirements that defined the purpose of the study. First, these families had relocated to the western suburbs within the last fifteen years. Second, they had children in the public school system at one time since their relocation to the state of Utah. Families were identified through professional and social networks of the research team. Eight of the ten families moved to Utah from California. One of the nine families re-integrated a family in the move, where the female and the children were in Mexico and relocated to Utah while the husband relocated from California. One other family relocated from Illinois to Utah.

Data collection partly included one semi-structured interview with parents and, at times, children who joined in the conversation as participants. Children participated in four of the ten interviews as part of a family interview. Elements of the interview included questions pertaining to the relocation, settlement, and employment, of the family as well as children's school attendance history. Questions were also structured to determine decision-making processes in selecting neighborhoods. Specifically, we included questions about mechanisms (i.e., finance, information points and sources, employment) and people (i.e., informational hubs) that facilitated and/or constrained the decision making process in selecting neighborhoods, and in how, if at all, they interjected schools or other services into the decision making process. The interview also probed into parents' and childrens' experiences with their schools, seeking to determine if and to what degree the quality of the experience in the school setting had an effect on decisions to stay or leave the school's boundaries.

The authors also collected and analyzed Geographical Information System (GIS) data. This comprised of gathering 1990, 2000 and 2010 census data focused on the metropolitan region. The data set included demographic information focused on race, ethnicity, and social-economic class, along with data focused on home ownership and cost. This data helped the research team create a twenty-year portrait of the regional shifts and socio-structural clustering along these various axes.

We employed a grounded theory/constant comparison approach in analyzing the interview data. Teams of two analyzed the data moving from open coding, where themes and codes were developed, to axial coding, or a fine-grained analysis around specific themes (Charmaz, 2014). Analyses and interpretations were cross-checked through subsequent whole group analysis. Some codes were discarded and maintained through subsequent analyses of new data. Codes that remained in the analysis were those that had a high level of presence and saturation across the data collected.

GIS maps of the region were analyzed for patterns of clustering along the axes of racial and ethnic group as well as social class. A comparison of maps from 2000 and 2010 was done in order to determine degree of demographic shift.

PORTRAIT OF A SUBURBAN SHIFT

The demographics in the Salt Lake metropolitan region have undergone a shift over the past 20 years as minoritized groups have moved into suburban neighborhoods. The convergence in the movement of ethnic populations from central Salt Lake City, an increase in refugee resettlement, and the inflow of Latinos/-as from inter-state and international destinations into suburbs has rapidly altered the complexion of the region. Yet, these demographic changes have cohered into historical patterns of residential segregation found in other medium to large metropolitan regions (Lichter, Parisi, Taquino, & Grice, 2010). The area has become bifurcated by an east-west divide, marking the region with the consolidation and clustering of populations by income, race and ethnicity. Structural relations (i.e., residential markets, religious institutions) have organized Latino, Asian, and Pacific-Islander families in a manner that has brought about an ethnoburbanization (Li, 2009), or the transformation of suburban cities into ethnic enclaves.

The portrait of the region has cohered into one where the western portion of the region—the cities of West Valley City, Taylorsville and South Salt Lake City—has seen a dramatic shift between 1990 and 2000 of the percentage of Latinos in Salt Lake County. These cities have gone from 7–13% composition of people of color—an aggregate construct comprised of Asian-American, Latino, African-American, and Pacific Islander—to a range of 25–30% in a 10-year period. Prior to 1990, these suburban cities were largely White.

While median household incomes in the suburban cities surrounding Salt Lake largely grew between 1990 and 2010, the racial/ethnic bifurcation also adhered to a class divide. An example of the increase in income can be seen in the city of West Jordan. Its residents experienced a significant income jump over a ten-year period. In 1990, residents' median household income ranged between $29,712.01 and $36,896.00. Incomes increased to $59,255–$73,125 by 2000. Suburban cities on the eastern portion of the district experienced a similar pattern. In suburban cities that had the highest concentration of people of color (i.e., Kearns, West Valley), household incomes lagged compared to the rest of the county and its eastern, suburban peers by approximately 9% to 16%. Home values serve as one indicator demonstrating the income gap. The median value of a home in 2007 in West Valley was $197,950 compared to $266,000 for the surrounding Salt Lake City counties. Table 1 demonstrates the trend of steady increases in West Valley. Yet these figures paled in comparison to the properties in eastern cities, by a margin of approximately 15%.

Table 1. Housing prices in West Valley

Year	Homes Sold	Median Sales Price	Average Sales Price	Average Days on Market
2000	593	$127,500	$128,077	61
2002	674	$130,500	$132,088	61
2004	928	$130,000	$133,862	54
2006	1297	$168,250	$175,191	29
2008	772	$190,000	$197,725	63

Source: Salt Lake County. Summary of analysis of impediments to fair housing (2013)

238

FINDINGS

Latino families' relocation narratives all included pivotal trust networks that facilitated their relocation into the suburban city of West Valley City. These networks were comprised of family members and close friends who functioned as gateway agents. Table 2 shows the relationship of gateway agents to relocating families. The location of these friends and family members in suburban cities pre-determined the neighborhood selection for transplants, setting neighborhood characteristics outside of the consideration process. The established status of friends and families within the relocation city, as well as the high levels of trust between the parties, linked the distances of space by providing informational and material resources that helped to attract and settle relocating families to the suburban city and neighborhood where they resided.

Table 2. Origin city and gateway relationship

Family name*	Initial relocation region	Gateway member relationship
Aguero	California	Husband's cousin
Bonilla	California	Wife's sister
Felix	California	Wife's sister
Gil	California/Mexico	Husband's sister
Juarez	California	Wife's brother
Moreno	California	Wife's brother
Ortiz	California/Mexico	Wife's sister
Padilla	Illinois	Husband's cousin
Portes	California	None
Valdez	California	Wife's brother

Pseudonyms

The provision of housing was paramount in these processes. Relocating families identified gateway family members and friends who facilitated their housing in all but two instances. Gateway agent(s) eliminated any need for families to research city or neighborhood specifics such as schools or other services. They brokered information and material resources that left families with only the preoccupation of relocating to the new city. A marker of the level of trust families bestowed upon agents was the fact that only two of the ten families indicated that they had visited the region prior to relocation. The case of the Juarez exemplified how families' networks facilitated the transition to Utah and, consequently, narrowed the scope of neighborhood for new arrivals. The Juarez family, comprised of Rosa, Antonio and their three daughters, relocated to West Valley City from southern California in 2004. Rosa narrated the manner in which her brother, who relocated to Utah eight years prior, assisted the family in identifying a residence prior to their arrival. Track in the following excerpt the manner in which her brother made available material and informational dimensions:

Rosa: *I lived in San Bernardino [California] for about a month, then I moved to Taylorsville. All of my family lived here. I came and lived with my brother.*

Interviewer: *Where did you find yourself, in a house or an apartment?*

R: *In a basement apartment that he had rented for us.*

I: *How did you learn about it?*

R: *My brother lived in Taylorsville and he told my husband about the opportunity to rent it. It was close by to him.*

The trust between family members permitted Rosa and her husband to turn over the search process to her brother. This pattern of residential facilitation by familial or close friends held for most families in our sample. Of equal importance, all housing that was not within the same residence of the gateway agent was in close proximity to the family or friends engaged in structuring settlement. While we did not probe this dimension, the pervasiveness of this pattern prompted us to speculate that the spatial clustering was intentional, possibly seeking to keep family members in close proximity as well as within a familiar geographical region.

Gateways agents' facilitation in five out of the ten cases involved a comprehensive approach, opening up access to employment opportunities alongside housing. These, too, remained within a confined area of the suburban region, maintaining the spatial boundaries in which families circulated. Many of these jobs were within the same place of employment. Leticia Bonilla, a six year resident of West Valley City, explained, like many with whom we spoke, how her sister arranged employment for her husband.

Interviewer: *How did you decide upon Utah?*

Female: *Through my sister. We came here and stayed with her. She got here because of my brother. He was gone when I got here, though.*

I: *What was she doing here in Utah?*

Female: *She worked in a factory building filters. My husband worked there, too. She got him the job.*

Leticia makes evident the chain relocation pattern that spatially situated families, as well as how gateway agent's social networks expanded to a host of other necessities. An abundance of factory work in the industrial area of West Valley City provided family members access to low-skilled jobs that had minimal prior experience requirements.

The facilitative processes in which these networks engaged also translated into relocations into neighborhoods that were pre-sorted along the axes of race, ethnicity, and social class. The demographic profile of the suburban neighborhoods and cities where all of these families settled were composed principally of other Latino/Hispanic families that were situated in the lower- to middle-socio economic ranks. Map 1 shows the economic portrait of the various cities in the metropolitan region. The inhabitants of the cities of Kearns and West Valley City were slotted in the bottom quartile of the median household income across the region, ranging between $38,000 and $48,000. These areas, as evident in Map 2, became the most Latino concentrated cities over the last thirty years. In municipalities such as West Valley, the concentration of Latinos rose to approximately 30% of the population by 2010. The pattern over these two decades showed a southern migration to other suburbs.

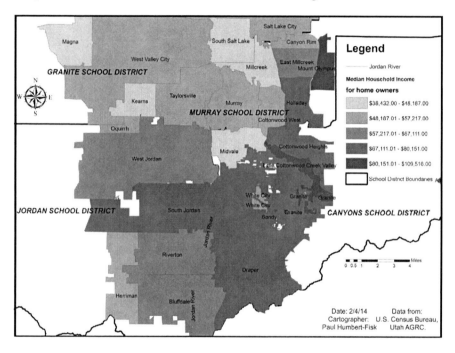

Map 1. Regional economic division

Basics First

While the twenty-year portrait of the suburban region demonstrated a pattern of economic and racial segregation across the region, the majority of the families in our sample had no knowledge of these divides when they moved into the region. Similar to the pattern which others have documented (Rhodes & DeLuca, 2014; Weininger & Lareau, 2014), the majority of families moved with solely the information from family and friends; only a few engaged in any research about the particulars of the city or its social institutions. Moreover, eight out of ten of the participants deemed the quality of the neighborhood or city schools as tertiary in importance in relation to securing the basics of finding housing and employment.

Per. of Hispanics in Suburban Salt Lake City, 1990-2000

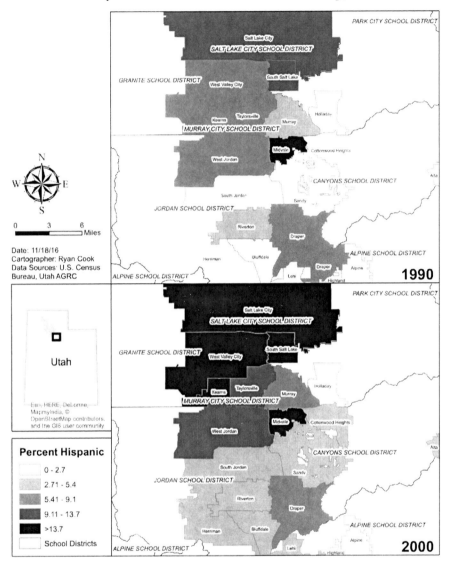

Map 2. Regional distribution of Latinos over twenty years

The majority of families were not in a financial position to attend to matters of school quality, particularly for the four families who left California at the height of the 2008 great recession.

Flor Aguero, a seven-year resident of Kearns, West Valley City's suburban neighbor, conveyed how families prioritized as they made their move. She identified how the lack of financial resources, signaled in her conversation by the second appearance of the term "economy," relegated neighborhood quality markers as peripheral:

> I: We want to ask you about your decision of moving here to West Valley? Did you move to this apartment influenced by the reputation of the schools? And, how did you end up deciding to live here instead of other areas in the city?
>
> FA: We were not even thinking about moving to Utah, but because of the economy, we came to Kearns. And you start living in one room with other people in the same house, and there were six of them. You start thinking, "I have to get out of here." You know the income [rent] is not much, so you start looking for something that is more comfortable and it doesn't really matter where. At that moment, you don't think about the city, or "Oh! I am going to move to the East where schools have a better reputation", because you don't have the economy [resources], and everything is decided around your economy. I mean, West Valley is the cheapest city to live in. And this apartment was cheap, when we moved in, because that's what we could afford.

Mrs. Aguero identified how the basic need of having a residence of their own drove the list of priorities. Her family's initial relocation to the area involved moving in with family friends from California who also had children, as well as to the low-income area of Kearns. She noted in the process of finding their own residence how the spatial and quality nuances of the region, demarcated by her mentioning the affluent east side of the metropolitan region, were not a consideration in the relocation.

For many, the information that trust networks provided was focused on employment. The quality of services in the new city was far removed from the necessities of making a living. The majority of participants in our sample were low-skilled laborers who had prior job experience in warehouses or agricultural related fields. Again, Mrs. Aguero's narrative encapsulated what many experienced in leaving a tumultuous California economy. She highlighted in the following explanation how employment was the principal topic:

> FA: My husband was out of a job for an entire year. We had no other option but to look elsewhere in other states. My husband had some cousins that lived here. So he called his cousins and they told us, "Come here. There are jobs, but they pay minimum wage."

What is significant is what Flor's relatives did not foreground, that the social or educational infrastructure might be satisfactory or strong, or that the city was clean and safe. A similar sentiment about securing employment was conveyed by David and Alicia Ortiz. David arrived in West Valley from California first and moved in with his sister-in-law and her husband. Alicia and their three children arrived from Mexico a year later reuniting the family in one home and city. David stated, "I had to find a job, that's what brought me here. I wasn't thinking about schools or neighborhoods. The fact that my brother-in-law could find me work and house me was enough."

The experiences of the outliers in the group are worth noting. The two families who moved to this suburban city earlier than 2006 identified also having had minimal information about the neighborhoods' schools, even though one family out of the two worked with a real estate agent. The latter family visited the area as well as the neighborhood to view prospective properties. They did not inquire about schools in making their selection nor did the real estate agent provide them with information about the neighborhood school. The second family left the Los Angeles metropolitan region to escape the population density and pollution. The husband visited the area prior to making the decision to move. The focus of the visit was appraising employment opportunities and the city's density and general sense of safety.

Transitions to Home Buyers

While understanding the initial move for these families is significant in drawing out the relationship between facilitated relocation, chain migration, and place segregation, it represents an event that is couched in a configuration of family and structural dynamics (i.e., employment, economic, family size) that imposes a temporary facet to the settlement. The first residence for eight of the ten families was not a long-term situation, due to the residence's size or its proximity to employment opportunities. Families' relocation to their second residence is insightful in demonstrating the shift in the prioritization of schools in the decision-making processes of Latino suburbanites. The majority of the participants became homebuyers within two years of their initial relocation to West Valley City. This is noteworthy in that they were poised to make another decision about neighborhood selection after living in the region for a period of time where they had acquired more information and first-hand experience about schools, neighborhood services, and neighboring cities.

Neighborhood schools surfaced as a significant dimension in their selection processes as families approached a home purchase. School quality was not the primary attribute parents identified in coupling schools and neighborhood, however. Rather, their children's continuity with the school where they first enrolled was the principal factor in neighborhood selection. That is, parents sought to avoid moving their children out of the school and into another. Consequently, parents' residential choice rationales accentuated the distance of a prospective neighborhood to the school that their children were attending. Note in Map 4 the proximity of the second home purchase to the initial residence of seven of the ten families. Many are within a few miles of the schools their children were attending—Five of seven purchased houses that were in the same catchment boundaries. Parents' determined these boundaries from information from the property's listing.

The home purchasing experience of the Padilla families exemplified the manner in which the dimension of school continuity shaped the distance parameters of a

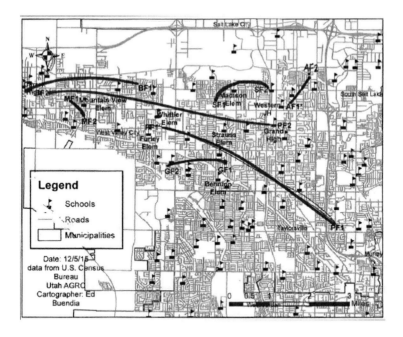

Map 3. Family intra-city relocation

home purchase. At the time of this interview, the Padilla family was living in their third residence in the West Valley region. The first was a rented basement apartment of a relative who facilitated their transition to Utah. The second was a house three blocks away from the neighborhood school in which their two children were enrolled upon starting school. The third residence was in the neighboring suburban city, approximately eight miles away from their second residence. The purchase of their first home in the region, or their second residence after arriving, demonstrates how residence and school distance factored in the decision. Their two children had enrolled in an elementary school after moving to West Valley City from Chicago. Eight months after their arrival they began searching for a home to purchase close to their children's school. The following excerpt demonstrates how the distance to their children's school factored in the home purchase decision.

> Mr. Padilla:　We first moved in with them [wife's cousin], then we started looking for houses in that same area and she knew some people who were renting their basement. So we lived in the basement, which was about 40th west. And after about eight months of renting, I, in that same area, since the kids were already going to a school in that area, Wright [Elementary], I, we all started to look at houses. So we bought there.

I: *Why was that important to stay close to school that they were attending?*

MP: *The neighborhood. Also children don't like to be moved from their schools. I really didn't like West Valley City, which my wife and I discussed quite often, but (shrugs).*

The logic of child-school continuity was a common theme in the neighborhood selection process for six of the participants. The decision to stay in the area was to avoid educational disruption. This priority was accentuated in the Padilla case considering that one of the two adults, the male, was not enthusiastic about the aesthetics or amenities of the city.

For the six parents who factored in schools in their relocation decision, school reputation was a non-issue as the dimension of continuity foregrounded proximity of the home to the school in subsequent moves. Three of the six parents had peer-group information or first-hand experience with the schools as they considered residential relocation. Even though the information that they had did not paint a flattering portrait, maintaining their child's, or children's, continuity with the school prevailed. Mrs. Moreno, a sixteen-year transplant from California, highlighted how school reputation was relegated to a tertiary level of importance.

Interviewer: *Have you always lived in this neighborhood?*

MM: *We lived somewhere else before, but on this street.*

I: *How did you find this place?*

MM: *We were looking for houses around 3500 Avenue. And they asked us if we wanted to see where they were building houses, and that's when we came here. And looking at the prices and everything, we decided to find out if we qualified.*

I: *When you looked in this area, did you do so because of the schools?*

MM: *Yes, because the houses were close to their schools, and they could take the bus in this area-the schools were Uintah (middle-school) and Summit (high school).*

I: *Did the reputation of the schools influence you in buying in this area?*

MM: *No, we never thought of the reputation when we bought this house. We always heard that Uintah and Summit had a bad reputation, but I think it depends on the students and the education they bring from home.*

The element of continuity prevailed in the face of reputation. The external factors of transportation and distance to school, as opposed to the school's annual reporting card drove the Moreno's decision-making processes. In addition, Mrs. Moreno rationalized that home culture would temper the negative elements of the school context.

Child Safety

Child safety concerns were also a prominent theme that brought schools and residential choice in alignment. Five of the participants, or half of the families studied, indicated that school safety prompted them to weigh heavily the distance between the school and their residence. Parents held as a priority the ability to quickly access their child's school in the case of an emergency. The Felix family illustrated how the safety dimension played into selecting the houses that they rented. The Felix family had moved twice since moving from California to West Valley City. Each relocation involved moving between two cities that were adjoined. The key factor in the selection process was the proximity of the dwelling and neighborhood to the school that their son was attending—not continuity. Mrs. Felix asserted that quick access to the school in the event of an emergency was central:

I: *So your children attended the schools they did because they were neighborhood schools. In making the choice to live here, did it factor the schools?*

MF: *Well, when we moved from Taylorsville to West Valley, I did contemplate the proximity of the location to the schools. It, first, the house had to be close to the primary school, then the junior high.*

MF: *Why was that necessary?*

MF: *So that I could be close by in case of an emergency.*

I: *Do you drive?*

MF: *No, I don't drive. That's why I want to live close by. That way I can be there quickly if there's ever a situation.*

Ms. Felix was without a vehicle, so the subsequent move to West Valley City prompted her to factor in the distance between her child's primary school and their home. Parent's concerns of gun violence surfaced pointedly in three of the interviews. To bolster this point Mr. Valdez, a parent of two sons, respectively 16 and 20 years old, elaborated on how the purchase of their home was predicated on the ability of one of the parents to walk their sons to school. The issue of peer bullying was at the heart of this decision. Note how this shapes the rationale:

I: *Did you drive your sons to school?*

MV: *No. My wife always walked them to school. It was a good arrangement. There was always one child, or group, who seemed to terrorize the other kids. She managed all of this.*

I: *The school is that close from here?*

MV: *Yes, it is. That was one of the attractions to this location. After living in Los Angeles, the distance to the school became more important to us. It always amazes me how children are able to get a hold of guns and bring them into school.*

For the five parents who noted the significance of access in the case of emergencies, the choice of house selection was very strategic. Safety and protection for their children was not completely handed over to school agents, but, instead, involved choices in residence that ensured that vigilance could still be maintained through proximity.

DISCUSSION

The manner in which the Latino families constituting our sample approached the relocation to suburbs involved a process in which family members inserted them into a vast array of social and spatial relationships. Similar to what Rhodes and DeLuca (2014) and others have chronicled, these gateway agents were crucial in facilitating the move and subsequent settlement. Yet, a nuance for the families interviewed was how family networks continued to link transplants to their material networks, expanding beyond the realm of housing. These networks reterritorialized family members, tethering them to a place partly though the mechanisms and relationships of employment, residence and, eventually, schools.

The manner in which schools became part of the reterritorialization process for these Latino families is significant to our understandings of neighborhood choice. The findings presented here indicate that schools clearly matter in the process of long-term settlement. However, the timeline is an extended one, ranging from a few months to a few years. While educational researchers have begun to explore the settlement of immigrants and the working poor in metropolitan regions in a robust manner, our approaches have not framed the issue within a timetable to understand how neighborhood selection and settlement processes emerge over time and within space to include schools. Based on the findings here, the field needs to consider settlement processes within an expansive time and spatial scale than we are currently employing to include as well as go beyond the initial arrival. Unlike the experiences of the white, middle, and upper-middle class (Holme, 2002), as well as those of working class African-Americans populations documented in the literature (Rhodes & Deluca, 2014), the neighborhood choice processes expand beyond the initial arrival point as families transition from their first location of residence to other long term housing.

The relationship families in this sample had with their schools also prompt the field to redefine the idea of school reputation as a key focal point. As this study, and others focused on lower to lower-middle socioeconomic populations show, and argue, school reputation is not a primary consideration for many within these populations. Instead, the social, spatial and psychological dimensions of proximity, networks, and access repeatedly surface as key variables. We should begin to see these as dimensions constituting market choices. These function as metrics for the Latino/a community just as school reputation does for the white upper-middle classes when considering neighborhood. The selection processes are embedded across these spatial and educational dimensions in tacit, yet impactful, ways. Family members are both situated within these relationships and equally constitute them. This suggests to us that the field might amplify and, quite possibly, employ different starting points to studying and planning for the neighborhood selection processes of immigrant populations. For example, it may be important to consider how families factor transportation infrastructure or neighborhood design (e.g., walking friendly designs) in decisions pertaining to their second or third residence. The socio-psychological dimensions of neighborhood safety for this population seem to suggest that it is partly a spatial property. Further research propelled by a spatial theory accounting for the socio-psychological is clearly needed.

Finally, the findings emerging from this study also bolster the arguments for conceptualizing choice as emerging at the intersection of the individual and the structural domains. Across the school and neighborhood literature, a resounding argument is that people, institutions, and social structures are central in these processes. Here, too, the facilitative actions of family members in accommodating and settling immigrants engaged in interstate relocations were all conducted within durable structural relationships that re-instantiated demographic and residential arrangements. They reproduced a historically recognizable spatial order. Individual choice needs the contextualization of the structural constraints of regions, particularly for populations not situated in relationships of economic or racial privilege, in order to properly situate mitigating factors.

REFERENCES

Berube, A., Frey, W. H., Friendhoff, A., Garr, E., Istrate, E., Kneebone, E., & Wilson, J. H. (2010). *State of metropolitan America: On the front lines of demographic transformation.* Washington, DC: Brookings Institute Metropolitan Policy Program.

Buendia, E., & Fisk, P. (2015). Building suburban dreams: School district secession and mayoral control in suburban Utah. *Teachers College Record, 117,* 1–48.

Castles, S., & Miller, J. J. (2003). *The age of migration: International population movements in the modern world.* New York, NY: Palgrave Macmillan.

Charmaz, K. (2014). *Constructing grounded theory: A practical guide through qualitative analysis.* Los Angeles, CA: Sage.

Fry, R. (2009). *The rapid growth and changing complexion of suburban public schools.* Washington, DC: Pew Hispanic Center. Retrieved from www.pewhispanic.org

Harvey, D. (1996). *Justice, nature and the geography of difference.* Boston, MA: Basil Blackwell.

Holme, J. J. (2002). Buying homes buying schools: School choice and the social construction of quality. *Harvard University Press, 72*(2), 177–206.

Holton, R. J. (1992). *Economy and society.* New York, NY: Routledge Press.

Katz, M. B., Creighton, M. J., Amsterdam, D., & Chowkwanyun, M. (2010). Immigration and the new metropolitan geography. *Journal of Urban Affairs, 32*(5), 523–547.

Kruse, K., & Segrue, T. (2006). *The new suburban history.* Chicago, IL: University of Chicago Press.

Lareau, A. (2014). Schools, housing, and the reproduction of inequality. In A. Lareau & K. Goyette (Eds.), *Choosing homes, choosing schools.* New York, NY: Russell Sage Foundation.

Li, W. (2009). *Ethnoburb: The new ethnic community in American.* Honolulu, HI: University of Hawai'i Press.

Lichter, D. T., Parisi, D., Taquino, M. C., & Grice, S. M. (2010). Residential segregation in new Hispanic destinations: Cities, suburbs and rural communities compared. *Social Science Research, 39*(2), 215–230.

Polanyi, K. (1957). The economy as an instituted process. In. K. Polanyi, C. M. Arensberg, & H. W. Pearson (Eds.), *Trade and markets in the early empires: Economies in history and theory* (pp. 243–270). Glencoe, IL: Free Press.

Reardon, S. F., & Bischoff, K. (2011). *Growth in the segregation of families by income, 1970–2009.* New York, NY: Russell Sage Foundation.

Rhodes, A., & DeLuca, S. (2014). Residential mobility and school choice among poor families. In A. Lareau & K. Goyette (Eds.), *Choosing homes, choosing schools* (pp. 137–166). New York, NY: Russell Sage Foundation.

Robson, C. (2011). *Real world research: A resource for users of social research methods in applied settings* (2nd ed.). New York, NY: Wiley.

Salt Lake County. (2013). *Salt Lake County summary analysis of impediments to fair housing.* Salt Lake City, UT. Retrieved from http://ucdp.utah.edu/reports/HUD_Portal/AI/Salt_Lake_County/SLSummaryAIJune2013.pdf

Singer, A. (2004). *The rise of new immigrant gateways.* Washington, DC: The Brookings Institution. Retrieved from http://www.brookings.edu/~/media/events/2004/4/15demographics/20040415_singer.pdf

Suro, R., Wilson, J. H., & Singer, A. (2011). *Immigration and poverty in America's suburbs.* Washington, DC: Brookings Institute Metropolitan Policy Program.

Tienda, M., & Fuentes, N. (2014). Hispanics in metropolitan America: New realities and old debates. *The Annual Review of Sociology, 40,* 499–520.

Weininger, E. B., & Laureau, A. (2014, February 22). *Sleepwalking into neighborhoods: Social networks and residential choice.* Eastern Sociological Society, Baltimore, MD.

Wells, A. S., Ready, D., Duran, J., Grzesikowski, C., Hill, K., Roda, A., Warner, M., & White, T. (2014). Still separate, still unequal, but not always so "suburban": The changing nature of suburban school districts in the New York metropolitan area. In W. F. Tate (Ed.), *Research on schools, neighborhoods, and communities: Toward civic responsibility.* New York, NY: Rowman & Littlefield Publishers for the AERA.

Edward Buendía
University of Washington – Bothell

Analiz Ruiz
University of Utah

Andrea Garavito Martinez
University of Utah

Eliot Sykes
University of Utah

Paul Fisk
University of Utah

AFTERWORD

DAVID A. GREENWOOD

TELLING OUR OWN STORIES

A Provocation for Place-Conscious Scholars

The early nineteenth century philosopher Arthur Schopenhauer famously wrote, "The task is not so much to see what no one yet has seen, but to think what no body yet has thought about that which everyone sees." This aphorism aptly describes how our eyes might be opened wider to the many ways that everyday social and ecological relationships can be revealed, clarified, and potentially transformed through geographic thinking, specifically through diverse enactments of an activist critical geography. The contributing authors and editors of *Deterritorializing/Reterritorializing: Critical Geographies of Education Reform* are each in their own way demonstrating new ways of seeing what is open to plain view, if only we keep learning from one another how to look. From the title page onward, this volume challenges educators at all levels to rethink our assumptions about the purpose of our collective work with respect to a wider activist project to reclaim space, place, land, and territory for life and learning.

That geographical thinking and doing is difficult is evidenced by the diversity of perspectives toward place and space represented in this volume, a diversity that is but a sample of an even more diverse and dispersed global public, if such a thing can even be said to exist. Geographical thinking—as a mode of perception, thought, and action—is made even more difficult by practicing it in the field of education, which suffers deeply and widely from the very placelessless, homogenization, and spatial control that critical geographers seek to interrupt. The chapters in this book challenge simplistic and unifying notions of place, while also sharing a common concern about how various visions of education reform are revealed through spatial focusing. All of the authors here are interested in asking the crucial question raised by Eve Tuck and Allison Guess (Chapter 3)—whose place are we talking about? This does not necessarily make them collaborators or allies with one another, though this is an attractive possibility. At a time when the movement politics of the left is suffering from the major setbacks of an exclusionary nationalism in Europe and the U.S., one wonders whether progressives and radicals can coalesce into a political force strong enough to subvert the growing power of the neoliberal fascist state.

But the sense I get from reading this book is that it is precisely our tendency to focus on global and national movements that obstructs our vision from the particular places where people live, learn, and die. As an antidote, or an experiment,

N. Ares et al. (Eds.), Deterritorializing/Reterritorializing, 253–255.

the temptation toward metatheory and blanket pronouncements about saving the world from the fascists, the neoliberals, the racists, and the settlers, needs to be resisted in favor of more detailed and nuanced attention to how actual lives are ordered and disordered in actual places. In order to know ourselves and to develop relationships with others that are not merely expedient, exploitative, or oppositional, we continually need to remind ourselves to ask, from where do I dare to speak and for whom? Answering this question requires a personal honesty and commitment that is almost unheard of in academe. Yet we see it everywhere in activism, as revealed, for example, in place-centered, non-violent resistance to the Dakota Access Pipeline on the Standing Rock Reservation, or in the deeply principled Black Lives Matter movement as it organizes around the particular locales and White Supremacist conditions of The New Jim Crow (Alexander, 2012). These are gathering places for storytelling, personal stories and collective stories. My hope is that the stories in the current volume will exemplify and inspire, for a broader public of educators, the kinds of disclosures necessitated by a politics of place focused on both learning and becoming. Education reform, in the context of critical geography, must involve reinserting the particularities of time, place, identity, and circumstance into a conversation that is too often based on generality and assumption.

We have our work cut out for us. Beyond the pressures surviving in the neoliberal state, scholars and activists seeking change also face the problem of developing political traction when their work is constrained by an identity politics that often emphasizes difference rather than correspondence, and opposition rather than collaboration. Furthermore, what makes an activist critical geography so complex is the contingent and shifting nature of "place."

The late Doreen Massey, whose critical vision of the power of geographical thinking has inspired many, for several decades worked to communicate the complexities of place and space. It is worth pausing, in remembrance of her life and her gigantic contributions to geographic thought, to reflect that these seemingly simple concepts could remain so compelling and elusive, even for someone whose celebrated career revolved around investigating their slippery contours. In her book, *For Space*, Massey (2005) problematizes place with a phrase that at once clarifies and confounds: she speaks of "the event of place" (p. 138). I find this phrasing particularly illuminating in its simplicity, as well as full of paradoxical tension. Places are not static entities to be defined; they are happening, they are events in some stage of unfolding process. Similarly, anthropologist Keith Basso, in his classic 1996 text, *Wisdom Sits in Places*, proposes that a *sense* of place is properly understood not as a noun, but as a verb: as the act of *sensing* places. The event of place thus becomes the intricate combination of the forces that created it and the consciousness that encounters and perceives it. This is the principle of reciprocity: we are. formed, or deformed, by place just as we form, and deform, places. The question that flows through the chapters of this book—from where do I dare to speak and for whom?—thus demands the difficult work of attempting to know oneself as a central feature of place-consciousness.

Increased self-consciousness—knowing one's own story and how to tell it—seems to me to represent the vanguard of critical geographical thought and activism. Wherever academic authors risk such self-disclosure breathes life into whatever places are and are becoming. The benefit of such storytelling is not merely that it unveils a major aspect of place-consciousness by going public with the substance of the perceiving body. Even more importantly, such storytelling can reveal a wider spectrum of what it means to be human than can the common, default register of the academic, authorial voice, however politically geared it may be. Storytelling allows authors to reveal themselves emotionally, spiritually, and physically, as well as intellectually; it potentially fosters empathy, understanding, and relationship. Critical geography needs this infusion of life force.

In her highly acclaimed 2015 book, *Trace: Memory, History, Race, and the American Landscape*, Lauret Savoy weaves her own life history as a descendent of slaves, colonists from Europe, and people indigenous to North America. She describes her emplacement in social and ecological space through personal narratives that function in two vital ways. First, they trace the author's biographical and geographical past, a process that informs both writer and reader about how landscape and mindscape are intimately intertwined. Second, the revelations of self-disclosure, rendered through story, challenge readers to examine in specific place-based detail how their own ways of seeing have been shaped by their own personal relationships to land and community. To rephrase Schopenhauer, Savoy's narratives help us to see what we haven't yet seen about that which we've always known.

All I am suggesting, as a forward-looking postlude to the current volume, is that critical geography, like place, is a concept in process. As the contributions here demonstrate, critical geographies are events. They are a series of active encounters fashioned out of making and re-making, perceiving and remembering, telling and retelling. Applied to education and educators, critical geography calls out assumptions about our purposes by recasting our analyses of our practices as spatial relationships that take place somewhere with particular and uneven effects that need to be unveiled. Applied to ourselves as a community of scholars, it raises the challenge posed by Lauret Savoy in *Trace*: that is, to know a place, and to speak of it with any authority, we need to know and speak about ourselves. And we need to learn to do this together. Because just as place and space can only be found on the move, the self can only be found in a community of its own becoming.

REFERENCES

Alexander, M. (2012). *The new Jim Crow: Mass incarceration in the age of colorblindness*. New York, NY: The New Press.

Basso, K. H. (1996). *Wisdom sits in places: Landscape and language among the Western Apache*. Albuquerque, NM: UNM Press.

Massey, D. (2005). *For space*. London/Thousands Oaks, CA/New Delhi: Sage.
Savoy, L. (2015). *Trace: Memory, history, race, and the American landscape*. Berkeley, CA: Counterpoint.

David A. Greenwood
Lakehead University

INDEX

CPSIA information can be obtained
at www.ICGtesting.com
Printed in the USA
FFOW01n1733300417
35097FF